T5-CRK-585

Elusive Origins

Elusive Origins

The Enlightenment in the Modern Caribbean Historical Imagination

Paul B. Miller

University of Virginia Press
Charlottesville and London

University of Virginia Press

Printed in the United States of America on acid-free paper
First published 2010

9 8 7 6 5 4 3 2 1

Library of Congress Cataloging-in-Publication Data
Miller, Paul B., 1965–
Elusive origins : the Enlightenment in the modern Caribbean historical imagination / Paul B. Miller.
p. cm. — (New World studies)
Includes bibliographical references and index.
ISBN 978-0-8139-2979-8 (cloth : alk. paper)
ISBN 978-0-8139-2980-4 (pbk. : alk. paper)
1. Caribbean literature—20th century—History and criticism. 2. History in literature. 3. History and literature—Caribbean area—History—20th century. 4. Caribbean area—Intellectual life—20th century. 5. Caribbean Area—In literature. 6. Enlightenment—Caribbean area. 7. Modernism (Literature)—Caribbean Area. I. Title.
PN849.C3M56 2010
810.9'9729—dc22

2009046815

A book in the American Literatures Initiative (ALI), a collaborative publishing project of NYU Press, Fordham University Press, Rutgers University Press, Temple University Press, and the University of Virginia Press. The Initiative is supported by The Andrew W. Mellon Foundation. For more information, please visit www.americanliteratures.org.

For Nathalie and Noemi
For my parents

Contents

Acknowledgments

Recently, as I was in the final stages of preparing this book, I became engrossed in C. L. R. James's "Lectures on *The Black Jacobins*" and was surprised to come across the following sentence by the great Trinidadian writer: "You don't know the famous artist who has immortalized the struggle of the Spaniards against Napoleon, that helped to defeat Napoleon far more than Wellington? A man of the day, one of the most famous European artists, a man called Goya." I felt I had come full circle. More years ago than I care to remember, this book had its genesis in my fascination with the art of Francisco Goya and its relationship to the Enlightenment. Today, two hundred years after Goya, I believe we would still be hard-pressed to find an utterance that captures the complex and conflicted legacy of the Enlightenment with the poetic precision of Goya's formulation "El sueño de la razón produce monstruos." Like Esteban crossing the Atlantic (and contemplating the guillotine aboard) in *El siglo de las luces*, I was led, through circuitous routes, to the Cuban author Alejo Carpentier, whose novel about the French Revolution imported to the Caribbean abounds in epigraphs from Goya's etchings *Los desastres de la guerra*.

Once I was rooted, or anchored, in the Caribbean, and with my training as a comparatist, the connections between Carpentier and James seemed clear and worthy of exploration. This book has taken shape from these initial constellations.

This long journey was not traveled alone. Carlos Rojas first sparked my interest in Goya in a series of unforgettable graduate seminars at Emory University. Also at Emory I was fortunate enough to benefit from the teaching and friendship of the late Jean-François Lyotard, who encouraged me to think and work against the grain and across disciplines. I especially owe a debt of gratitude to Carlos J. Alonso, who fostered my interest in Carpentier and Caribbean literature and has never wavered in his support and wise counsel, from the beginning stages of the project up to the present time.

It is safe to say that, whatever the flaws or virtues of this book, without Kevin Meehan, a virtual human sounding board for most of the ideas I have struggled to elaborate here, I would have written a far poorer book. Over the years he has worn the variegated masks of my collaborator, bibliographer, librarian, native informant, editor extraordinaire, and administrative assistant. I am grateful for his help in all these areas, but even more for his friendship.

I would also like to thank Nick Nesbitt, *il miglior fabbro*, whose thoughtful reading of and commentary on the manuscript not only helped me to improve it but also provided an inspiring example of intellectual generosity I strive to emulate.

I am indebted and grateful to Micheline Debrauwere, whose perennial kindness, hospitality and nurturing made it possible for me to work virtually without interruption on the revisions of the manuscript.

Finally, I would like express my deepest gratitude to my wife, Nathalie, and our daughter, Noemi, whose steadfast love and patience make this, and everything that I am, possible.

Chapter 1, on Alejo Carpentier, first appeared in *Latin American Literary Review* 29, no. 58. It is reprinted here, in expanded form, by permission of the publisher. Chapter 2, on C. L. R. James, also expanded, first appeared in *MLN* 16, no. 5 (December 2001): 1069–90. It is reprinted with permission of The Johns Hopkins University Press.

Unless otherwise specified, the translations of all foreign-language quotations in this work are mine.

Elusive Origins

Introduction

The Structure of the Enlightenment

While the questions of modernity and postmodernity have been posed with regard to Latin America and the Caribbean on numerous occasions and in a variety of forms, less discussion has been generated in this context about the putative origins of Occidental modernity, the Enlightenment. Moreover, while conversations about modernity and postmodernity in Latin America and the Caribbean often take place in a highly theoretical realm, the Enlightenment in the region is usually discussed in a much more concrete language of economic, administrative, military, and penal reforms. If the idea of modernity in Latin America and the Caribbean can be described as a burden, something simultaneously (or alternately) wished for and rejected[1]—or, in García Canclini's memorable formulation, as something that in these regions has not entirely arrived while tradition lingers on—then by examining modern interpretations and representations of the Enlightenment from this perspective, we gain insight into how recent Caribbean writers view the origins, with all their metaphysical trappings, of their own modernity. The specific texts by the writers discussed in this monograph question, through a historico-fictive representation of the Caribbean during the ages of reason and revolution, these elusive origins of their Caribbean modernity.

The wide divergence of forms and articulations of the Enlightenment among the various European countries was retained and reproduced among the colonial societies of the Caribbean, making a coherent definition or outline of the Enlightenment in either hemisphere a challenging endeavor. If classic studies such as those by Ernst Cassirer and Lucien Goldman already emphasized important ideological differences rather than uniformity among the ranks of Enlightenment thinkers, more recent interventions such as those by Jonathan Israel, Louis Sala-Molins,

Tzvetan Todorov, Sankar Muthu, and, in a specifically Caribbean context, by Nick Nesbitt delineate even more forcefully the distinction between Enlightenment philosophers of a timid ilk, ideologically speaking, and those who advocate, overtly or by extrapolation, what Nesbitt calls "universal emancipation." For Todorov, even the idea of an inherent faith in historical progress, which seems like such a commonplace legacy of the Enlightenment, was not something viewed with unanimity among the *philosophes*. Rousseau especially, who was probably the most influential of the *philosophes* in Latin America and the Hispanic Caribbean, viewed human progress ambivalently.[2] For Sankar Muthu too, "Rousseau looms over the latter half of the eighteenth century as an ambiguous figure who both impedes and enables the development of anti-imperialist political thought." Muthu devotes a monograph to the perhaps surprising idea that several Enlightenment thinkers, especially Diderot and, more arguably, Kant were essentially anti-imperialists. Despite the fact that, according to Muthu, there was no precedent for this anti-imperialist thought prior to the Enlightenment, nor were there any clear and prominent anti-imperialist successors in the nineteenth century (Muthu characterizes Marx's thought as "agnostic on the issue of imperialism"),[3] the anti-imperialist tendencies of the Enlightenment are mostly viewed with skepticism by the Caribbean writers studied here. In a text that I will have occasion to discuss in detail in chapter 2, C. L. R. James refers to the tirades in the *Encyclopédie* against slavery in the colonies to physicians who can only prescribe invectives against the malady from which the patient is suffering. This skeptical attitude toward the universal applicability of the Enlightenment might be said to constitute a founding principle for the historical imagination of especially Hispanic Caribbean writers, taking their cue from Alejo Carpentier.

The complexity of the reforms in the Caribbean colonies in the eighteenth century and their mixed results exacerbate the difficult of characterizing "the Enlightenment" there. Despite national, regional, and linguistic differences (delineated by Arthur L. Stinchcombe),[4] for *modern* Caribbean writers of disparate languages and traditions, I argue, the idea of the Enlightenment implies first and foremost a reckoning with the structural dynamic that emerges when Latin America and the Caribbean are included within the Enlightenment's ambit (and vice-versa). To elucidate this structural situation, it is helpful to hearken back to a key moment of this philosophy and historical epoch, crystallized in Immanuel Kant's 1784 essay "Was ist Aufklärung?" This essay is not only core reading for the Enlightenment; Michel Foucault has traced the very origins of European modernity back to this notoriously ambiguous text: "[This text] . . . marks the discreet entrance into the history of thought of a question that modern philosophy has not been capable of answering, but that it has never managed to get rid of either. . . . What, then, is this event that is called the *Aufklärung* and that has determined, at least in part, what we are, what we think, and what we do today?"[5] Kant defines Enlightenment as "man's emergence from his self-incurred immaturity."[6] The word that has been translated as "emergence" is *Ausgang*, which Foucault retranslates as an "exit" or "way out," thus emphasizing the highly negative and differential quality of the Enlightenment.[7] If the Enlightenment can be defined as an "emergence" or "exit" from a world informed by error, myth, and superstition, what has replaced these older, undesirable components that will not be merely their mythic repetition? As Fredric Jameson has said in another context, "we cannot be content with a merely negative account of the whole Enlightenment demolition programme, but must also attempt to convey what 'positively' was set in place in the moment of desacralization."[8] Even more to the point, one might ask to what extent have these older discredited modes of thought survived or been sublated into the post-Enlightenment era, in a kind of syncretic or hybrid modernity that is particularly attractive to the Caribbean historical imagination.

Kant stresses that this so-called immaturity is not an intellectual one, but rather "spiritual," due more to laziness and pusillanimity than to a deficiency of intellectual capacity. (Not coincidentally, laziness and cowardice are also keywords Kant uses to characterize people living outside of Europe.) As I hope to show, when Kant's prescription is read through the lens of the modern Caribbean historical imagination, a series of structural paradoxes emerges that effectively "trap" the modern Caribbean writer in a series of binary relationships such as center/periphery, master/slave, leaders/masses. These binary traps reemerge in these writers like a tenacious return of the repressed, undermining their efforts to articulate an escape route; at the same time, this structural situation provides a matrix within which some of the Caribbean's most creative writing and historical reflection have taken place.

The discernment of the emergence of these antinomies in the Caribbean historical imagination is not intended, however, to reduce the complexity of Enlightenment thought in general to a reductive series of binary relations. In a fascinating observation, Slavoj Žižek remarks that underlying the thinking of both Kant and Descartes is the uninterrogated and unreflective acceptance of societal custom as a given authority, an irrational but necessary guarantor of the conditions for rational thought:

> "Reason about whatever you want and as much as you want—but *obey*!" That is to say: as the autonomous subject of theoretical reflection, addressing the enlightened public, you can think freely, you can question all authority; but as part of the social "machine," as a subject in the other meaning of the word, you must obey unconditionally the orders of your superiors.[9]

For Žižek, the unreflective continuity of social conventions and customs is the "obverse" of Enlightenment rationality. He also observes this intertia functioning as a "fissure" in Descartes' cogito: in the *Discourse on Method*, Descartes specifically names "customs and laws of the country" as a "first rule" that must be obeyed without question.[10] Now, it is precisely this kind of internal contradiction, this "obverse of Enlightenment," that writing from the Caribbean will expose and explode as outright paradoxes and incommensurabilities. I argue that a generation of modern Caribbean writers, represented primarily here by C. L. R. James, Alejo Carpentier, and Marie Chauvet, are cognizant of the Enlightenment's "collective unconscious" (so to speak) and strive to bring it to the surface in order to expose the internal contradictions. But at the same time, these writers also engage the Enlightenment on its own terms, both in their manner of representing history as well as in the ideological underpinnings of their critique of the Enlightenment. They therefore perform the oscillating gesture of exposing to the light of day the Enlightenment's dark side while simultaneously or subsequently repressing it anew. As I will show, a more recent generation of Caribbean writers, represented here by Maryse Condé, Reinaldo Arenas, and Edgardo Rodríguez Juliá, building on the foundations of Caribbean modernity as articulated by James, Carpentier, Chauvet, and others, also write in a historical vein in an attempt to extricate themselves even further from Enlightenment paradigms. It might be said that nothing describes with more precision the impetus of Reinaldo Arenas's and Edgardo Rodríguez Juliá's historical fiction than the term "Enlightenment's obverse" since they posit societal irrationality, and especially the irrationality of the eighteenth-century Caribbean (and, for Arenas, by allegorical extension, Cuba in the 1960s) as the prominent backdrop that precludes the possibility of rational thought. For both Arenas and Rodríguez Juliá, who might be described as postmodern or post-Carpenterian writers, this "obverse" is tantamount to a full inversion, with the irrational occupying center stage and "rational thought" receding to the background.

For Louis Sala-Molins, another articulation of the "obverse of the Enlightenment"—the blind acceptance of the conditions of contemporaneous social custom as a necessary milieu within which even radical thought might take place—was condensed for the French Enlightenment in the figure of the black slave in the Caribbean. In a rhetorically charged critique that is in some ways strikingly similar to the strategies employed by Caribbean writers, Sala-Molins approaches the Enlightenment in a diametrically opposed manner from Muthu. By placing the question of slavery at its core, Sala-Molins exposes the Enlightenment's incommensurabilities. In an essay on one of the most progressive of the *philosophes*, Condorcet, whose *Réflexions sur l'esclavage des nègres* advocated a gradual phasing out of slavery, Sala-Molins flourishes: "The rhetoric of the Enlightenment and the Revolution is worth absolutely nothing when judged against the only reality that matters: the master is guilty, the slave trade is a crime, slavery is the crime of all crimes: let's do away with it! Do away with it? Wait a moment!"[11] Why wait? Because slavery had so infiltrated the economic and institutional foundations of eighteenth-century Europe that its sudden disappearance was inconceivable even for those thinkers daring enough to envisage abolition: "Raynal was a court favorite, while Diderot enjoyed a pension from a shipping company involved in trade—who knows what kind?—between Africa, the Caribbean, and France."[12] In chapter 2, I discuss how at crucial moments during the Haitian Revolution Toussaint L'Ouverture hesitated—a gesture that C. L. R. James reenacts in his famous text *The Black Jacobins*. Sala-Molins lays bare how these hesitations are structurally endemic to Enlightenment thought. "Societal custom" may be the unconscious, irrational, and unreflective backdrop against which the thought of the Enlightenment unfolds, but when that backdrop is nothing more or less than the institution of slavery, the machinery of the Enlightenment breaks down under the weight of its internal contradictions. Sala-Molins: "To interpret the Enlightenment without them [the "Negro" slaves] is to play the game of the Enlightenment: it is tantamount to limiting universal philanthropy to one's little neighborhood."[13] Regarding this quotation, Nick Nesbitt asserts that Sala-Molins, while claiming to critique the Enlightenment from the point of the view of the slaves, in fact "ventriloquizes" them and is overly concerned with "the white European thinkers of the Enlightenment."[14] But this criticism is also an apt description of the general Enlightenment "trap," at least from the point of view of the Caribbean writers I discuss. Because of the ways in which its episteme is articulated, the Enlightenment machinery of representing others remains a ventriloquism. This is particularly evident in Carpentier's representation of the slave Ti Noël in *The Kingdom of This World* as well as in C. L. R. James's problematic evocation of "the masses" in *The Black Jacobins*.

Part of the crux of the Enlightenment problem lies, therefore, in who and what qualifies as a person and what precisely are the Enlightenment "rules" for representing her. These questions lead us back to Kant's *Aufklärung* essay. The word translated as "man" or "mankind" is *Menschheit*. Foucault asks: "Are we to understand that the entire human race is caught up in the process of Enlightenment? In that case, we must imagine Enlightenment as a historical change that affects the political and social existence of all people on the face of the earth."[15] Kant describes Enlightenment as humanity's emergence from or coming out of a state of extended immaturity into one in which it will be able to think for itself, "without the guidance of another." Is this de- or pre-scription (for Kant, *Aufklärung* is somewhere between a state of things and a becoming) to be a purely spontaneous movement on the part of multitudinous individuals or populations, or can it be disseminated, bestowed, enforced? This "emergence" of these "men" is vague, begs the question of the subject, since in the imperialistic and colonizing practices of the so-called enlightened nations of Europe, people from other continents were deemed to be in need of guidance in order to think for themselves. In the case of Latin America and the Caribbean at the end of the eighteenth century, this dynamic between enlightened and unenlightened echoes, even in its use of the metaphor of light, the Christianizing mission of the conquistadores and colonizers of the three prior centuries. Todorov, too, discerns this parallelism: "The Spanish and Portuguese colonists of the sixteenth century acted in the same way when, to justify their conquests, they invoked the need to expand the Christian religion."[16] Todorov asserts this parallel between the Enlightenment colonialism and the Iberian conquest of America in order to demonstrate that in both cases, the colonizers and conquistadores used the reigning philosophies of the day as "alibis," or *détournements*, to justify their brutal acts. And yet if we observe closely what some of the *philosophes* had to say about race and conquest, there can be little doubt that many of them laid the epistemological groundwork for the colonial activities from the eighteenth to the twentieth century.

Sankar Muthu argues that when Kant refers to "people" (*Humanität, Menschheit*), he is speaking about reasoning, cultural beings and by extension every person living on the face of the earth: he quotes Kant's assertion of our "equality with all rational beings, whatever their rank" as a foundation of "humanitarian moral sensibility."[17] Nick Nesbitt also makes the case that, despite some of Kant's unfortunate remarks about slavery and his reactionary view of revolution, slavery and imperialism were entirely antithetical to Kant's systematic understanding of what qualifies as a person: "Kant repeatedly construed his conception of universal moral reason as applicable to *all* reasoning beings. . . . In an age where Europeans increasingly came to define Africans as bestial Others, Kant reversed this order of attribution."[18] For Nesbitt, Kant characterizes freedom as an essential trait of all reasoning beings, a first principle, and not something derived from empirical criteria. Slavery, therefore, would be anathema to Kant's systematic understanding of human beings. For Muthu, this understanding of "humanity encompasses Kant's entire philosophical worldview."[19]

And yet despite this interpretation of Kant's expanding view of humanity and the convincing demonstration of the anti-imperialist and antislavery verve in his thought, it is not at all clear that when Kant employs the term *Menschheit* in the Enlightenment essay, he is including people of other races living outside of Europe. More importantly for the purposes of this study, the writers I discuss have a skeptical view about the relationship between Caribbean subjectivity and the capaciousness of Enlightenment categories. And yet much of the history of the Caribbean in the seventeenth and eighteenth centuries could be characterized by slave rebellions and the formation of autonomous societies (*palenques*) of runway slaves or maroons (*cimarrones*). What could be a greater example of Enlightenment, or a refusal to accept arbitrarily someone else's authority? As we shall see, this is precisely how C. L. R. James interprets the Haitian Revolution (1791–1804), a globally seismic event that began only seven years after the publication of Kant's essay. And yet the historians and theoreticians of European modernity, including those both contemporaneous to the events at the dawning of the nineteenth century as well as twentieth-century intellectuals—as Sibylle Fischer has demonstrated in her book that explores the cultural and ideological reverberations of the Haitian Revolution throughout the Caribbean in the nineteenth century—have generally reacted to the Haitian Revolution not as a manifestation of Enlightenment but as an aberration generating silence. While perhaps it is not surprising that, among Creole and European contemporaries of the ousting of the French from their wealthiest colony, "there was a consensus . . . that Haiti was not a commendable model of emancipation," as Fischer expresses it,[20] it is harder to explain away the fact that even in recent interventions in European historiography and philosophy, the events in the Caribbean at the end of the eighteenth century and slavery in general are interpreted as excess or disturbance and not as something particularly noteworthy in the general trajectory of modernity.[21]

Susan Buck-Morss proclaims authoritatively, though perhaps too categorically: "The Haitian Revolution was the crucible, the trial by fire for the ideals of the French Enlightenment. And every European who was part of the bourgeois reading public knew it."[22] If so, there were too many internal conflicts preventing this "knowledge" from assuming a conscious form. And too often when it did, the slaves themselves were unwittingly recruited, to echo David Scott's language, into the cause of these ideals, and often to their detriment. The multifaceted implications of this dynamic form a cornerstone of the Caribbean historical imagination.

Fischer's apparently unassuming quote from C. L. R. James—"slaves have always wanted to be free" [23]—underscores a somewhat Hegelian paradox: on rhetorical, material, and ideological levels (as "obverse" or foil) slavery was necessary for the Enlightenment's unfolding; but the slaves themselves never needed (*pace* Nick Nesbitt)[24] Kant, Condorcet, Diderot, or Raynal to envisage or articulate their own desire to be free. This differend or noncorrespondence is an irony that is not lost upon the Caribbean writers I discuss. In a vignette the emblematic nature of which is such that I have numerous occasions to refer back to it, Carpentier depicts the old slave Ti Noël seated upon several volumes of the *Encyclopédie* eating sugarcane, an ironic image of casual, noncausal contiguity.

Fischer's precursor in discerning the general silence and discursive erasure regarding the Haitian Revolution was Michel-Rolph Trouillot, whose *Silencing the Past* posits the revolution as an event for which the Occidental world had no prepared epistemological categories to comprehend. That slaves of African descent could mobilize into an armed revolutionary force capable of defeating Europe's greatest military forces was simply inconceivable, unthinkable, an absurdity. "The Haitian Revolution thus entered history with the peculiar characteristic of being unthinkable even as it happened."[25] And yet, if we tend intuitively to be more tolerant toward the silence of the past while condemning more harshly that of the present, since we naturally expect those in our day and age to know better, Susan Buck-Morss ingeniously reverses this intuition: "But there is a danger in conflating two silences, the past and the present one, when it comes to the Haitian story. For if men and women in the eighteenth century did not think in nonracial terms of the 'fundamental equality of humanity,' as 'some of us do today,' at least they knew what was happening; today, when the Haitian slave revolution might be more thinkable, it is more invisible, due to the construction of disciplinary discourses through which knowledge of the past has been inherited."[26] Buck-Morss's well-known thesis is that of course "Hegel knew"—knew about the slave rebellion in the French colony of Saint Domingue, knew precisely what modern plantation slavery was, and understood the historical implications of the founding of an independent Haitian nation. And yet despite this knowledge, Hegel, in Buck Morss's words, conceded to the continuation of the slave trade and, though attempting to enhance his knowledge about Africa after 1820, Hegel was in fact "becoming dumber."[27] As though to complete an articulation of a universal history, which is in fact nothing more than an extension of European variety, Hegel elaborates on why in fact it does not include America: "Regarding America, especially Mexico or Peru, and its degree of civilization, our information indicates that its culture expires the moment the Spirit draws near. . . . The inferiority of these individuals in every respect is entirely evident."[28]

The pattern emerges in both Kant and Hegel that though the belief in human emancipation from oppression is expressed abstractly and philosophically, an irreconcilable expression of European racial superiority and African inferiority persists in their concrete language. Though Trouillot does not mention Kant's essay and the ambiguity surrounding the word *Menschheit*, he does discuss the Enlightenment context in which the philosophes, the French assembly, and other European powers were not entirely sure what a "man" was: "A French memoir of 1790 summarized the issue: 'It is perhaps not impossible to civilize the Negro, to bring him to principles and make a man out of him: there would be more to gain than to buy and sell him.'"[29]

The thorny questions of precisely what Kant (and, by extension, the Enlightenment) meant by "people" and the nature of his thought regarding race, slavery, colonialism, and imperialism are emblematic of the unsettled legacy of the Enlightenment right up to the present moment. Even a cursory glance at the pendular swings of interpretation concerning these questions might leave the student of intellectual history bewildered, to say the least. On the one hand, Emmanuel Chukwudi Eze is right to point out that "when writings on race by the major Enlightenment figures have been noted in traditional scholarship, it is often to dismiss them as journalistic, or as having little that would be of serious philosophical interest. While some of the works are dismissed as popular, or recreational, others resilient to such convenient dismissal are interpreted as 'cast in an ironic tone.'"[30] On the other hand, one might object that Eze's approach—assembling in one volume the abundant damning references to race made by Enlightenment thinkers—might also lend itself to misinterpretation, since these isolated fragments can account for neither context (both the larger work from which they were extracted as well as the contemporaneous debates and notions about race) nor the evolution of an individual thinker's body of work over time. This is partially the line of defense employed by both Muthu and Nesbitt in their attempt to rehabilitate the philosopher from Königsburg.

For Kant, as we have seen, unenlightened immaturity is characterized by laziness and cowardice, and, in his explicit declarations on these matters, these are the two qualities that he attributes to Europe's outsiders. If Enrique Dussel asks: "Ought one to consider an African in Africa or a slave in the United States in the eighteenth century to be culpably immature? What about an indigenous person in Mexico or a Latin American mestizo at a later period?"[31] Kant, in *Physical Geography*, points to the "Indian" and the "Negro" as the prime examples of "cowardliness" and "laziness," and seems to give a direct answer to Dussel's question:

> All inhabitants of the hottest zones are exceptionally lethargic. . . . Indians are also very indecisive. . . . The weakening of their limbs is supposedly caused by brandy, tobacco, opium, and other strong things. . . . Montesquieu is correct in his judgment that the weakheartedness that makes death so terrifying to the Indian or the Negro also makes him fear many things other than death that the European can withstand.[32]

Or, if there were any doubt about Kant's classifications:

> Humanity is at its greatest perfection in the race of the whites. The yellow Indians do have a meagre talent. The Negroes are far below them and at the lowest point are a part of the American peoples.[33]

While attempting to provide a blueprint for autonomy, Kant at the same time epitomizes the "Negro" as cowardly and as embodying the antithesis of Enlightenment. As opposed to the "lethargy" and "cowardice" of Africans and Native Americans, the "white" race for Kant is upheld as the embodiment of temperance, intelligence, restraint, even beauty: "The inhabitant of the temperate parts of the world, above all the central part, has a more beautiful body, works harder, is more jocular, more controlled in his passions, more intelligent than any other race of people in the world. That is why at all points in time these peoples have educated the others and controlled them with weapons."[34] While the Enlightenment was actually something fragmented and contradictory rather than consolidated and monolithic, many of the primary philosophical players of the Enlightenment betray a surprising solidarity in their opinions on race. In fact, as Kant's reference to Montesquieu attests, there is even a kind of incestuous cross-referencing—something Eze, somewhat tongue-in-cheek, refers to as "intertextuality"[35]—among Kant, Diderot, Hume, Jefferson, and others to support their mutual opinions on race. These opinions regarding those living outside of Europe became a kind of pseudoscientific "fact" once they found the mutual support of these authoritative voices, and we are one step away from an outright imperialist program. Trouillot points out, "By the time of the American Revolution, scientific racism, whose rise many historians wrongly attribute to the nineteenth century, was already a feature of the ideological landscape of the Enlightenment on both sides of the Atlantic."[36] In "Idea for a Universal History," Kant posits Greek history as subsuming and "authenticating" other prior or contemporary histories. Following the Greeks, of course, came

> *Rome*, then the "*Barbarians* who in turn destroyed it, and if we finally add the political history of other peoples *episodically*, in so far as knowledge of them has come down to us through these enlightened nations, we shall discover a regular process of improvement in the political constitutions of our continent *which will probably legislate eventually for all other continents.*[37]

For Muthu, Kant's pronouncement on the imperial destiny of Europe is not so much a colonialist judgment as a Cassandrian prophecy. If the Occidental notion of history (starting with the Greeks) subsumes all others, and in fact the European continent is destined to "legislate" for all others, where is the space for the other continents to "emerge" from immaturity? How do we reconcile Kant's *in flagrante delicto* statements regarding race and ethnocentrism with the views of Muthu, who meticulously demonstrates that Kant "defends the right of peoples to order their collective lives as they see fit, and thus he explicitly defends the rationality and freedom (the cultural agency, and thus the fundamental humanity) of nomadic and pastoral people in the course of attacking European imperialism"?[38] Muthu minimizes, though does not entirely dismiss, Kant's declarations on race as an appropriation of David Hume's notoriously racist statements regarding people of African descent.[39] He identifies those texts of Kant's that express a disparaging opinion of people living outside of Europe as belonging to his early lectures, which are informed by climate-based notions of racial difference. During the latter stages of Kant's production, Muthu argues, Kant abandons the climate-based views in favor of an understanding of humanity as cultural agency and reasoned being, which in turn permits him to articulate an anti-imperialist thought. In none of Kant's later works does he reiterate his earlier views on race and moreover "vehemently attacked European empires and conquest." One of the most interesting aspects of this anti-imperial critique, from the Caribbean perspective, is Kant's rebuttal to John Locke regarding the nature of land ownership. For Locke, only those who exploited the land agriculturally could rightfully claim ownership, providing ready-made justification for European imperial practices. Kant bolsters his anti-imperialist credentials by rigorously opposing this view, asking, "In order to acquire land is it necessary to develop it (build on it, cultivate it, drain it, and so on)?" His response is an unequivocal "No." Despite the fact that the question and answer can be read ambiguously (as either a condemnation or a defense of imperialistic land acquisition), Muthu (and Nesbitt) make a compelling case not only to defend Kant against the charges of racism but to portray him as a full-fledged anti-imperialist advocate. And yet it would all be that much more convincing were we to find in Kant's anti-imperialist thought an explicit repudiation in equally concrete terms of the language of racial inferiority with which he had at one time characterized non-Europeans. For even when Kant does unequivocally denounce the practices that led to the acquisition and colonizing of the lands belonging to the "American Indians" and the "Hottentots," he still mentions that these actions were unjust despite "our superiority" (188).[40] This disjunction between the concrete language of racial inferiority in tandem with the *abstract* expression of human freedom is one of the fundamental characteristics of the Enlightenment that Caribbean writers exploit in the deployment of their historical imagination.

It seems to me that whether or not a particular Enlightenment thinker can be seen as progressive or reactionary regarding questions of race, imperialism, and colonialism, the dynamic that emerges is that the center constitutes itself as such, as enlightened civilization, precisely through a differentiating mechanism that hinges on a periphery that must embody the general qualities of "immaturity" that inform unenlightened barbarism. For the Caribbean writers I discuss in this book, this dynamic results in a representational "structure" that defines and defies the limits and excesses of the historical imagination.

Walter Benjamin's once surprising thesis on the philosophy of history—that each document of civilization is at the same time one of barbarism—from the perspective of the Caribbean now seems axiomatic. In the structural relationship between European Enlightenment and Latin America and the Caribbean, the former laid the epistemological foundation for declaring itself center while subsequently relegating the latter to periphery. This Ptolemaic relationship has haunted the question of modernity in Latin America and the Caribbean and is the bête noire of many of the writers discussed in this study. If the Enlightenment upheld the periphery as the embodiment of unenlightened immaturity, it relied on such a differentiation for its own identity as enlightened center. This reliance assured that the periphery would be kept in a prolonged state of tutelage, or enforced dependence. The discursive vicious circle in which the periphery was placed was scripted in the following fashion: "You are unenlightened and therefore incapable of autonomy; how can you make claims to enlightenment without being autonomous?" This was the ideological groundwork for Kant's prediction that Europe would legislate for the other continents. This structural knot of the Enlightenment with Latin American and the Caribbean forms the context or point of departure from which modern Caribbean writers will approach the idea of the Enlightenment in the Caribbean. The challenge or vocational call of their writing can be described as a Caribbean intervention in and critique of the discourse of Enlightenment, which at the same time attempts to salvage or reconstitute a Caribbean subjectivity.

The Enlightenment in the Caribbean and Latin America

María Ángeles Eugenio Martínez points out three disparate phases of the Enlightenment in Ibero-America in the eighteenth century: the first is far more Hispanic than French, notable for the influence of the Benedictine ilustrado Benito Jerónimo Feijóo and the persistence of the scholastic method in colonial universities. In this timid expression of Enlightenment thought, ideas of progress, the scientific method, and the supremacy of reason commingled with traditional notions of religious faith. And yet these strange bedfellows came to blows in a second phase, in which the Bourbon reforms of Carlos III aimed at diminishing the power and influence of the church, culminating in the expulsion of the Jesuits from the Spanish holdings in America. It was not until the third phase, though, in the final decade of the eighteenth century, that the more revolutionary ideas of the French encyclopedists and Jacobins, emanating directly from France or indirectly through Spain or the French colonies, impacted Spanish America.[41] It is certainly this final phase, with its epicenter of the Haitian Revolution, that will have an immediate impact on Caribbean civilization and the unfolding of its culture, politics, and demographics and that will prove most attractive to modern writers such as Alejo Carpentier and C. L. R. James.

The Enlightenment in Latin America and the Caribbean has alternately been interpreted as a lack or failure, or, inversely, as an entirely successful diffusion or extension of the European variety. Part of the so-called "leyenda negra" was to suggest that there was *no* Enlightenment in either Spain or Spanish America, where an Inquisitional mentality reigned well into the nineteenth century. The historian Ronald W. Harris represents this point of view: "In Spain alone in western Europe did the Catholic faith keep the irreligion of Enlightenment at bay."[42] Even Octavio Paz, one of the most authoritative voices in Latin American letters, overstates the lack of the Enlightenment in Latin America. In *Los hijos del limo*, Paz observes that the Enlightenment in Spain was an ineffective imitation of the "authentic" French variety and provided insufficient reform of Spain's outdated institutions: "[T]he two nations that began the epoch of expansion, Spain and Portugal, soon were relegated to the margin of capitalist development and did not participate in the movement of the Enlightenment."[43] For Paz, Latin America was even further removed from the influence and benefits of European Enlightenment; he refers to it as "a reflection of a reflection."

Taking an opposing point of view, Germán Arciniegas argues that among the European nations embracing the Enlightenment, "if there was one nation that could greet these happenings with the youthful enthusiasm accorded a revolution, that was the Spain of the eighteenth century."[44] So whereas Octavio Paz sees an already weak or practically nonexistent movement of the Enlightenment diluted even further in the American colonies, Arciniegas discerns an opposite paradigm, wherein an enthusiastic reception of the Enlightenment in Spain gathered intensity in the Americas: "America had become the university of the world."[45]

The essays comprising *Latin America and the Enlightenment*, edited by Arthur Whitaker, also attempt to overturn the commonly held view that there was no Enlightenment in Latin America. Roland Hussey attributes the origins of the "no Enlightenment" thesis to a statement ascribed to the so-called enlightened despot Carlos IV, that "it is not fitting to have Enlightenment generally in America."[46] It is true that the Inquisition—in all senses the very antithesis of the Enlightenment—was still a force to be reckoned with in the eighteenth century. Ronald Harris asserts that Carlos III tolerated the Inquisition because it was not in conflict with the power of the king, and cites the Bourbon monarch as saying, "The Spaniards want it, and it does not bother me."[47] Hussey observes that "the Index of 1790 prohibited the works, or the important part of the works, of Bayle, Bossuet, Brisson, Brissot de Warville, Burlamaqui, Diderot, the Encylopédie, Helvetius, Holbach, La Fontaine, Marmontel, Montaigne, Raynal, Rousseau, and Voltaire. It laid restrictions upon Bodin, Bayle, Condillac, Jansen, and Moreri's *Dictionnaire*."[48] And yet, despite these restrictions, there is abundant evidence from personal libraries and correspondences of the period that many of these works or the ideas contained in them circulated in colonial Latin America rather freely. Hussey notes: "Officials, merchants, emigrants, and scientists went constantly from Spain or Portugal to America and Americans as constantly visited the Peninsula, and often France and other parts of Europe. . . . Ideas were ineradicably carried in migrating heads, and scientific apparatus and books made part of many men's baggage to America."[49] Arciniegas identifies some of the ships that "entered Spanish ports loaded with chocolate and sailed back to America carrying books by Montaigne, Voltaire and Rousseau."[50]

For the purposes of this study, it is worth observing that the names of these restricted authors often frequent the historical imagination of many modern Caribbean writers: Rousseau inhabits the pages of Carpentier's novel *The Kingdom of This World*; since the earliest accounts of Toussaint L'Ouverture's biography, Abbé Raynal has been considered a determining influence on Haiti's founding father; Bossuet's sermons resonate in Marie Chauvet's *Dance on the Volcano*. According to Michel-Rolph Trouillot, Denis Diderot, more than a collaborator, was a veritable ghost writer of Abbé Raynal's *L'Histoire des deux Indes*, wherein appear the famous passages about the "Black Spartacus," the "courageous chief" awaited by the black masses of the West Indies to deliver them from bondage. According to legend, hammered home by C. L. R. James, Toussaint L'Ouverture "read and reread" these passages, though Trouillot casts doubt on the historical veracity of the assertion.[51]

But as Sibylle Fischer shows, it was not just a question of the dissemination of the ideas of the *philosophes* in the Caribbean; the specter of the Haitian Revolution also lingered on in neighboring lands well into the nineteenth century. José Antonio Aponte was arrested in 1812 and accused of spearheading a conspiracy to overthrow slavery in Cuba. Part of the evidence used to inculpate Ponte was the fact that among the possessions found on his person "were portraits of Toussaint L'Ouverture, Henri Christophe and Dessalines,"[52] the heroes and "founding fathers" of the Haitian Revolution. Moreover, there is an interesting parallel in this episode: just as the French and Haitian revolutions are connected through a complex web of material and ideological links, Fischer points out that the Aponte affair came about as a result of rumors in Cuba that the Cortes of Cádiz, perhaps the most enlightened nineteenth-century institution in Spain, had abolished slavery.

Despite the resonance of the Enlightenment figures and thought in the Caribbean historical imagination, the refutation of the "no Enlightenment in Latin America" thesis often amounts to a mere litany of names and publications. While *Latin America and the Enlightenment* and, to a lesser extent, Arciniegas fail to define or critique the Enlightenment sufficiently to make it clear whether or not Latin America ever "had" it, nor do they go so far as to explore the institutional, social, economic, and epistemological transformations that would support the thesis that the Enlightenment "happened" there, the compilation of titles and names associated with the Enlightenment, plus the association of these names with changes in university curricula (Bacon, Locke, Gassendi, Descartes, Newton, and Condillac were standard texts in Spanish universities by 1769–87)[53] is enough to cast doubt on the sweeping nature of Paz's remarks about the total lack of the Enlightenment in Latin America. And yet the opposing thesis, that Latin America and the Caribbean fully partook of the universal movement of the Enlightenment, neglects to take into account the structural dynamic of center and periphery, along with its attendant differentiating mechanism, that makes the Enlightenment's "clean" exportation from the former to the latter problematic. A posterior essay by Whitaker attempts to document the changing (and unchanging) views of the Enlightenment in Latin America;[54] he takes note, for example, of the conflicting interpretations of the wars of independence as either a reaction against or a product of the Enlightenment—but the author does not waver in his generally uncritical view of the Enlightenment itself as an active and positive force in Latin America and the Caribbean. The same could be said to characterize an essay by Arciniegas, who sees a direct link between Rousseau (and especially *The Social Contract*) and the independence movements in Latin America at the beginning of the nineteenth century. For example, Arciniegas describes Bolívar as "a character that comes out of the pages of Rousseau, a revolutionary, an ideologue. His point of departure is the *Encyclopédie*, in France."[55]

Paz, in contrast, comments in greater detail in *The Labyrinth of Solitude* on the so-called "failure" of the Enlightenment in Latin America and echoes a similar thesis by Harris:

> The reforms undertaken by the Bourbon dynasty, especially by Charles III (1759–88), improved the economy and made business operations more efficient, but they accentuated the centralization of administrative functions and changed New Spain into a true colony, that is, into a territory subject to systematic exploitation and strictly controlled by the center of power. . . . The Bourbons transformed New Spain from a vassal kingdom to a mere overseas territory. . . . The impulse given to scientific investigation, the development of humanism, the construction of monumental public works, even the good government of various Viceroys, were not enough to reanimate colonial society. The colony, like the metropolis itself, was now only a form, and empty body.[56]

Paz's analysis is more penetrating here than in the prior quotations; his observations are a sobering response to those who enthusiastically enumerate the abundance of texts and names associated with the Enlightenment in Latin America, like Whitaker and Arciniegas, but who do not go so far as to question why the concurrent material and political benefits failed to appear in the wake of all this intellectual and institutional reform, which is, in part, the essence of the "problem" of modernity in Latin America. This psychological compensation has been pointed out by John Beverly in similar context, wherein the modern literary developments in Latin American history have been overvalorized in an attempt to compensate for the less spectacular achievements in social, economic, and institutional aspects of modernity.[57]

But at the same time, it is important to point out that this "failure," left unhistoricized, fallaciously connotes an ontology. Dependency theory is only one among many discourses that note the active role of the developed nations, the birthplaces of the Enlightenment, in maintaining the periphery as both "unenlightened" and underdeveloped. This is one of the most fundamental features of the structure of the Enlightenment. And yet Paz does not go so far as to actually critique this aspect of Enlightenment itself; he seems rather to embrace it as something desired though unachieved for Latin America. In other words, Paz seems to loosely buy into a triumphalist philosophy that can envisage no other notion of social well-being than the Western European variety—a philosophy that can hardly be complementary to the Caribbean, and that many of the cultural practitioners of the region are eager to revise. One of Paz's precursors on this score is Edmundo O'Gorman, who was a pioneer in discerning the "invented" (rather than "discovered") nature of Latin America reality, but, in a surprise ending of his seminal *La invención de América*, applauds the historical denouement or *telos* of this "invention": "[A]mongst all the life projects that have been imagined and attempted throughout universal history, this program [of 'Ecumenical Occidental Culture'] is the only one with a real possibility of congregating all the peoples of the earth together under the sign of freedom."[58] In the apocalyptic final paragraphs, O'Gorman suggests that the Occidental notion of liberty is desirable even if we must run the risk of "nuclear holocaust" to achieve it.

When Paz speaks about Enlightenment as something monolithic and homogeneous, as something that "didn't happen" in Spain, and that should have, he commits a more subtle fallacy. Whatever the Enlightenment may have been, it was most certainly something fragmented, heterogeneous, and conflicted, represented not only by Rousseau and the *Declaration des droits de l'homme* but by Sade and the Code Noir[59] as well, characterized both by revolution and reaction, republicanism and monarchy, reform and corruption. This discrepancy—between those who treat the Enlightenment not unlike Paz, as a coherent historical embodiment, and those who acknowledge its basically heterogeneous and fragmented nature—is echoed in the two phases of the Caribbean historical imagination that I discuss in this book: modern authors, who, though they may assail or critique Enlightenment tenets, are playing on the Enlightenment's "turf," so to speak, and a younger, postmodern generation of Caribbean writers for whom the categories of Enlightenment thought have already been partially dismantled, largely in thanks to the work of their predecessors.

The Historical Imagination in the Caribbean

Despite the historical contextualization of the Enlightenment in the Caribbean and Latin America, the precise focus of this book is not strictly historical. Rather, by interrogating the modes of representation that many modern Caribbean writers have employed to articulate their vision of the Enlightenment in the Caribbean (and of the Caribbean in the Enlightenment), I hope to call into question the relationship between our understanding of history itself and the way that it is—consciously or unconsciously—underwritten by the rules of causality and historical unfolding that we have interpreted from the Enlightenment. Awareness of this condition, which is yet another articulation of the paradoxes of modernity in the Caribbean, greatly complicates the best-intentioned decision to seek out "other histories" that would ideally be free from the grasp of a Eurocentric understanding the world. Yes, it is true that "Caribbean writers cannot adopt the history and culture of European modernism . . . but neither can they escape from it because it has overdetermined Caribbean cultures in many ways,"[60] as Simon Gikandi has expressed it; nevertheless, it is also worth stressing that the Caribbean, along with other cultures on the periphery of Europe, have also contributed in their own right to underdetermining, so to speak, modern and postmodern metropolitan culture.

Germán Arciniegas argues, in what seems like a blueprint for Alejo Carpentier's historical imagination, "The Caribbean was the first place where the old ideas, the vested interests, came into conflict with American ambitions, the theories of illuminism [i.e., the Enlightenment], enlightened despotism and the desire for independence."[61] Though in this introduction I have been using the terms "Latin America" and "the Caribbean" in tandem, Arciniegas's observation about the historical primacy of the Caribbean in America's collision with the Enlightenment helps clarify my categorical focus on the Caribbean and its historical imagination. The Caribbean encounter with the Enlightenment provides a provisional template for understanding the ways the "Age of Revolution" would later reverberate throughout Latin America.

This study constellates modern Caribbean writers who represent the origins of this situation: the encounter between, on the one hand, European rationalism, Enlightenment, and the "Age of Revolution," and, on the other hand, an evolving autonomous Caribbean society that had already begun to emerge with its own features, including social organization, spiritual practices, and historical consciousness in the Caribbean by the eighteenth century. If the kind of modern historical writing about the eighteenth century I am asserting can be considered a subgenre of Caribbean literature, then surely one of the founders is the great Cuban novelist Alejo Carpentier (1904–1980). Among the many contradictions of Carpentier's life and work[62] is the fact that this self-proclaimed practitioner of the baroque and anti-Cartesian seemed preoccupied with the century of Enlightenment, depicting the Caribbean in the eighteenth century in *Explosion in a Cathedral* (*El siglo de las luces*), *The Kingdom of This World* (*El reino de este mundo*), and *Baroque Concert* (*Concierto barroco*). It was through the example of Carpentier that I became aware of this kind of writing about the late eighteenth and early nineteenth centuries in the Caribbean, of the correlation between the French Revolution and the burgeoning movements of Latin American independence, as a kind of topos of Caribbean historical writing in general.[63] In addition to Carpentier, the other Caribbean writers I discuss who have embarked on this theme are C. L. R. James (Trinidad), Marie Chauvet (Haiti), and, more recently, Maryse Condé (Guadeloupe), Edgardo Rodríguez Juliá (Puerto Rico), and Reinaldo Arenas (Cuba). By grouping these writers together under the rubric of this study, I hope to extract from each case a particular interpretation of the Enlightenment and its relevance to and impact on the Caribbean. It is my contention that a first group of writers, including Carpentier, James, and Chauvet, have as their point of departure a response or rebuttal to the center/periphery dynamic discussed above. These writers may attempt to articulate this relationship in different ways, or draw different conclusions from it. Carpentier, for example, sees the Caribbean as testing ground for the Enlightenment that exposes the failure of the latter. For C. L. R. James and Marie Chauvet, the Caribbean and specifically the Haitian Revolution represent a victory of the Enlightenment values in the Caribbean that have been betrayed in Europe. And yet, despite these writers' attempts to circumscribe a Caribbean autonomous subjectivity, this attempt is in the final instance thwarted, in a kind of return of the repressed, by that original historical structure that posits Europe as the central matrix within which the tenets of Enlightenment came about, and the Caribbean as receiving periphery, poised as it may be to accept, modify, or reject the imported ideologies.

Another notable effect of this structural rapport with the Enlightenment is its treatment as a discernible, coherent body of thought in the first place. Not only does the second group of writers—Condé, Rodríguez Juliá, Arenas—call into question the originary center/periphery structure that characterizes the Enlightenment in the Caribbean, they also, by the very virtue of this decentering, expose the fallacy of a monolithic Enlightenment and European modernity in general for the Caribbean. This being the case, the center/periphery structure can no longer hold, and the historical novelist is free to reinterpret and recast the historical detritus from both Europe and the Caribbean in a kind of phantasmagoric historico-fictional space. This alternative hinges on the negation from the outset of the center/periphery dynamic. In its place, these writers attempt a reconstitution of Caribbean subjectivity in a way that does not involve an outright *rejection* of Enlightenment's tenets (which would still be an acknowledgment of the original dynamic), but rather acknowledges the historical influence and importance of the European Enlightenment and at the same time reinterprets the level of its causality to an evolving Caribbean subjectivity (as in the case of Maryse Condé) or as something transformed unrecognizably through a kind of baroque metamorphosis once exported into the Caribbean, where the very idea of historical subjectivity properly speaking is no longer applicable (Rodríguez Juliá). It may seem at times that I valorize the more recent generation of writers at the expense of their predecessors. But if it appears that the more recent generation of Caribbean writers has at least partially broken free from some of the ideological traps that entangled their elders, the fact remains that Carpentier, James, and, to a lesser extent, Chauvet were the pioneers and innovators. The contradictions stemming from the Enlightenment may infuse their writing, but they also supply a seminal moment for a foundational expression of the Caribbean historical imagination thanks to which their successors enjoy a more extravagant and unshackled view of history. It remains to be seen whether the younger generation of writers—who call into question the signifying structures of modern historical representation—embody a more progressive or conservative view of the Caribbean historical imagination.

Regarding the first group of writers (Carpentier, Chauvet, James), for whom there is a structural historical consciousness that involves a relationship of periphery to center, my task is to bring out the point of contact or mediation between the two structural poles. For Carpentier, I examine the role of music in his writing as a discursive figure that signifies and contains an incommensurability between Europe and the Caribbean, not only historically, but also for Carpentier personally in such a way that has major ramifications for his writing project. For Marie Chauvet, as for her protagonists, the understanding of the events leading up to the Haitian Revolution, and the role of the *affranchi* class reside in a certain undecidability, one that attempts to repress the historical linkage between, on the one hand, European art, music, and literature, and, on the other hand, slavery, racism, and colonialism. Chauvet's undecidability is embodied not only in the figure of her mulatto protagonists and their historical predicament in Saint Domingue, but also in the history of Saint Domingue's theater groups, whose memory Chauvet is attempting to revive. Artists, like mulattoes, had an ambiguous or intermediate social status: neither full citizens nor entirely subalterns or outcasts. Moreover, as Joan Dayan points out, the theater in eighteenth-century Saint Domingue was not only a venue for well-known European operas and bel canto. There increasingly appeared "local pieces" with an intended public of mixed racial heritage (which will figure in Chauvet's novel); and Moreau de Saint-Méry describes a public execution that was presented as theater in 1777.[64] Therefore, the social and racial complexities that plagued prerevolutionary Saint Domingue and its theater scene also infuse Chauvet's novel.

For C. L. R. James, it is perhaps no surprise that a certain faith in a liberational spirit arose from the Enlightenment—even if it was perhaps betrayed by those who originally articulated it. For James, it was this spirit that was exported and embodied in Haiti, in the figure of Toussaint L'Ouverture and his "Black Jacobins." And yet James avails himself, curiously, of one of the most ancient European literary notions, the *hamartia*, or tragic flaw, to frame the historical situation of Toussaint L'Ouverture for his readers, thus occasioning a series of textual contradictions that problematize his discursive and ideological aims.

With respect to Edgardo Rodríguez Juliá, Reinaldo Arenas, and Maryse Condé, the second (or "postmodern") group of writers I am positing, it is no longer a question of drawing out the point of mediation between center and periphery as a key to interpreting their texts since that is no longer the structure that underwrites the historicity of their writing. It is now a matter of a ludic reinvention of the historical self. For Rodríguez Juliá, this involves a parodic operation that insists on a radical indistinction between testimony, myth, and fiction, resulting in a kind of pastiche of history and identity. For Condé, in both *Tituba* and other novels such as *Segu* and *Crossing the Mangrove*, the Caribbean historical self finds its origins in Africa rather than Europe, especially with regard to medicine, community organization, and the interpretation of the visible. In Condé's dramatic text *In the Time of Revolution*, the question of the historical legacy of the Haitian and French Revolutions as well as Louis Delgrès's rebellion in Guadeloupe are explored. This text makes clear Condé's lineage with the earlier writers and establishes her as a transitional figure in the evolution of the Caribbean historical imagination.

For Reinaldo Arenas, a point of contact between his own historical vision and that of his eminent precursor Carpentier is a certain anxiety of influence resulting in a generational opposition that I attempt to locate in the Cartesian cogito. Since Arenas views Carpentier as an authoritarian figure of quasi-Cartesian dimensions (despite Carpentier's own misgivings about Cartesian rationality), his oppositional mode of self-expression takes the form of a gesture of antirationality.

It may seem that the two-tiered organization of this study bears an uncanny structural resemblance, especially given the themes and problematic that constitute its substance, to the historical and cultural dualism that we know as modernism and postmodernism. After all, if writers such as Carpentier, Chauvet, and James are locked into a dialectic or dialogue with the Enlightenment, which is commonly understood, and which the writers in question understand as the origins of modernity, the more recent generation of writers can justifiably be depicted as posterior to this engagement. Despite Octavio Paz's quip that the postmodern represents yet another *grand récit* imported into the region, the term does appear to appropriately describe the second group of authors discussed here. It is not merely a question of Latin America finding its own terms of periodization,[65] but rather a question of transforming the original conceptualizations and associations since the term "postmodern," used in this specific context, not only ties the Caribbean to a global cultural and historical situation, but also can take on its own level of specificity if we understand the dividing line between modern and postmodern in the Caribbean as the Cuban Revolution. In a very palpable sense, the historical libido (to borrow a term from Antonio Benítez-Rojo) that drives the writing of C. L. R. James in *The Black Jacobins* and Alejo Carpentier in *Explosion in a Cathedral* reaches a kind of culmination in the Cuban Revolution. Carpentier himself, when accused of a certain historical pessimism in his novel, suggested the connection:

> If the French Revolution was a failure to a certain extent, I could not, historically, appear very optimistic about it. History is the way it is and can't be otherwise. But regarding revolutions in general, all I have to do is observe the results of the Cuban Revolution, its great realizations, the magnificent

> changes it has brought to the lives of my compatriots, to realize that not all revolutions betray those that make them.[66]

Presumably Carpentier wrote these words in the 1960s. And C. L. R. James, in the epilogue to *The Black Jacobins*, asserts the direct lineage between Toussaint L'Ouverture and Fidel Castro, though unfortunately James desists from elaborating on his view of the Cuban Revolution. In any case, the postmodern moment in the Caribbean historical imagination is characterized by a much more tempered if not disenchanted attitude toward the Cuban Revolution. Not unlike a possible reading from the more metropolitan versions of postmodernism, the post–Cuban Revolution writers I examine, regardless of their varying viewpoints on revolution and resistance in general, certainly have a more detached and skeptical relationship with the idea of the state and the traditionally dialectical notion of historical progress. This skepticism is quite in keeping with more commonplace notions of postmodernity. Neil Larsen discusses the tendency of postmodern practitioners and defenders to inextricably link Marxism to "Enlightenment modernity": "It is not all 'Western' modes of thought and being that must now be discarded, but more precisely their Enlightenment or *modern* modalities, *founded* on the concept of *reason*."[67] Though Larsen is critiquing and perhaps parodying the postmodern "position" here, it would be difficult to find a more apt description of the kind of discourse that underwrites the fiction of Reinaldo Arenas and Edgardo Rodríguez Juliá, even if the rejection of Marxist reason is more explicit in the text by the Cuban author. Irrespective of whether Caribbean postmodernity is a progressive or reactionary cultural practice, using the term in this context, with the understanding of the Cuban Revolution as a generational and ideological divide, rather than diluting the Caribbean specificity of the topic, may in fact bestow the term with a more concrete referentiality and historicity that render its general metropolitan usage more meaningful. Toward this end, in the conclusion I recap these issues in a brief discussion of the Cuban filmmaker Tomás Gutiérrez Alea, who may be constellated in this study thanks to his film depicting the late eighteenth century in Cuba, *The Last Supper* (*La última cena*). Gutiérrez Alea's critique of the Enlightenment resonates with that of his Caribbean predecessors Carpentier and James; yet Alea's later film *Strawberry and Chocolate* (*Fresa y chocolate*) represents an ideological shift away from the *grands récits* of revolutionary progress and historical trajectory toward the "intimist" micropolitics of personal sexuality.

Finally, despite the already daunting challenges of incorporating literature from three different linguistic traditions from the Caribbean, a disclaimer is still in order for the unfortunate exclusion of a representative writer from the Dutch Caribbean. It would be a worthwhile endeavor to determine if the Enlightenment has similar implications for the modern historical imagination in Surinam, Curaçao, Aruba, Saint Eustatius, Bonaire, and Saint Maartin as it does for the writers discussed in this monograph, whose nations were directly or indirectly impacted by the Haitian and French Revolutions, but there can be no question that the eighteenth century in the Dutch Caribbean was characterized especially by slave rebellions and maroonage, which are seen as manifestations of the Enlightenment elsewhere in the Caribbean.

Narrative of an Expedition against the Revolted Slaves of Surinam, by the Scotsman John Gabriel Stedman, exerted an influence on later generations of writers similar to the thematic and historic impact that figures such as Moreau de Saint-Méry, Père Labat, and Baron de Wimpffen had on the modern Caribbean historical imagination.[68] In the 1972 preface to Stedman's text, Van Lier mentions at least three literary works in English, German, and French that were influenced by Stedman's *Narrative*.[69] Richard Price's discussion of eighteenth-century Surinam quotes amply from Stedman and also makes clear the connections between this history, so rife with slave rebellions, and the same period in other parts of the Caribbean. Stedman speaks of "The Celebrated Graman Quacy . . . one of the most Extraordinary Black men in Surinam, or perhaps in the world."[70] Similarly, Price discusses Alabi, one of the eighteenth-century founding figures of the Saramaka in Surinam, in such a way that is reminiscent of descriptions of other leaders of slave rebellions from the period in the Caribbean, such as Boukman, Mackandal, and especially Toussaint L'Ouverture himself. The Saramaka Peace treaty, written in 1762, a year that corresponds with the British occupation of Havana, resonates with the historical and thematic framework of this study and invites a comparative reading with Caribbean texts such as Toussaint's "Letter to the French Directory" which C. L. R. James discusses at length.

According to Hilda van Neck-Yoder, the first novel from the Dutch Caribbean was *Mijn zuster de negerin*, or "My Black Sister ," by Cola Debrot (1935).[71] In Debrot's text, a plantation owner bequeaths to his son, Fritz, not only the plantation itself but a half sister, Maria who is the product of his affair with a black servant who died in childbirth. The revelation of this secret kinship between Fritz and Maria disrupts the erotic attraction between the two and renders it taboo. In the novels I discuss by Marie Chauvet and Maryse Condé, there are also important characters that issue from the violation of a black woman by a white man. Therefore the potential for a comparative linking between Debrot's novel and those by the Francophone women novelists I discuss is clear. Nevertheless, Debrot's foundational text, in which there figures a complex web of interaction among race, sex, and nationhood, describes an emerging postcolonial moment in nineteenth- and twentieth-century Caribbean culture rather than the period corresponding to the Enlightenment, which is the historical and thematic focus of this monograph.

The same could be said of John de Pool's *Bolívar en Curaçao*, written in Spanish and published in Panama in 1946. Nevertheless, though Bolívar the liberator is more commonly associated with the nineteenth century and the foundation of the Latin American republics, he is certainly a figure with strong ties to both the Caribbean and the Enlightenment, whose "point of departure is the *Encyclopédie*" to reiterate a quote from Germán Arciniegas. Just as Bolívar sought and was granted logistical support by Alexandre Pétion, the leader of the new nation of Haiti, so the liberator received assistance in Curaçao. Ineke Phaf elaborates:

> Bolívar was accustomed to contacts with Caribbean islands. When he needed money and other support for his liberational struggle, he appealed to Jamaica as well as to Haiti and Curaçao. Several young men from Curaçao had already studied in the Netherlands, had written their dissertations there, or had even become involved in the political events surround the Batavian Republic. After their return, their "republican" spirit did not seem to be extinguished, certainly not in Brion's case. He personally offered Bolívar his hospitality and apparently also felt himself bound to Bolívar's political ideal.[72]

The connection between Bolívar and the islands of the Caribbean, including Curaçao, as well as John de Pool's textual portrait of Bolívar, would certainly be among the keys to linking the writing of the Dutch Caribbean to the Enlightenment in the modern Caribbean imagination that I discern in this study. Though I have not been able to pursue these connections here, I hope that my approach is capacious enough for future scholarship to elaborate on them and to expand the comparative intertextuality of Caribbean culture.

Part I

Inaugurating the Modern Caribbean Historical Imagination

1 Carpentier and the Temporalities of Mutual Exclusion

> The character of Victor Hugues fascinated me, because it answered to an old ambition of mine, which was to bring European characters to America or to take Americans to Europe. That is to say, to establish a powerful symbiosis of cultures and not to enclose ourselves within a limited milieu with no penetration of ideas coming from the outside.
>
> Alejo Carpentier, *Afirmación literaria americanista*

THE IMPORT/EXPORT operation that Carpentier describes in this epigraph does not amount to a "symbiosis" characterized by mutual benefit to the parties involved. Symbiosis implies compatibility, whereas much of the force of Carpentier's writing stems from the incongruity of different peoples and civilizations that occupy the same space at a given historical moment. Perhaps no image is more characteristic of Carpentier's description than that of the old slave Ti Noël seated on several volumes of the *Encyclopédie* eating sugarcane: even more than the narrative engine itself, this kind of juxtaposition amounts to a vignette whose poetic force owes almost entirely to its incongruity rather than its status as an image of symbiosis or mutual benefit.

Those familiar with Carpentier's writing will perhaps have taken notice of a binary manner of thinking that informs his narration: oppositions such as black/white, Caribbean/Europe, baroque/classical, and oral/written are not so much terms locked into a dialectical engagement promising synthesis as they are entities whose incommensurability results in an irresolvable play reminiscent of the baroque. Whenever one of these realms infiltrates the opposing camp, it seems that the result is not so much a symbiosis or synthesis as it is a grotesque spectacle or caricature. This dualistic penchant is at once Carpentier's flaw as well as his discursive and creative impetus.

Carpentier wavers or hesitates, then, between two possible cognitive frameworks: a positive fusion or synthesis, on the one hand, brought about by the convergence and exchange of European and Afro-Caribbean cultures; and, on the other, a Manichean irreconcilability. In the latter scenario, a blending or miscegenation between Europe and the Caribbean results in a kind of monstrous progeny, underlining the incommensurability between the two worlds in question. In this chapter, I trace the evolution of Carpentier's conceptual undecidability in his early fiction. Though there has been no shortage of critical commentary on the opposition between Europe and America, black and white in Carpentier, it is my view that revisiting these issues in detail in his early work demonstrates a perhaps surprising direct historical lineage of many of the more contemporary discussions in postcolonial and Caribbean studies that are similarly preoccupied with questions of hybridity and Manichaeism. In many ways, Carpentier's narration anticipates this dialectic or dynamic, suggesting an intellectual kinship not only with Frantz Fanon and Fernando Ortiz, but also schools of thought such as those associated with third cinema, the subaltern studies group, Said, *créolité*, Stuart Hall and cultural studies, and the ongoing interpretative struggles over Rigoberta Menchú and Latin American testimonial. If, as Alberto Moreiras has pointed out, there is a genealogical line in Latin American thought from notions of transculturation (Ortiz) to heterogeneity (Cornejo Polar) to hybridity (García Canclini), with each subsequent notion opposing while supplementing the former, we can view Carpentier's writing as a precursor of these discourses of Latin American modernity.[1] And yet Carpentier's conflicted attraction to Manichaeism also suggests an imminent comparability with Fanon. Though the world conjured by Carpentier's fictive version of the eighteenth century is historically and geographically removed from the decolonization process that Fanon describes so powerfully, the latter's description of the Manichean mechanism is certainly applicable to the conceptual framework of Carpentier's project: "Thus we see that the primary Manichaeism which governed colonial society is preserved intact during the period of decolonisation; that is to say that the settler never ceases to be the enemy, the opponent, the foe that must be overthrown."[2]

What Carpentier calls "symbiosis" can also be considered a precursor to more recent discussions on transculturation and "hybridity." Fernando Coronil suggests that "it is significant that two critics of imperialism [Edward Said and Fernando Ortiz] developed, independently of each other and fifty years apart, a contrapuntal perspective for analyzing the formation of cultures and identities."[3] Perhaps a more appropriate juxtaposition with Ortiz would have been Carpentier himself, who also avails himself of a contrapuntal technique that may formally allegorize a unity of cultural development but which, within its formal totality, also dramatizes a cultural opposition and division. Just as Coronil asserts that, in Ortiz's contrapuntal opposition between tobacco and sugar, both terms are not "fixed qualities" but already "hybrid products," so the same might be said about the European Creole and the Afro-Caribbean, the opposing contrapuntal terms in Carpentier's early fiction.

"¡El bongo, antídoto de Wall Street!"

Both the earliest commentators on Carpentier and the more recent have discerned, in one form or another, what Juan Marinello described in 1937 as a "central fissure" ("la grieta central") separating the black interior from the ethnographic desire of the white Creole.[4] In a more recent intervention, Antonio Benítez-Rojo rearticulates this Carpenterian divide in psychoanalytic terms, as a triangular Oedipal conflict between the absent father (France, discourse) and the desired mother (America, music).[5] Music in Carpentier's texts, among other roles, serves as an index signaling the presence of Carpentier's dilemma, his undecidability between the frameworks of hybridity and Manichaeism, as well as the gap between Europe and America, since music represents for Carpentier both a chasm resulting in a binary world and at the same time a suture promising an elusive reconciliation, a category that gathers fragments into a totality. As I will show, the ideal platform for Carpentier to explore these psychological and historical antinomies is his historical fiction set in the eighteenth century. By shifting back in time, Carpentier seemed to find his "true voice" (witnessed by his repeated excursions into the century of Enlightenment) while at the same time founding a subgenre of historical writing in the Caribbean that deals specifically with the problems of modernity issuing from the eighteenth century. While the Enlightenment could be said to have ushered in a new phase of colonialism, with a consolidated administrative, military, and political center and periphery, Carpentier's and subsequent authors' emphasis on the geographic and historical specificity of the Haitian Revolution bestows on this subgenre a specifically Caribbean ethos. Carpentier's other great novel about the period was *Explosion in a Cathedral* (*El siglo de las luces*). Both of these historical novels about the Haitian Revolution and the impact of the French Revolution on the Caribbean employ a strategy that is key to Carpentier's success in writing historical fiction. If Carpentier claims in the prologue to *The Kingdom of This World* that the novel was written with rigorous attention to the exactitude of names, dates, events, and chronology, then what distinguishes the novelist from the historian is the introduction of a fictive protagonist. If the names and places such as Boukman, Mackandal, Henri Christophe, San Souci, La Ferrière, and Victor Hugues come straight out of the pages of such colonial chroniclers as Moreau de Saint-Méry, Carpentier introduces Ti Noël as the slave who gains his freedom only to suffer forced labor under the regime of the black king Henri Christophe. Ti Noël, along with Esteban in *Explosion in a Cathedral*, are the fictive "keys" to Carpentier's historical imagination insofar as they serve as passive witnesses to the momentous historical events in the Caribbean, such as Mackandal's execution or Victor Hugues's introduction of the guillotine in the French Caribbean. Ti Noël and Esteban, passive observers of historical phenomena, supply Carpentier with a vantage point that is at once subjective and objective, "remedying" an old problem that was evident in his first novel, *Ecue-Yamba-O*. After a brief discussion of this novel, I show how Carpentier attempted to overcome ideological impasses by transferring some of the similar paradigms of the earlier novel to the late-eighteenth-century setting in the Caribbean in *The Kingdom of This World*.

The problems of *Ecue-Yamba-O*, written while the author was incarcerated in a Havana prison in 1927, are well known. I have already cited what Marinello identifies as Carpentier's narrative crack, the rupture resulting from the narrator's desire to represent the Afro-Cuban from both the inside and the outside simultaneously. Carpentier's own criticisms seem like a reiteration of Marinello's analysis: "After twenty years of research about the syncretic realities of Cuba, I realized that the deep, the true, the universal aspects of the world that I had wanted to depict remained outside the reach of my observation."[6] Marinello's "inside," in Carpentier's articulation, is the "deep, the true, the universal," unempirical phenomena that are not accessible to an outside "observer." Unlike Borges's Aleph, which contains all possible perspectives simultaneously, this outside observer by definition can only occupy a single vantage point at a time.[7] In his prologue to a reprinted version of the novel, Carpentier expresses another view of this crack or dividing line: "It was necessary to be 'nationalist,' while attempting at the same time to be 'vanguardist.' That's the question. . . . a difficult proposition, since all nationalism depends on the veneration of a tradition while 'vanguardism' indicated, necessarily, a rupture with tradition."[8] The author of *Ecue-Yamba-O* desires access to the profound interior of the Afro-Cuban being, and yet is limited to the outside because his techniques of representation—including, among others, the form of the novel itself and the limited maneuverability of the observer—are inextricably tied to the Western tradition for which he is seeking an alternative. Fernando Coronil's discussion of Malinowski in the context of Fernando Ortiz is relevant to Carpentier's situation as well: "In *Argonauts of the Western Pacific*, Malinowski argues that an anthropological vision requires the perspective of a detached observer, capable of seeing the functioning of the whole society."[9] In short, Carpentier's desire to access the profundity of his object of study was thwarted by his perspective as an outsider—anthropology's perennial occupational hazard. Thanks to Anke Birkenmaiers's valuable study, we can understand with greater contextual accuracy Carpentier's anthropological mind-set at the time he wrote *Ecue-Yamba-O*. Birkenmaier quotes a revealing review Carpentier wrote of an ethnographic study of the Ivory Coast by William Seabrook. In the review, Carpentier laments the expression of an ethnocentrism endemic to ethnography, the sense of belonging to a "superior race" with which most ethnographers approach their objects of study. This distance between the ethnographic subject and object results in an unfortunate and unintended "irony."[10] However, Carpentier's desire to overcome this irony by bridging the gap novelistically between ethnographic observer (or narrator) and his Afro-Cuban protagonists tended to exacerbate this thorny ethnographic and philosophical problem rather than remedying it.

Amy Fass Emery also contributes documentary contextualization for interpreting *Ecue*. She cites an article Carpentier wrote for the journal *Bifur* called "Lettre des Antilles" documenting his attendance of a *ñáñigo* ceremony. In the letter, the Cuban author speaks "as both native informant to a European audience and as a detached ethnographer." Emery also quotes a letter to Alejandro García Caturla in which Carpentier urgently requests information about *ñáñigo* funeral rites. This information bolsters the argument that in fact the existential and methodological problem of *Ecue* is the fissure that Marinello identified between internal access and external observation.[11] Emery also asserts that "Carpentier's novel wavers between an emerging view of the Other as creative hybrid and a residual portrait of the Other as having a primitive mentality that is socially dangerous."[12] Nevertheless, though a young Carpentier does portray Menegildo and other Afro-Cubans as unwitting "conscripts of modernity" (to echo the title of David Scott's book about C. L. R. James), he does so only in an urban setting that is portrayed as inauthentic and corrupting. The Afro-Cuban "authentic" space for an oppositional ontology in the anthropological imagination of the author of *Ecue-Yamba-O* is the countryside, or *el monte*, where blacks occupy their "rightful" place of pure opposition to a decadent Occident.

Carpentier's reference to the novel as a "failed attempt"[13] is especially striking when compared to the satisfaction he expresses about his subsequent works: "If I had to write *The Kingdom of This World*, *The Lost Steps*, and *Explosion in a Cathedral* all over again, that is to say, my entire body of work beginning with 'Journey Back to the Source,' I would do so in exactly the same fashion, without removing or adding a single comma."[14] If, looking back on his oeuvre, he would leave each comma unchanged beginning with the 1944 short story "Journey Back to the Source," then this means that the only major work that does not fall into this august category is, in fact, *Ecue-Yamba-O*. Evidently Carpentier seems to consider the difficulties of representation, of the unbridgeable gap between inside and outside, subject and object, to be ones that were remedied in his subsequent works. And so it is somewhat surprising that many of these same issues that created problems in Carpentier's first novel resurface in *The Kingdom of This World* and are especially noticeable when music is prominent in the text. I therefore briefly comment on the role and importance of music in *Ecue-Yamba-O* as a way of establishing a thematic link with *The Kingdom of This World*, which will subsequently receive a more detailed analysis. Music is, in fact, another articulation of the fissure that Marinello mentions, in that, on the one hand, it is an empirical phenomenon readily accessible to the observer, while at the same time an aperture promising access to a profound interior. Music is the common thread through Carpentier's oeuvre that reveals that the same consciousness, though significantly evolved over time, is at work, in that as a highly discursive figure it represents that incommensurable split between the written and the oral, history and presence, Europe and the Caribbean. But music also represents the point of contact between these incommensurabilities, and thus suggests the possibility of an elusive and illusive reconciliation.

Ecue-Yamba-O narrates the birth, adolescence, and short adulthood of Menegildo, an Afro-Cuban born and raised in the all-encompassing shadow of sugar, involving the labor of every individual in that world in the harvesting of sugarcane, its transport, its processing and refining in the demonic sugar mills (whose geometry and mechanization lend themselves to many of the novel's incongruous "futuristic" metaphors that Carpentier would later lament). Menegildo falls in love with Longina, battles and slays the Haitian migrant worker Napolión for his beloved, and as a result is briefly incarcerated in an urban penitentiary. He joins a secret *ñáñigo* underworld society, succumbs to the decadent temptations of the city, and falls victim to a rival gang. After his death, Longina leaves the city and returns to the countryside, where she gives birth to Menegildo's child, thus, as González Echevarría emphasizes, "beginning another cycle."[15] Despite what may seem like a rather straightforward plot structure, *Ecue-Yamba-O* at times employs unorthodox chapter organization, outlandish descriptions using similes and images that Carpentier himself later described as being of a "detestably futuristic bad taste,"[16] and employs a narrator that vacillates in a disconcerting fashion between detached omniscience and engaged political commentary, a "flaw" decried by some critics.

Music in the novel does not delay in making an appearance. One of his first rites of passage involves Menegildo's musical initiation:

> It was true that Menegildo didn't know how to read, and was even ignorant of the art of signing one's name with an X. But on the other hand he had an advanced degree [*era doctor*] in gestures and cadences. The sense of rhythm pulsated through his blood. . . . Vibrating drumsticks imitated a dry collision of tibias . . . the chewing-gum box now a drum. Music of leather, wood, bones and metal—music of elemental materials.[17]

Condensed in this citation are the principal binary oppositions that pervade the novel and much of Carpentier's oeuvre. First of all, the dualism is made explicit between the fact that Menegildo is illiterate and that he has a certain innate rhythm. The implication is not only that Afro-Cuban mastery of music and rhythm serves as a compensation or valid equivalent of the kind of mastery acquired from an Occidental education, but it is also clear that the "knowledge" inherent in and stemming from these rhythms amounts to a language, a mysterious "writing" unto itself to which Western man is denied access: "Menegildo learned the drum riffs, including the secrets."[18] That Afro-Cuban music contains a secret, or is a kind of secret language, is not a Carpenterian invention. In Fernando Ortiz's *La música afrocubana*, there is a brief discussion on the difficulty of transcribing Afro-Cuban music into standard musical notation. Ortiz cites at least a half dozen musicians and composers who attest to this difficulty. Raimundo Valenzuela, the nineteenth-century musician "of color" is cited as refusing to explain the rhythmic figure called the *cinquillo*, calling it "a secret." Valenzuela adds that it would spell doom for Cuban artists if foreigners were able to "decipher" the *cinquillo*. Torroella is reported to have said that Afro-Cuban music cannot be written down, "don't you know that with Black people there's always a secret?"[19] Moreover, in Carpentier's review of Seabrook's book, he praises the ethnographer precisely for not revealing the secrets of the people he has studied.[20] (Nevertheless, Carpentier transcribes and discusses at length the "secret" rhythmic figure of the *cinquillo* in *La música en Cuba*.)

It is also known that in African music linguistic or verbal messages are conveyed via instrumental means: "the sounds of drums [in African music] are interpreted in three different ways according to the type of drum and the mode of drumming employed. They may be interpreted as 'signals'—call signals, warning signals, or as 'speech,' in which case words, phrases, and sentences would be attributed to them. . . . That is to say, what is heard as music sometimes conveys a verbal message."[21] The "secret" of Afro-Cuban rhythms is a doubly articulated one: on the one hand, these rhythms are secret because they can communicate specific linguistic messages that are inaccessible to the outsider; on the other hand, the secret resides in the fact that the rhythms themselves resist transcription into standard notation. Hence the fascination for Carpentier of this secret that is at the same time a paradox: Afro-Cuban rhythms cannot be written down, and yet at the same time they are themselves *a kind of writing*: "Moreover, Cristalina knew it. She knew stories with music, of the kind that almost no one was capable of narrating any longer in traditional rhythm." It is easy to see how this paradox—writing which is not writing or which cannot be written—would hold a special interest for Carpentier; it is a discursive figure that acts as a dividing line, crack, or rupture which beckons while barring access to a non-discursive profundity. This tendency in his thought to valorize the unmediated "true tradition" as opposed to an Occidental culture flooded with the mediation of written signs reveals a certain Platonic streak in Carpentier's early writing.[22]

Anke Birkenmaier suggests that the Afro-Cuban weltanschauung in *Ecue-Yamba-O* is described in such a way as to "equate white science [or knowledge] with that of the blacks."[23] Yet it seems to me that the descriptions of Afro-Cuban artistic expression, while certainly intended to valorize cultural practices that had heretofore been underappreciated, clearly draws a sharp distinction between the two worlds. The transcribability of Afro-Caribbean music would connote its universal fungibility or commodification; the impossibility of transcribing these secret rhythms seems to suggest for Carpentier that they occupy a sacrosanct and "authentic" space impenetrable to a Westerner's roving eyes and ears. Michel Foucault's description of the evolving characteristic of the semiotic sign within the classical episteme captures precisely that which is diametrically opposed to Carpentier's notion of the Afro-Caribbean understanding of the sign: "It is the task of words to translate the truth if they can; but they no longer have the right to be considered a mark of it. Language has withdrawn from the midst of beings themselves and has entered a period of transparency and neutrality."[24] In Carpentier's vision of the Afro-Caribbean understanding of cultural transmission, writing and truth are contained in rhythms; visual representations have an organic or "seamless" connection to the thing or person represented. For the Carpentier of *Ecue-Yamba-O*, Afro-Caribbean rhythms are the bearers of a certain knowledge, and yet they cannot be separated out from that knowledge as their mere indicators; they form an organic unity with it (to borrow Benjamin's well-known simile) like a fruit with its skin.

If the Afro-Cuban musical ceremonies are intended to convey a certain kind of secret knowledge, "from fathers to sons, from kings to princes, from initiators to initiated," then Occidental or Creole music, passed on not as part of an oral tradition but constituted by "ciphered messages," takes on the status of a cultural artifact floating in time that has become detached from any authentic communication of knowledge through continuity. Western music, at least in *Ecue-Yamba-O*, is part and parcel of the decadent side of the binary equation that includes cosmopolitanism and the influx of explicitly decried consumer items like "orange crush" and "hot dogs" and is specifically associated with the metropolis. The narrator also names in this list "symphony tempos" among so many of the imported consumer items to Cuba contributing to a fragmented and inauthentic temporal reality. When Menegildo is taken prisoner and arrives from the country to the city, one of the first things he sees is a group of music students awaiting the arrival of their music professor, who is wearing a sash with the words "¡Viva la música!" engraved in silver letters.

Afro-Cuban rhythms are involved in a concrete, "authentic" historicity through a tradition that is specifically rural and therefore suggestive of the autochthonous. Consider the significance of the flashback passage describing Menegildo's grandfather Juan Mandinga: "Despite his allegiance to the master he was able to decipher, like all those of his kind, the secret drum riffs that announced the forthcoming uprising on the neighboring plantations. Juan Mandinga sniffed the air in silence, perceiving an ancestral sympathetic link to those who had the audacity to modify the rites of African telegraphy with those drums that smelled of blood. He thought to himself that if the desperate effort yielded no fruit, at least the societies of runaway maroons would swell in number."[25] This passage permits us to take issue with a commonplace in Carpentier criticism, that the Afro-Cuban notion of time is circular and repetitive, while the European temporal experience is historical, linear, and progressive.[26] Carpentier himself, in his revealing prologue to the reprinted edition, admits that he had not taken into account his characters' "ancestral beliefs and practices that in reality signified a resistance against the overwhelming power of external factors."[27] And yet, despite this confession, this description of the episode involving Juan Mandinga confirms, in fact, that the liturgical signification of music and rhythm in Carpentier's Afro-Cuban world is tied to a concrete historical process whose purpose is not merely preservation and repetition with no telos, but rather liberation and progress as well: the drums beating in the countryside forebode an imminent slave revolt that, even if unsuccessful, will swell the ranks of the maroon societies with more runaway slaves and contribute to the promise of a society free of slavery. Juan Mandinga experiences an ancestral connection with those audacious enough to modernize, to rejuvenate, or bring up to date (*remozar*) the ancient rhythms by adapting them to contemporary circumstances, connoting that the performance of these rhythmic rites is not a mere atemporal repetition of those that may have taken place centuries before, but rather an attempt to transmit and apply ancient knowledge to a specific and contemporaneous context, a context that, incidentally, requires innovative musical techniques in order to convey this new information as precisely as possible.

Understood in this fashion, the return of widowed Longina, obeying the instinctive call of an "obscure duty" to the countryside to give birth to Menegildo's son, does not necessarily represent the beginning anew of a circular pattern but rather an escape from the tainted metropolis, where even Afro-Cuban musicianship suffers from the corrupting influence of professionalism and its trappings, to carry on the multigenerational struggle for liberation. Read thus, it is clear that to characterize Afro-Caribbean temporality in Carpentier as circular and repetitive is not entirely accurate since there are contemporary social circumstances that require an evolution of techniques of representation—musical and otherwise. But Carpentier does not go so far as to suggest a linear or progressive march of time, either. Correspondingly, the author opposes to the "authenticity" of Afro-Caribbean culture a notion of Western music and culture that is inseparable from the insidious penetration of foreign capital in Cuba. And yet the narrator avails himself of a vocabulary pertaining to the decried Western tradition to describe Afro-Cuban music, betraying a confusing set of ideological registers. What this process reveals is not so much a growing complexity in Carpentier's thought as much as the fact that the Manichean division in *Ecue-Yamba-O* was perhaps not so Manichean after all. The narrator in the novel never opposes *explicitly* Afro-Cuban music to the European classical tradition; to the contrary, he more often than not borrows metaphors from the European tradition to describe Afro-Cuban music: "counterpoint," "philharmonic," "*allegro primitivo*." Such rhetorical devices were probably intended to be disconcerting in the vanguardist tradition of the time. Unfortunately, they betray a narrator who has difficulty deciding. If such great lengths had been taken to valorize the Afro-Cuban tradition as autonomous or even autochthonous, what function could it serve to introduce terminology from the classical tradition, with all the cultural hegemony that it implies, to describe it?

It is perhaps not so surprising, then, that, over a decade after writing *Ecue-Yamba-O* and now armed with historical knowledge acquired through research for *Music in Cuba* (1946), Carpentier, for his next major fictional project, would go back in time to the epistemological and material encounter between European Enlightenment and the Caribbean world in the late eighteenth and early nineteenth centuries. If the problem in the first novel had not been so much a question of binary opposition or Manichaeism but rather a false or unsymmetrical opposition, Carpentier will now distill out the complexities of contemporary culture in order to represent the encounters of Europeans and Africans and their descendants in the Caribbean as pure incongruence or opposition in *The Kingdom of This World* (1949).[28] Carpentier will now consolidate the incommensurability of Europe and the Afro-Caribbean through both historical and rhetorical devices, narrating in *The Kingdom of This World* a much more clearly elaborated portrait of differing notions of temporality revealed especially through musical references.

Music in the Enlightenment

Since Carpentier's second major fictional undertaking, *The Kingdom of This World* (as well as his later *Concierto barroco* [1974]) is so replete with musical references from the eighteenth century, it would be worthwhile to briefly recapitulate some of the Enlightenment attitudes toward music to see how they come to bear on Carpentier's understanding of musical expression. During the Enlightenment, the great debate of the period, according to Cynthia Verba's study, was between Rameau and Rousseau and was primarily concerned with whether harmony or melody could be considered the essential element of musical expression: "Both agreed that the doctrine [of imitation from Aristotle's *Poetics*] applied to music as well as to the other arts—that music had to express something, that it had to have a meaning."[29] In Carpentier's understanding of Afro-Caribbean music, neither melody nor harmony is the essential component, but rather rhythm; moreover, meaning is a much more concrete affair in Afro-Caribbean music than in the Enlightenment debate, in which music had to signify merely *something*. The meanings in Afro-Caribbean music can include signals, warnings, calls to battle, or the actual transmission of precise linguistic messages.

Though there were heated disagreements among the Enlightenment philosophers concerning such topics as the ontological status of music and the analysis of its formal means,[30] there was agreement when it came to proclaiming the superiority of European civilization—epitomized by music—over that of other continents. Rousseau proclaimed that European music, "our music," is "but empty noise to the ear of the Caribbean." The context of this statement was part of the harmony/melody debate. Whereas Rousseau acknowledges that there are natural rules that predetermine the effects of harmony, he insists, taking issue with Rameau, that expression and pleasure from music can derive only from melody, which is socially and culturally determined and therefore infused with meaning. While Rousseau is famed for championing the "noble savage," a romantic valorization of a natural state of life without the corrupting influences of society, his opinions on music seem to reveal a contrary and contradictory set of criteria. Rousseau's musical xenophobia begins close to home, in northern Europe and the "barbaric invasions" during the Roman Empire. "These crude people who were a product of the North accustomed everyone's ears to the roughness of their speech; their voice harsh and bare of accent was noisy without being sonorous."[31] For Rousseau, the natural condition of need was incompatible with the civilized and cultivated state of poetic feeling. His remark about "our most moving music" being only "empty noise for the Caribbean," is therefore not entirely a commentary on music alone. By the same token, "a Caribbean" is supposedly incapable of comprehending European music, since the feelings that are stimulated by music issue from a moral source that can only be the product of an advanced civilization. Thus what seems like an innocuous aesthetic polemic on the virtues of melody versus those of harmony in fact reveal that the structural dynamic of the Enlightenment, whereby negative criteria (another's "immaturity," "laziness," "inferiority," or, now, "insensitivity") are employed to proclaim oneself the enlightened center, extended into the domain of European music as well. It could be said, perhaps with some exaggeration, that Carpentier in *The Kingdom of This World* practically dramatizes Rousseau's proclamation about the illegibility or incomprehensibility of European music in the Caribbean. What is surprising is that Carpentier is not interested in overturning Rousseau's judgment, but rather reiterates it from the point of view of the Caribbean. European music is incomprehensible for the Afro-Caribbean, but Carpentier introduces rhythm as an element that is overlooked by Rousseau and the *philosophes* and that is, in turn, equally mystifying for them.

Mental Counterpoint

If, as has been suggested,[32] the shortcomings and criticisms of Carpentier's first novel resulted in a prolonged silence, it would then be worthwhile to scrutinize the strategies by which a remedy for these shortcomings was attempted. Carpentier was contracted to write *Music in Cuba* by the Fondo de Cultura Económica in Mexico, and the volume appeared in 1946, thirteen years after *Ecue-Yamba-O*. His approach to the material was strictly historical, based on the meticulous perusal of manuscripts and scores that were stored away and forgotten in "cathedral archives—principally of Santiago and Havana—of capitulary records of churches and city halls, of parish closets."[33] Carpentier takes special pride in his discovery, "in an old cabinet," of the forgotten musical scores of Esteban Salas, to whom he attributes great importance in the history of Cuban and Latin American music. Though he was clearly drawn to the novelistic or anecdotal aspects of history that lend themselves to narrative, the proclivities of the novelist or storyteller were held in check by the historical record itself. In other words, Carpentier's tendency to essentialize in *Ecue-Yamba-O* was moderated by the discovery in *Music in Cuba* that historically, in fact, the line was not so clearly drawn between Occidental and Afro-Cuban culture. As early as the sixteenth century, Carpentier finds that, "From the outset, the Christian church exercised a powerful attraction for the blacks brought to America. The altars, the accessories surrounding the cult of worship, the images, the religious garments, were crafted to seduce souls strongly attracted by a sumptuous world of rites and mysteries. . . . Ogún, Changó, Elegguá, Obatalá and many others continued thriving in the hearts of many. . . . The African transplanted to the New World never believed that these two worlds, Catholic and African, could not be shared in admirable harmony."[34] And so if

Carpentier the novelist had not yet sought to establish a cultural symbiosis between Europe and America, the history of musical development in Cuba is in fact a testimony to the real cultural "hybridity" between Occidental and African music. Despite Carpentier's valorization of the rhythmic modifications that the Afro-Cubans conferred on the traditional Creole-European musical forms, such as the *contradanza*, one can also detect a certain note of nostalgia or regret at this incursion of the Afro-Cuban into "white music" during the nineteenth century: "blacks played and created white music, without enriching it further, except with their atavic rhythmic sense, where they uniquely accentuated certain kinds of danceable compositions. . . . When they wrote a melody they did not seem to remember for the moment the rich treasure of their ancestral African heritage. . . . If the drum made the innermost fibers of his heart resonate in sympathy, he did not admit it. It is possible that at times he would attend the ritual drum beating of the Carraguao neighborhood. But in the dances where he performed his professional duties, he played the courtly minuet."[35] Detectable here are echoes of the narrator of *Ecue-Yamba-O*. The rhythmic modifications with which the nineteenth-century Afro-Cubans reinvented *contradanzas* and *minués de corte* may have revolutionized world music, but these "atavistic" rhythms no longer amount to the same secret language that communicated with the invisible world and transmitted the knowledge from prior generations, a historical development that Carpentier seems to regret. While the historical record in *Music in Cuba* demonstrates that in nineteenth-century Cuba a real if tenuous merging, blending, or hybridity of Afro-Cuban and white-Creole music took place, then Carpentier seems to hesitate, to waver between embracing this integration—a symbiosis that was, he was later to claim, his "fascination and old aspiration"—and the conceptual framework of oppositional exclusion that informed *Ecue-Yamba-O*. What is interesting is that rather than revising his basic conceptualization of characters and cultures, rather than attempting to portray a kind of transculturation that would have more faithfully corresponded to the contemporary setting of *Ecue*, Carpentier, in *The Kingdom of This World*, will go back in time to revisit that originary epistemological and material encounter between European Enlightenment and the Afro-Caribbean world of sugar and slavery in the late eighteenth and early nineteenth centuries to more effectively portray his preferred paradigm of mutual exclusion.

In *The Kingdom of This World*, the applied solution is history itself, the placement of the events within a specific historic context. By representing actual Caribbean history of the late eighteenth and early nineteenth centuries within the framework of a fictional or narrative presentation, Carpentier was able to suture the "crack" from which *Ecue-Yamba-O* suffered into the very theme of his narration. If in the early novel there persisted an ethnographic divide between subject and object in the author's portrait of Menegildo, it is interesting to note that in a preliminary sketch of *The Kingdom of This World* published in 1944 and reprinted with a commentary by Verity Smith, the witness-observer was a modern traveler that, for Smith, stood in for the author himself. In the 1949 novel, of course, this witness to the events of the late eighteenth and early nineteenth centuries will metamorphose into the slave Ti Noël, a transformation that is further evidence of Carpentier's ongoing reflection on the ethnographic subject/object divide.[36]

If there is a hint of nostalgia in *Music in Cuba* when the narrator seems to lament the cultural miscegenation of the nineteenth century, then by returning to the late eighteenth century, the author is able to recuperate that moment in his historical imagination of pure opposition between Afro-Caribbean and Enlightenment epistemology. Part of the purity of this opposition resides in the relationship of master to slave along with its attendant dialectics. Ti Noël and Lenormand de Mézy now embody the kind of pure opposition that evaded the portrait of Menegildo in *Ecue-Yamba-O*. The role of Occidental music in this oppositional schema is now more refined than in *Ecue-Yamba-O,* where classical music was simply part and parcel of a vaguely portrayed consumer society. In *The Kingdom of This World*, the temporal, historical, and cultural associations of classical music and Occidental culture in general are more clearly delineated.

Emil Volek suggests that the structure of *The Kingdom of This World* is basically contrapuntal,[37] certainly an undeniable claim. One way to interpret the components of this counterpoint is through the divergent—retrospective and prospective—expressions of temporality. A textual juxtaposition demonstrates this expression. At one point in the novel, Mackandal, the rebel slave of Jamaican descent, has been discovered to be the source of the poison that has devastated the colony of Saint Domingue. The soldiers commissioned to track down the Mandingan rebel chant songs that "recounted the feats of grandfathers who had taken part in the sack of Cartagena."[38] These songs represent the past as history, as an irretrievable bygone. The soldiers evoke this distant past in which "the edicts issued in Paris and the gentle reprimands of the *Code Noir*" (40) were not forceful enough to establish rule of law. Meanwhile, though the slaves are aware that their savior Mackandal is a marked man, their music is free of this retrospective orientation: "Nevertheless, the slaves displayed a defiant good humor. Never had those whose task it was to set the rhythm for the corn-grinding or the cane cutting thumped their drums more briskly" (41).

The drums are played in order to establish a rhythm to accompany the grinding of corn or the harvesting of cane as before, yet the fact they are played with a special impetus or driving force underlines an anticipation of a liberating intervention that will free the slaves from the cycle of forced labor. The passage that closes this section of the text explicitly ties hearing and music to this refusal to despair, or to accept Mackandal as history, as part of an irredeemable past: "The anxious wait lasted four years, and the alert ears never despaired of hearing, at any moment, the voice of the great conch shell which would bellow through the hills to announce that Mackandal had completed the cycle of his metamorphosis" (43). This juxtaposition, between a retrospective Occidental culture and a prospective Afro-Caribbean culture, heralds the prime contrapuntal theme of the novel.

In the opening chapter, Ti Noël views the latest prints displayed by the bookseller. When he learns that a certain print depicting African royalty is actually the portrait of "the king of [his] country," he makes an imagined comparison of royalty in Africa (whose description is informed by Mackandal's songs he has heard) and European royalty. The comparison reveals much about the intersection between power, representation, and music: "They were kings, true kings, and not those sovereigns wigged in false hair who played at cup and ball and were gods only when they strutted the stage of their court theaters, effeminately pointing a leg in the measures of a rigadoon" (14). From the Afro-Caribbean perspective, European power is decadent because it is more concerned with mediation and play, in all the senses of the word, than with the exercise of power properly speaking. Mackandal points out to Ti Noël that the European king is incapable of fighting his own battles and is powerless to arbitrate litigation. Instead, games, theater, and music are the pastimes of European sovereigns. In this portrait of a decadent West, music has become divorced from ritual, work, and battle and occupies a separate domain of entertainment that is alien to Carpentier's notion of the Afro-Caribbean world. In Mackandal's version of an African kingdom, on the other hand, the numerous musical instruments that abounded in *Ecue-Yamba-O* have been distilled to a rhythmic essence in the figure of the drum. The rhythms they produce are not separate phenomena from the essential elements of social life, including warfare, food distribution, and rites of passage. The metaphors employed imply an organic inseparability of rhythm from nature: "sonorous stones were thumped to produce a music like that of tamed cataracts" (20), and the drums themselves, "mothers of drums," are anthropomorphized in appearance. By the same token, the description of European sovereigns and music underlines a divorce from nature; kings wear "false hair" and listen to songs that issue from the beaks of "stringed birds." The rhyme between *sinfonías* and *chifonías* ("symphonies" and "whisperings of gossip") underlines the superficiality of the former.

Along with other realms of Occidental representation, music is portrayed as a historical object, destined to become mere passing fashion that, since it is always in reaction to the past, even in innovation is retrospective. Seen in this way, the appropriate Freudian text to characterize Carpentier's version of Occidental history is not necessarily *Totem and Taboo*, as Benítez-Rojo suggests, for whom music in general in Carpentier's texts represents a suppression of historical discourse.[39] Benítez-Rojo's interpretation of the crack or dividing line in Carpentier, which separates discourse and history on the paternal side from music and the absence of meaning on the maternal side, overlooks the fact that there is in Carpentier, and especially in *The Kingdom of This World*, another important fissure within music itself, polarizing Afro-Caribbean rhythms and European music. Perhaps the Freudian text that more appropriately describes Carpentier's version of the latter world is *Moses and Monotheism*. In a parricidal series of historical successions, the rigadoon is succeeded by the minuet which in turn succumbs to the waltz, each new formal innovation requiring a violent suppression of its historical precursor.[40] In contradistinction to this understanding of Occidental history, Carpentier portrays Afro-Caribbean music in this schema not as a formal object of history that is doomed to the vicissitudes of fashion, but rather as a mode of signification congruent with history's unfolding. Afro-Caribbean music is therefore prospective, in that it permits an application of the past's knowledge to the organization of social life in the present and the future. This retrospective/prospective divide between Afro-Caribbean and European worldviews is the axis or hinge on which the novel turns. This motif could not be more clearly laid out than at the conclusion of chapter 1, when M. Lenormand de Mézy and Ti Noël are returning to the plantation from their visit to the Cap Français: "Old memories of his days as a petty officer stirred in the master's breast, and he began to whistle a fife march. Ti Noël, in a kind of a mental counterpoint, silently hummed a chanty that was very popular among the harbor coopers, heaping ignominy on the King of England" (16). The play or opposition that establishes the counterpoint in the passage is a temporal one. While the master, literally "assaulted" by nostalgia for his days as a soldier, whistles a fife march, Ti Noël quietly (or "mentally") hums a sailor's tune, thus rendering the march a kind of ideological and temporal fugue. The retrospection or nostalgia that informs the master's performance is thematically opposed to the slave's rendition, which insults the king of England, but which, by explicit extension, also applies to the king of France or Spain, and thus any European figure that represents tyrannical authority, not the least of which is the master himself. Ti Noël's second theme or motif therefore constitutes a temporal counterpoint, since the meaning with which he instills the sailors' tune reflects a longing to overcome his contemporary situation of arbitrarily imposed authority and is therefore forward-oriented in anticipation of future resolution.

Mackandal's capture and ceremonial execution represents a climactic confrontation of the opposing retrospective and prospective worlds. Here, too, there are drums, but they are now in service of the adversary: "military drums rolled a solemn beat." Whereas the drums of the Afro-Caribbean ceremony had the function of evoking the presence of Mackandal as his apparition rose above the torch flames, the military drums are now mere background to accompany his burning at the stake and final metamorphosis and elimination. Whereas that which predominately characterizes the Afro-Caribbean rituals and ceremonies is music evoking presence, the narrator emphasizes that the ceremony organized for the execution of Mackandal is a spectacle, (the word *espectáculo* is employed repeatedly), appealing to a visual rather than auditory sense that highlights distance and detachment. The scene seems to be suggesting that Occidental representation as spectacle, involving distance and generating a relationship of (seeing) subject and (seen) object, is the essential mechanism by which aesthetics is used politically to relegate its object to an irretrievable past or absence. After Mackandal's execution, the narrator reports that "Ya no había nada que ver," meaning not only that there was nothing left to see but also that there was no longer any relevance, clearly not the case for the mass of slaves who frequented the scene. Spectacle, representation, history, and the collusion among the three are anathema to the Afro-Caribbean understanding of temporality and presence, and this primary opposition represents the main theme or motif, established in part 1, on which the novel's contrapuntal composition is carried out.[41]

While the masses only see Mackandal escape from the flames, calling out "Mackandal sauvé," very few saw, the narrator reports, the ten soldiers who seized Mackandal and shoved him headfirst into the flames. The whites, having eliminated Mackandal from the realm of the visible, are convinced that the matter has been decisively concluded. Meanwhile the slaves, for whom invisibility is no sign of absence, are convinced that Mackandal has remained in the "kingdom of this world." The white colonists wish to represent Mackandal's execution as spectacle, representation, and history (as part of the past), while the black slaves perceive the event as immediacy and continuation. The distance between observer and observed that is the sine qua non of spectacle is eliminated or overcome, since Mackandal rises from the flames and "sinks into the black wave of the slave masses." Mackandal can be compared to the point on a time line, with the opposing camps stemming from that point and extending in different directions. We may interpret "the kingdom of this world" as referring not only to the terrestrial world down here as opposed to the celestial world of the afterlife, but also as a temporal connotation, this world in the present time as opposed to the bygone world of the past, reified as history.

Mackandal's execution sets the stage for various repetitions and recurrences throughout the novel that elaborate the principal theme of a binary or adversarial split. In them, the Occidental world will invariably attempt to impose a finality on events through specular techniques of representation, a tactic that will also consistently prove ineffectual in its attempt at mastery since the Afro-Caribbean is portrayed as rejecting it in favor of a rhythmically grounded notion of temporality that is oriented to present and future time.

There is a description early in the novel of the slaves whose ears did not despair of hearing the voice of the great conch shells. The voices of these shells, or *lambis*, do finally appear in part 2, as a result of the "pact" resulting in the uprising led by Mackandal's successor, Boukman:

> From far off came the sound of a conch-shell trumpet. What was strange was that the slow bellow was answered by others in the hills and forests. And others floated in from farther off by the sea, from the direction of the farms of Milot. It was as though all the shell trumpets of the coast, all the

> Indian *lambis*, all the purple conchs that served as doorstops, all the shells that lay alone and petrified on the summits of the hills, had begun to sing in chorus. Suddenly, another conch raised its voice in the main quarters of the plantation. Others, higher-pitched, answered from the indigo works, from the tobacco shed, from the stable. (73)

Up to this point, the drum had the function of animating the rhythms accompanying work and of summoning the intervention of a liberating force, but tonality now makes its appearance in the form of the idiophonic conch shells. Whereas the slave labor had been performed with a drum accompaniment whose rhythm promised a future deliverance, the tonality of the conch shells now announces that the awaited moment has arrived. What stands out from this extraordinary description is the fact that the various pitches and timbres produced by the striking variety of different shells (especially in the original text) enter the "chorus" at different moments and at different pitches, resulting in a radical counterpoint or fugue.

If, in *Ecue-Yamba-O*, the narrator had borrowed terms from Occidental music ("allegro," "philharmonic," etc.) to describe Afro-Cuban music, creating a disconcerting and conflicted juxtaposition, he now applies a comparable terminology to achieve a more deliberate and pointed effect. Paralleling this chorus of conch shells is another chorus in the Santiago Cathedral, directed by Esteban Salas. While M. Lenormand de Mézy, "growing older by the week," prays in the Santiago Cathedral, Ti Noël has the opportunity to listen to the chorus under Salas's direction: "It was really impossible to understand why this choirmaster, whom everyone seemed to respect notwithstanding, was determined that the singers should enter the chorus one after another, part of them singing what the others had sung before, and setting up a confusion of voices fit to exasperate anyone" (86). Ti Noël identifies strongly with the "Voodoo" warmth of the baroque cathedral, including the human hair of the Christ and the wealth of "symbols, attributes, and signs" that are "seductive for their presence." This religious affinity felt by the Afro-Caribbean for Spanish Catholicism had been observed by Carpentier in *Music in Cuba* as something that existed as early as the sixteenth century. Ti Noël "never encountered this [Voodoo] warmth in the Sulpician temples of the Cap," an indication that Carpentier considers the hybrid culture of the Afro-Hispanic world a New World baroque alternative to the imported European Enlightenment of the late eighteenth century.

The similarity between the two descriptions of musical phenomena resides not only in the fact that in both the call of the conch shells and the baroque chorus the voices enter the "group singing" at different times and registers. What highlights the connection between the two scenes as one that is not merely casual is the specific audience indicated for both "choruses" and their respective reactions. For on closer inspection, we realize that the two scenes bear an inverse relationship, since it is Ti Noël, slave, who responds to the music of Esteban Salas, and none other than M. Lenormand de Mézy, master, who hears and reacts to the call of the conch shells. This crisscross or chiasmatic relationship amounts to a commentary or response on the part of the narrator not only to Rousseau's remark about Occidental music being "empty noise to the ear of a Caribbean" (a Rousseau aria is mentioned explicitly in the novel) but to Diderot's observation as well that "the melody of primitives will be too simple for us, and our music too complex for them ."[42] Were Carpentier truly interested in a synthesis or symbiosis between Occidental and Afro-Caribbean worlds, he would have taken steps to overturn or reverse the *philosophes*' differentiation. To the contrary, through this chiasmus, Carpentier seems ultimately to reinforce or complete the opposition by representing the music of both worlds as mutually incomprehensible.

For Ti Noël, "it was truly impossible to comprehend" the canonic or contrapuntal technique involved in Salas's *villancico*. And yet, as we have seen, this technique is not so different from that of the call of the conch shells announcing Boukman's uprising, where several voices of varying timbres and pitches also entered the mix in the form of call-and-response and, in fact, bears a striking resemblance to it. We may therefore conclude that this incomprehensibility is more a result of function and context than of formal technique. The chorus in the Santiago cathedral functions as accompaniment of Lenormand de Mézy's "groaning ejaculatories" in anticipation of his approaching demise. In fact, the entire chapter "Santiago de Cuba" that concludes with this scene amounts to an extended linkage of Occidental music with decadence and death, in a carnivalesque last hurrah of the ousted colonists from Saint Domingue: "All the bourgeois norms had come tumbling down. What mattered now was to play the trumpet, give a brilliant performances in a minuet trio, or even strike a triangle on the right beat for the greater glory of the Tívoli orchestra" (83). While the accelerated minuets are the precursors of the waltz, the latter also seal the fate of the former as yet more of history's detritus, of something that is soon to be irretrievably lost. It is within this historically retrospective context that

Ti Noël cannot comprehend the music that accompanies Lenormand de Mézy's last rites. It is fitting that the last lines of the chapter are yet again comprised of a song, but this time one chanted by Ti Noël himself, who had heard it from Mackandal, who, conversely, represents a prospective protomessianic intervention. Correspondingly—and this is where Carpentier radicalizes Rousseau's judgment—the so-called simplicity of Afro-Caribbean music also renders it incomprehensible to the ears of Lenormand de Mézy. If it was "impossible to understand" the canonic or fugal techniques of Esteban Salas's chorus for Ti Noël, then this impossibility is mirrored by the master's realization after Boukman's uprising and the near destruction of the Northern Plain of Saint Domingue that sometimes a drum might in fact be something more than a goatskin stretched over the opening of a hollow log. Unfortunately for Lenormand de Mézy, this understanding comes too late.

Once we have established this mutual incompatibility and miscomprehension of the retrospective and prospective worldviews, we realize that much of the novel is a variation on this motif. In a chapter entitled "The Daughter of Minos y Pasiphäe" (none other then Phèdre herself, of course), M. Lenormand de Mézy's second wife gives a drunken performance of this passage from Racine's tragedy for a public comprised of the plantation's slaves:

> *Mes crimes desormais ont comblé la mesure*
> *Je respire à la fois l'inceste et l'imposture.* (61)

The slaves do not comprehend the historico-mythical representation inherent in these verses and take the recitation at face value, as a confession of unspeakable crimes. They conclude that "the lady must have committed many crimes in days gone by, and that she was probably in the colony to get away from the police of Paris" (61). Contrary to such "immoralities, the slaves continued to revere Mackandal." Whereas this chapter begins with a description of the economic prosperity of the Cap Français twenty years after Mackandal's execution, a prosperity characterized by the appearance of a store selling violas and traverse flutes, the chapter concludes once again with a reference to "simple songs" that Ti Noël had composed to the glory of Mackandal, by which he "transmitted" to his children the exploits of the Mandingan warrior. The songs kept alive the memory of the one-armed man who "would return when least expected."

The narrative recurrence to music as a vehicle for expressing this absolute incongruence renders the split incomplete, since music, to echo the language of Naomi B. Sokoloff in her study of the novel's use of rhetorical tropes, is a metonymic device, suggesting a formal or inherent comparability even if the result is contrastative. In other words, despite the enormous differences between Afro-Caribbean and European conceptions of music, the very category of music is what brings the two sides of the equation into the same semantic field. *Blancas* (half notes) and *negras* (quarter notes) are visually antithetical, but, like the opposing voices of a fugue, are united within the totality of the musical staff. This being the case, it would be worthwhile to observe an occasion in the text in which synthesis *rather* than separation of the Enlightened Occident and the Afro-Caribbean takes place. Henri Christophe and the construction of Sans-Souci and the Citadel La Ferrière is one of the best-known episodes in the novel. Since Henri Christophe represents an attempt to implement a hybrid or syncretic world of Afro-Caribbean autonomous power with European aesthetic trappings, it is deserving of scrutiny as a possible countermotif or alternative to the overriding theme of mutual exclusion. The narrator goes to lengths to underline the kind of "symbiosis" or syncretism that, we will recall, Carpentier would claim was his objective: "Through an open window came the sound of a dance orchestra in full rehearsal. . . . But what surprised Ti Noël most was the discovery that this marvelous world, the like of which the French governors of the Cap had never known, was a world of Negroes" (115). But we soon realize that, rather than symbiosis, Henri Christophe's borrowing of European decor for his kingdom results more in a kind of grotesque monstrosity than in a cultural miscegenation. Monstrosity is certainly an appropriate way to describe the air that Carpentier lends the court of King Christophe. This incompatibility is especially revealed in Christophe's fondness for European music, and in the description of the gentrified musicians of his court: "Christophe noticed that the musicians of the royal chamber were crossing the entrance court, carrying their instruments. Each displayed his professional deformity. The harpist stooped, as though humpbacked under the weight of his harp; another thin as a rail, seemed pregnant with the drum that hung around his neck; another clasped a helicon" (142). This passage is reminiscent of Carpentier's wary judgments against the advent of the Afro-Caribbean professional musician in *Music in Cuba* and his negative portrayal in *Ecue-Yamba-O*. In fact, much of the mentioned "deformity" is linked to the fact that these are musicians by "profession." The instruments are described as utterly alien and cumbersome to the Afro-Caribbean body; the harp and the helicon, too, with their mechanistic architecture of strings, valves, and pipes, are in stark contrast to the "organic" or nonmechanistic idiophones, the drum and the conch shell, which had been played by the Afro-Caribbean musician up to this point. And so it is fitting that the uprising against Henri Christophe should involve a radical conversion of these oppressive musical instruments into the harbingers of revolution: "His Majesty took careful note of his grenadiers. . . . The untuned drums were not playing the prescribed call, but a syncopated tone in three beats produced not by the drumsticks but by hands against leather" (142–43). Since, in Carpentier's interpretation, the white world is represented by mediation and distance while the Afro-Caribbean world is best characterized by immediacy, then this discrepancy is allegorically depicted in this scene. The drumstick, the very mediator between hand and drum, is discarded in favor of immediate contact between fingers and drumhead.

Jean Jonassaint suggests (somewhat provocatively) that, in the Francophone Caribbean context, the translation from a literary-discursive realm of concepts such as indigenism, négritude, and *créolité* into the "real world" of political power results in a kind of "tropical fascism" embodied in the Haitian dictator Duvalier.[43] Carpentier portrays an opposing tendency in the figure of Henri Christophe, who eschewed nativism and the "African mysticism" of other of Haiti's first leaders in favor of a court with a "European air." For Carpentier it is precisely these European pretensions on the part of a black leader that result in a regime as tyrannical as those that preceded the revolution. Ti Noël, enslaved once more, makes the comparison explicit: "[T]he Negro began to think that the chamber-music orchestras of Sans Souci, the splendor of the uniforms, and the statues of naked white women soaking up the sun . . . were the product of a slavery as abominable as that he had known on the plantation of M. Lenormand de Mézy" (122). And so, ironically, though the miscegenation of European and Afro-Caribbean worlds was depicted as producing a monstrous progeny (like the daughter of Minos and Pasiphäe), once again overturning or problematizing Carpentier's stated aim of cultural symbiosis, this incongruous miscegenation does have the effect of elevating Ti Noël's consciousness. In yet another of the novel's repetitions or echoes, Ti Noël, enslaved anew, recalls a sailors' song that he had sung in "mental counterpoint" to Lenormand de Mézy's fife march in the novel's first chapter. But now Ti Noël experiences a revelation: "Staggering in the moonlight, he set out for home, vaguely recalling a song that in other days he had sung on his way back from the city. A song that was all insults to a king. That was the important thing: to *a king*" (132). In the first recitation of the sailor's song, Ti Noël underlined the fact that the maligned and effeminate king could be from England, France, or Spain, and contrasted him to the venerated African king. Now, it would appear, this rejection of tyranny has been universalized to become a categorical judgment against a king with no national or racial modifiers.

Pendularity

I have argued to this point that the entire framework of Carpentier's writing between *Ecue-Yamba-O* and *The Kingdom of This World* relied on cultural opposition, facilitated by the historical context of the Enlightenment as its motor. Carpentier questions the idea that so-called "Western progress" is temporally forward-oriented and replaces it with a portrait of the West that is retrospective and decadent, whereby each Western historical innovation—and music is Carpentier's privileged instance of this process—results in the irretrievable loss of what was replaced, creating a fragmentation in historical time the consequences of which were already lamented in *Ecue-Yamba-O*. The apt image for this temporal view is Benjamin's angel of history, who, turned to face the past, is blown backward by the storm of progress into the future, with the ruins of history piling up before it.[44] The Afro-Caribbean slave, caught in the same storm, is, to the contrary, facing forward, awaiting the Messianic reappearance of Mackandal and the call of the conch shells.

The repetition of events at different historical moments in *The Kingdom of This World* would seem to suggest a notion of history without progress, since tyranny reappears in Haiti even after the whites have been thrown out, and the basic social structure of masters and slaves remains intact. But despite this vision of history in which situations remain the same, Ti Noël nonetheless undergoes a transformation of consciousness by effacing the notion of race from his idea of the enemy (the unmodified king). Hence it can be concluded that through the elevation of consciousness or historical revelation, Ti Noël has taken the first step toward transcending or sublating the master/slave deadlock.

In the celebrated prologue to *The Kingdom of This World*, Carpentier explicitly opposes his notion of *lo real-maravilloso* (the marvelous-real) to "the return of the real. . . . the commonplaces of 'literary engagement' or the eschatological joy of certain existentialists,"[45] a not-so-subtle prod at Sartre and his notion of political engagement. While the prologue does identify "revelation" by name as one of the most privileged modes of *lo real-maravilloso*, Ti Noël's quasi-dialectical revelation in fact seems more akin to the maligned "eschatological" variety than to the magical or marvelous. And yet the advent of a dialectic, leading to a resolution of conflicts and a synthesis, would threaten to bring the entire Carpenterian edifice tumbling down. It is no surprise, then, that Carpentier closes the door on this burgeoning dialectic. For if an elevated consciousness suggests a dialectic, then surely the idea of nature as an even more powerful force than human consciousness signals a regression to a weaker term. Recalling the return to the countryside in *Ecue-Yamba-O*, Ti Noël returns to his former master's plantation "like an eel to the mud in which it was spawned" (127). And in fact, nature, not consciousness or history, has the last word in *The Kingdom of This World*, as a massive hurricane sweeps over the Cap Français and the Northern Plain, carrying away all trace of Ti Noël.[46] Nature completes the work of men rather than the reverse: despite the brief glimpse of a dialectic, of an emerging and autonomous human consciousness, the narrator's interpretive intervention as the novel concludes, in which "man's greatness resides precisely in wishing to better himself" despite adverse conditions, amounts to a compromise or undecidability, between a consciousness that, driven by a wish for betterment, evolves and progresses, and a world ruled by repetitive cycles. The fitting symbol for this undecidability is the figure of the spiral—the hurricane that determines the novel's denouement. The spiral, neither perfect circle nor straight line but rather a combination of the two, amounts to a tropological equivalent of this hesitation.

Remarkably, Carpentier will in the decade following *El reino de este mundo* (1949) repeat this historical and narrative back-and-forth movement, from the modern setting of *The Lost Steps* (*Los pasos perdidos*, 1953) back to the eighteenth century in *Explosion in a Cathedral* (*El siglo de las luces*, 1962 [written in 1959]). This double return will again serve the similar function of reversing or recasting what is essentially a psychological conflict—the modern protagonist's frustrated search to recover a lost utopia in *The Lost Steps*—into one that is once more concretely historical: Victor Hugues's frustrated attempt to bring the French Revolution to the shores of the Caribbean.

We could go even further and suggest that this movement between the twentieth and eighteenth centuries is repeated yet a third time in the 1970s, with *Reasons of State* (*El recurso del método*, 1974) and *Ba-*

roque Concerto (*Concierto barroco*, 1974). And yet the historical paradigm of mutual exclusion no longer seems entirely applicable in *Baroque Concerto.* In this, his final excursion to the eighteenth century, Carpentier now appears more interested in synthesis than separation; and music, which before had been the discursive figure that most clearly embodied mutual exclusion, will now be the very sign of this synthesis. The trumpet will replace the *lambi* shell as an emblem that temporally and culturally links jazz to the music of the eighteenth century. Despite his contention that this symbiosis was his age-old aspiration, only in *Baroque Concerto*—his third attempt at depicting the eighteenth century—does Carpentier gesture toward the possibility of a cultural and temporal synthesis.

And yet in the end it would seem that this longed-for synthesis in fact remains more gestural than realized. For if Carpentier attempted to overcome the barriers of temporality by catapulting characters from the eighteenth century to the setting of a Louis Armstrong concert, it is not surprising to find in *Baroque Concerto* echoes of Carpentier's earlier way of thinking about history and temporality as well. Twenty-five years after the publication of *The Kingdom of This World*, it is astounding to find yet again the precise formulation of a temporal divergence between a retrospective Europe and a prospective America:

> "You mustn't forget that great history feeds on fable. Our world seems like a fable to the people *over here* because they've lost their sense of the fabulous. They call everything *fabulous* that is remote, irrational, that belongs to yesterday." He broke off. "They don't understand that the fabulous is in the future."[47]

The reemergence of this temporal schism confirms the appeal that this rhetorical and conceptual paradigm consistently held for Carpentier. But more importantly it establishes the pendular undecidability between synthesis and opposition, between the twentieth century and the eighteenth, to be perhaps the most enduring—and therefore productive—trait of his writing.

Carpentier's historical imagination, in representing the eighteenth century, established a preponderant precedent of historical fiction for the Hispanic Caribbean. In subsequent chapters, I show how two more recent writers of the Hispanic tradition, Reinaldo Arenas and Edgardo Rodríguez Juliá, both explicitly acknowledge their debt to Carpentier and in some ways attempt to move beyond the parameters he established. Now let us turn to a writer and intellectual of the Anglophone tradition in the Caribbean who, despite uncanny similarities with Carpentier, never explicitly engaged in dialogue or intertextuality with his Cuban contemporary. The Trinidadian C. L. R. James will focus his narrative on Toussaint L'Ouverture, the most admired of the Haitian Republic's founding fathers. Despite the plethora of historical names that populate Carpentier's writing about the Francophone Caribbean, Toussaint L'Ouverture is strangely absent.

And yet there is a "Toussaint" that is mentioned in *The Kingdom of This World*. In the chapter "Human Guise" that describes the advent of Mackandal during an Afro-Cuban ritual invocation, there is an offhand reference to a certain "Toussaint, the cabinet maker." Verity Smith's compelling essay correctly points out that though Toussaint L'Ouverture was not a cabinet maker (*ebanista*), the invocation of the first name of the most famous of the Haitian revolutionaries is surely a historical "wink" to the reader on the part of the Cuban author.[48] For Smith, the fact that the house servant "had carved the Three Wise Men in wood, but they were too big for the Nativity" (45) is undoubtedly a reference to the three Black Jacobins of the Haitian Revolution: Toussaint, Dessalines, and Christophe.[49] Why precisely Carpentier chose to focus on Christophe at the expense of the other two is the question Smith poses. The answer probably has everything to with Carpentier's trip to Haiti in 1943, his visit to Christophe's citadel of La Ferrière and palace at Sans Souci as well as the author's architectural imagination. And yet it is also conceivable that in 1949 Carpentier was aware of C. L. R. James's *The Black Jacobins*, which had been published in 1938, and which, though not a historical novel about Toussaint L'Ouverture, Dessalines and the Haitian Revolution, does in fact treat these topics in a quasi-literary fashion (as I discuss in chapter 2). Carpentier's novel about the Haitian Revolution and his posterior *Explosion in a Cathedral* about the importation of the French Revolution, the guillotine, and the reinstatement of slavery in the French Caribbean complement James's authoritative and enduring account of the Haitian Revolution. Together they contribute essential pieces to assembling the puzzle of the modern Caribbean historical imagination.

2 Enlightened Hesitations

C. L. R. James, Toussaint L'Ouverture, and the Black Masses

> Laziness and cowardice are the reasons why such a large proportion of men, even when nature has long emancipated them from alien guidance . . . nevertheless gladly remain immature for life.
>
> Kant, "An Answer to the Question: What Is Enlightenment?"

In the previous chapter, I characterize the writing of Alejo Carpentier as being informed by a subtle contradiction at its core: the author's proclaimed intention to find synthesis and symbiosis between Afro-Caribbean and European Enlightenment culture is in fact belied by the narrative and psychological propensity to thematize their very incommensurability. In the case of the great Trinidadian writer and intellectual C. L. R. James, an inverse tendency seems to operate. James's towering contribution to Caribbean writing and scholarship, *The Black Jacobins*, also balances certain tensions that, left to themselves, might seem to be mutually canceling or exclusive. And yet, whereas for Carpentier an intellectual acknowledgment of the interpenetration and mutual dependence of Caribbean and European culture gives way to an almost libidinal attraction to incommensurability, in the case of James—at least the C. L. R. James who published *The Black Jacobins* in 1938—the specificity of eighteenth-century Saint Domingue is deemphasized in favor of a totalizing view tending toward universality. In 1971, James intimated that his thoughts when he wrote *The Black Jacobins* were in fact directed toward the cause of African independence: "Now, what did I have I mind when I wrote this book? I had in mind the writing about the San Domingo Revolution as the preparation for the revolution that George Padmore and all of us were interested in, that is, the revolution in Africa."[1] For James (in 1938), the Haitian Revolution had an almost allegorical and organic relationship not only to the French Revolution but to early-twentieth-century Africa; and European literary genres such as epic and tragedy were an intricate part of the historical unfolding. In this sense, James is a far more engaged partisan of historical and cultural "symbiosis" or interconnectedness than is Carpentier.

The Black Jacobins, more than a history of an eighteenth-century slave rebellion in the West Indies, is also a commentary and reflection on the Enlightenment. Toussaint L'Ouverture, the leader of the Haitian Revolution and Haiti's most prominent "founding father," represents for James the unequivocal figure of the autonomous Black Caribbean who has thrown off the yoke of extraneous authority in order to achieve maturity; by that very definition, Toussaint is for James the prototype of the Enlightened Man—a problematic and paradoxical categorization. The contradictions and tensions that the present study will bring out result not so much from a shortcoming on the part of James, but rather from the fact that the particular conceptual conditions within which he operates already contain an incommensurability—between leaders and masses, center and periphery, autonomy and dependence. James works simultaneously within the framework of Enlightenment thought while challenging or attempting to go beyond its tenets—a dual effort that could be described as emblematic of the modern moment in the Caribbean historical imagination. This effort to operate within the laws of Enlightenment historicity while transcending its borders might be seen as contradictory or counterproductive; at the same time, however, the paradoxes this situation occasions provide a matrix for some of the most notable achievements in Caribbean writing. James's identification with Toussaint is illustrative of the conflicts that characterize much of his writing, conflicts that, when read in the context of his lifelong production, come to a narrative climax in the form of a confessional in *Beyond a Boundary*, when James reflects on his decision to join the "white" cricket club, Maple: "I was teaching, I was known as a man cultivated in literature, I was giving lectures to literary societies on Wordsworth and Longfellow. Already I was writing. I moved easily in any society in which I found myself. So it was that I became one of the men whose 'surest sign of . . . having arrived is the fact that he keeps company with people lighter in complexion that himself.' . . . I had gone to the right and, by cutting myself off from the popular side, delayed my political development for years. But no one could see that then, least of all me."[2] This honest confession seems to contain the allegorical kernel of a critique of *The Black Jacobins*. As a response to those who would accuse James of deferring at times to the cultural icons of the West, there stands his solid record of indefatigable political labor, from his writing and activities on behalf of African Americans during his sojourn in the United States

(1938–53) [3] to his lifelong advocacy of African independence and Pan-Africanism. This ceaseless political activity and engagement, including political organization and collaboration, constant travel, the writing and editing of pamphlets and journals, the collecting of testimonials, and the organization of strikes and demonstrations, resulted in James's deportation from the United States in 1953 (after some fifteen years of residence) and, in 1965, his incarceration in Trinidad.[4]

Therefore, this chapter, while critiquing some of the cultural and ideological contradictions of *The Black Jacobins* (written, after all, in 1938, and revised in 1963), tells only part of the story. James's entire engagement and subsequent rupture with Trotsky (and Trotskyism) is another of its important chapters.[5] My focus on *The Black Jacobins* in this chapter to the exclusion of James's subsequent political work is due to the transcendent importance of both the text and the event it discusses within the context of this monograph and the intertextuality it provides with other modern historical reflections from the Caribbean. If there is any validity to the category of the "Enlightenment in the Caribbean," than surely the Haitian Revolution of 1791, at least for both James and Carpentier, is the paradigmatic event. James's text approaches the event precisely within this framework, vacillating between a critique of the Enlightenment that is fully conscious of its inconsistencies and an advocacy of its pretensions. This vacillation translates into a historical account that reenacts these tensions. My approach here is not so much to gauge these tensions culturally or historically, but rather, I am interested in transcribing the Jamesian dialectical tensions into rhetorical terms, in an attempt to locate James's text horizontally, within a Caribbean constellation of comparable rhetorical strategies for appropriating or repudiating the Enlightenment. In the introduction, I discussed what I see as the unsettled legacy of the Enlightenment, quoting critics who bemoan its inherent contradictions and conflicts of interest that impede the clear articulation of a vision and politics of freedom. Other commentators discern in the thought of certain Enlightenment philosophers the elaboration of an anti-imperial, anticolonial theoretical vision unrivaled in both its predecessors and successors. One of the sources of the enduring fascination that James's text exerts on us today is that it almost seems to dramatize within its pages these opposing tendencies. Even while consciously critiquing the limitations of the Enlightenment, James reenacts them in his portrait of Toussaint and the denouement of the Haitian Revolution.

To reiterate a point made in the introduction, one of the most notable hallmarks of the Enlightenment is the division of the world into "enlightened leaders" and "ignorant masses"; this dualism is certainly one that characterizes James's thought in general. Toussaint is such a fascinating figure for James precisely because he promises—and, as James is painfully aware, fails to deliver—a bridge or mediation between these popular masses and enlightened few. And yet James himself seems to both share in and reenact this failure. As Kara M. Rabbitt has astutely pointed out, "it should be noted that James's poetic and dramatic rendering of Toussaint in *The Black Jacobins* ironically seems occasionally to efface that very element: the people."[6] The generic interplay of fiction, history, and myth is one of the hallmarks of Caribbean writing. Rabbitt's essay demonstrates the "conscious use of Aristotelian tragic structure" in order to reveal how "James creates a dramatic figure out of a historical one." James's famous declaration of the literary genre at work in *The Black Jacobins* highlights this problematic operation, and is worth quoting at length:

> The hamartia, the tragic flaw, which we have constructed from Aristotle, was in Toussaint not a moral weakness. It was a specific error, a total miscalculation of the constituent events. Yet what is lost by the imaginative freedom and creative logic of great dramatists is to some degree atoned for by the historical actuality of his dilemma. It would therefore be a mistake to see him merely as a political figure in a remote West Indian island. . . . The Greek tragedians could always go to their gods for a dramatic embodiment of fate, the *dike* which rules a world neither they nor we ever made. But not Shakespeare himself could have found such a dramatic embodiment of fate as Toussaint struggled against, Bonaparte himself; nor could the furthest imagination have envisaged the entry of the chorus, of the ex-slaves themselves, as the arbiters of their own fate.[7]

Though James's reference recalls Aristotle and not Kant, this grafting of the tragic mode onto historical events betrays an Enlightenment criterion, much in the same way in which Horkheimer and Adorno traced the Enlightenment back to *The Odyssey*.[8] In the latter study, the Enlightenment could be described as a transhistorical emergence of the autonomous individual and the dissolution of myth, rather than as a specific body of thought linked to a historical epoch. The category of the "tragic" in James's study functions similarly, insofar as the emergence of the tragic individual is opposed to the faceless mass—"the ex-slaves themselves"—compared to the chorus in Greek tragedy. The almost insurmountable challenge that James will face in his narration is to maintain the tragic structure of the individual against the chorus or masses, with the latter themselves emerging as protagonists, "the arbiters of their own fate." In a revealing footnote that exposes this difficulty, James quotes at length from Georges Lefebvre, the historian of the French Revolution: "It is therefore in the popular mentality, in the profound and incurable distrust which was born in the soul of the people, in regard to the aristocracy. . . . [I]t is there that we must seek the explanation of what took place. The people and their unknown leaders knew what they wanted. . . . Who then are the leaders to whom the people listened? We would like to have the diary of the most obscure of these popular leaders."[9]

Despite the importance attributed to the masses or "people" by both James and Lefebvre, their very discernment of this framework—"leaders and masses"—marks the unrepresentable and unknowable quality of the latter. Lefebvre reveals this impasse by first positing the desirability or need to seek answers in the "popular," and yet when a pragmatic form of this inquiry is considered ("we would like to have the diary"), a schism occurs. From this popular mass, "unknown leaders" emerge, individuals, who are the only empirical entities who can serve as "authors" who produce the texts that historians scrutinize, and thus the original model of leaders and masses (with the former serving as synecdoche, representation [*Vertretung and Darstellung*][10] of the latter) is reproduced. The original dual framework therefore remains intact, and these vital masses subsist beyond representation, as an elusive referent or signified.

James's "effacement of the people" in *The Black Jacobins* requires qualification, then, since this effacement is not so much the result of an oversight on the author's part but rather an unavoidable consequence of a method, which is literary in form while employing categories inherited from the Enlightenment. In a series of lectures delivered in 1971 and reprinted in the journal *Small Axe* in 2000, James reflects on his writing of *The Black Jacobins*, elucidates his state of mind and intellectual influences at the time of its publication (1938), comments on the 1963 revisions, and even goes so far as to speculate about how he might have written the book differently in 1971. James recalls the quotation from Lefebvre cited above and underscores yet again the French historian's regret that we are not in possession of that "lost diary" of one of the obscure and forgotten leaders of the French Revolution. In 1971, however, James now takes issue with Lefebvre on one score: yes, a lost diary would be helpful, but not from some lost *leader*: "You see, in 1971, what I have to say about Lefebvre is that he is concerned with the obscure leader—*I am not*. I am concerned with the two thousand leaders who were there. That is the book I would write. . . . I would have something to say about those two thousand leaders."[11] James's one regret in these lectures seems to be precisely that which I uphold as the source of tension in *The Black Jacobins*: a top-heavy approach that overemphasizes the *leaders* at the expense of the *masses*. Nevertheless, he reiterates toward the end of the lectures the validity of the Aristotelian approach of the tragic figure with which he framed Toussaint. Thus some of these original tensions that abound in *The Black Jacobins*, and that, in my view, bestow the work with an enduring literary quality, resurface in the 1971 lectures.

Kant writes: "For there will always be a few who think for themselves, even among those appointed as guardians for the common mass,"[12] a sentence in many ways echoed in James's text. In fact, the notion of the masses, or the people—whether referring to the Haitian ex-slaves or the French masses that stormed the Bastille—is one of the narrator's recurring references and preoccupations. These two groups are inextricably linked in the narration, contiguous chapters being entitled "The San Domingo Masses Begin" and "And the Paris Masses Complete." The idea of the masses, then, rather than being ignored or effaced, ostensibly receives *heightened* discursive attention in the narration and constitutes James's privileged historical subject. But in a problem strikingly similar to that encountered by James's Caribbean contemporary Alejo Carpentier, it is a question of access and the phenomenological status of the anonymous masses. Carpentier accesses them rhetorically, so to speak, by creating fictional characters that serve as metonymies of the bygone masses in an imaginary realm. Despite James's literary approach to the topic, Carpentier's option is not available to the historian. More recent historiography emphasizes culture "from below," as Carolyn Fick, a disciple of James, terms it. Nevertheless, even historians who take this approach of reconstructing the Haitian Revolution by emphasizing slave culture and society encounter the trap of having to rely on sources "from above" for much of their information. Fick recurs to the chronicles and travelogues of Moreau de Saint-Méry, Père Labat, and the Baron de Wimpffen—the holy triumvirate of colonial sources about eighteenth-century Saint Domingue—for information about slave culture and society, just as Carpentier and James do. In his 1971 lectures, James specifically expresses remorse about his overreliance on travelogue sources. After reiterating a complimentary description of a slave written by the

Baron de Wimpffen, author of *Voyage à Saint Domingue*, one of the most important eighteenth-century travelogues, James declares: "That is again a description of an observer, a *sympathetic* observer. I wouldn't do that today. I would write the actual statements of the slaves telling *what they were doing*. . . . We have had enough of what *they* have said about us even when sympathetic. It is time that we begin to say what *we* think about ourselves." Naturally it is worth noting that in 1971 James uses the first-person plural to align himself unequivocally with the masses, with the slaves who had lived in Saint Domingue two hundred years before these lectures were delivered. This declaration of alliances marks a clear evolution of James's thought since 1938, and one might go so far as to extrapolate that were James to have written the *Black Jacobins* thirty years after its original date of publication, perhaps Toussaint L'Ouverture, who (as David Geggus points out, had not only *not* been a slave for some time at the start of the Haitian Revolution but in fact had been a slave owner himself), would not have played so prominent a role in the book.[13]

One pioneer of approaching Saint Domingue history and culture "from below" was the Haitian historian Jean Fouchard, and yet in his quest for popular sources to inform our understanding of the period, he relies on a colonial mediatic organ, the *Affiches Américaines*, in addition to the aforementioned colonial chroniclers, as major sources. In an interesting case of Caribbean intertextuality, James writes the preface to Fouchard's *The Haitian Maroons: Liberty or Death* (1972). Fouchard will also supply the major historical raw material for Marie Chauvet's *Dance on the Volcano*, a novel about the days leading up to the Haitian Revolution that I discuss in chapter 3. In these examples of Caribbean intertextuality "from below," it is interesting to note that the schism of masses and leaders reemerges through a perhaps unavoidable scrutiny and emphasis on characters, emplotment, and texts.

The high/low, leaders/masses divide pervades *The Black Jacobins* as it does the 1971 lectures that reflect back on it. Regarding Toussaint's fatal flaw or *hamartia*, James makes the following observation: "Toussaint, in his twelve years of politics, national and international, made only one serious mistake, the one which ended his career" (224). And yet what James's narration of the Haitian Revolution makes clear is that the series of misjudgments and errors leading up to Toussaint's demise are too numerous to be condensed into a single "tragic flaw." After the comparison of the ex-slaves to the chorus in a Greek tragedy, "as the arbiters of their own fate," the following cryptic sentence completes this key paragraph (it is intended, as a clarification of Toussaint's "miscalculation" or tragic flaw): "Toussaint's certainty of this as the ultimate and irresistible resolution of the problem to which he refused to limit himself, that explains his mistakes and atones for them" (292). This is one of the key sentences in *The Black Jacobins*, and also one of the most difficult. To which error is James referring? Toussaint's certainty of the ex-slaves as "arbiters of their own fate"? How can an error grave enough to be qualified as a "tragic flaw" be at the same time that which "explains mistakes" while simultaneously atoning for them? James again employs cryptic rhetoric: "His severity and proclamation reassuring the whites aimed at showing Bonaparte that all classes were safe in San Domingo, and that he could be trusted to govern the colony with justice. It is probably true, and is his greatest condemnation" (286). Though James is elusive when it comes to spelling out precisely what Toussaint's tragic flaw was, one of the greatest tactical errors was certainly the execution of his nephew Moïse, the commander of the revolutionary garrison at Fort Liberté. Yet at the same time it is clear, for both James and the reader, that Moïse's execution is more than a question of tactics or a strategic error. As James himself admits, apart from fear of his growing popularity, the reasons why Toussaint had Moïse shot are unclear, but the political differences between uncle and nephew reveal more about Toussaint's unarticulated "flaw" than the execution itself: "What exactly did Moïse stand for? Toussaint refused to break up the big estates. Moïse wanted small grants of land for junior officers and even the rank-and-file. Toussaint favoured the whites against the Mulattoes. Moïse sought to build an alliance between the blacks and the Mulattoes against the French" (278).

Toussaint favored the whites. But, since Moïse was opposed to the latifundia that Toussaint tolerated, their differences were not merely race-based. James reports that Toussaint "was now afraid of the contact between the revolutionary army and the people, an infallible sign of revolutionary degeneration." And yet this character flaw—which is not the same as a "specific miscalculation"—is one that appears in Toussaint well before any revolutionary degeneration.

James goes to great lengths to convince the reader that Toussaint was capable of performing an extraordinary balancing act, between acknowledging and emulating all that was good and desirable about European civilization, while at the same time maintaining at arm's length the barbarism and excesses of European imperialism: "It is Toussaint's supreme merit that while he saw European civilisation as a valuable and necessary thing, and strove to lay its foundation among his people, he never had the illusion that it conferred any moral superiority" (271).

James's text abounds with similar rhetorical flourishes. Perhaps it is here, in its engagement with the rhetoric of Enlightenment categories, as much as in the so-called tragic structure of the narration, where the literary interest of this book resides. Is this merit, this capacity to winnow out the bad from the good with regard to the legacy of European civilization, a tenable practice? Can the material be valorized in its own right as a category autonomous of the ideological? And equally to the point, did Toussaint truly possess, or strive to possess, this capacity? We need look no further than an early moment in James's own text to supply us with a pertinent starting point to answer the first of these questions: "The slave trade and slavery were the economic basis of the French Revolution. 'Sad irony of human history,' comments Jaurès. 'The fortunes created at Bordeaux, at Nantes, by the slave-trade, gave to the bourgeoisie that pride which needed liberty and contributed to human emancipation'" (47).

James's quotation of Jaurès points to the inseparability of these categories, the material or institutional (Jaurès's slave-trade), which, according to James, Toussaint saw as valuable and necessary, and the ideological (Toussaint's "moral"; Jaurès's "pride" and "liberty"), which, to borrow from a familiar model, serves as an inextricable superstructure to the material base. The long tentacles of the material and institutional benefits of slavery constrained well-intentioned *philosophes* such as Raynal, Diderot, and Condorcet, something that James understood clearly in 1938, well before Sala-Molins's *The Dark Side of Light*. James recognizes as well this unavoidable "linkage" as the source of the apparent hypocrisy in much of the thought of the Enlightenment concerning the colonial situation and slavery: "'Let the colonies be destroyed rather than be the cause of so much evil,' said the Encyclopaedia in its article on the slave-trade. But such outbursts neither then nor now have carried weight. The authors were compared to doctors who offered to a patient nothing more than invectives against the disease which consumed him" (24). Alexander von Humboldt once commented on precisely the same dynamic, so common during the years of the "Age of Revolution" and never quite so manifest as when applied to slavery in Saint Domingue: "One often sees men with their mouths full of beautiful philosophical maxims, who nevertheless violate the first principles of philosophy with their conduct, abusing slaves with a copy of Raynal in their hand, and speaking enthusiastically of the cause of freedom while selling the children of Negroes only a few months after their birth."[14] We have already established the de facto attitude of the Enlightenment vis-à-vis the periphery, which entails a prescription for autonomy while maintaining a subjectivity from this prescriptive vantage point. This is an attitude that, despite the heterogeneity of thought and positions among the ranks of Enlightenment thinkers, enjoys a surprising degree of unanimity among its members. The *philosophes* "thought of themselves as a *petite troupe*, with common loyalties and a common world view," as Peter Gay states it.[15] James demonstrates a clear understanding of the structural dynamic, and yet, as his portrait of Toussaint unfolds, it is also clear that for both the historian and his historical protagonist, the Enlightenment at times produced certain blind spots or lapses. By elevating Toussaint to the level of an extraordinary individual or historical protagonist, James shares in his flaw, which, in fact, though he hesitates in articulating it as such, consists of a distrust, alienation, or severance from the "masses," the ex-slaves themselves, and an overprivileging of the promises of the French (Revolution). In a curious slip, James reveals this prejudice or privileging at work:

> It was a crucial moment in world history. If the British could hold San Domingo, the finest colony in the world, they would once more be a power in American waters. Instead of being abolitionists they would be the most powerful practitioners and advocates for the slave trade, on a scale excelling anything they had ever done before. *But there was a more urgent issue.* If the British completed the conquest of San Domingo, the colonial empire of revolutionary France was gone; its vast resources would be directed into British pockets, and Britain would be able to return to Europe and throw army and navy against the revolution. (137, emphasis added)

James in effect claims in no uncertain terms that the fate of the French Revolution in Europe (at the hands of the British) is *more important* than the fate of the slave trade in Saint Domingue and by extension the emergence of the independent republic of Haiti. In the 1971 lectures, James makes this point even more forcefully when he claims that the French Revolution, "in my opinion is still the greatest historical event in the last thousand years of history—the French, not the Russian Revolution, the French Revolution."[16] Without underestimating the importance of the French Revolution, James's privileging of it in this context is surprising, especially when one considers James's own account of the degeneration of revolutionary principles under Napoleon—*including the reinstatement of slavery* in the French Caribbean—as well as the referential horizon of *The Black Jacobins*, which was the independence movement in Africa. James, like Toussaint, perhaps reveals an excessive fidelity or fascination with France in this passage at the expense of the Haitian masses, for whom, in the final instance, the fate of the French Revolution was of little consequence.

James's vacillations amount to a mirror image of Toussaint's flaw. He, too, as he claims for Toussaint, has a kind of historical faith in the masses to determine their own destiny, and yet he chronicles the Haitian Revolution first and foremost by focusing on the emergence of a particularly enlightened individual who takes precedence over the masses themselves. We need go no further than the title itself for evidence of this divergence. Does "The Black Jacobins" refer to the masses of nameless slaves who guaranteed the success of the Haitian Revolution, or the cadre of leaders, including Dessalines, Christophe, Rigaud, and Moïse, in addition to Toussaint? The subtitle, "Toussaint L'Ouverture and the San Domingo Revolution," makes clear that the subject of James's study will not be so much these masses but rather the individual who emerged as their leader.

Many are the passages that attest to this particular dynamic—of Toussaint as a shining star rising above the homogeneous masses. For example, "In describing the great figures of the French Revolution and Napoleonic era, one finds this note of astonishment, this 'I can't believe my own eyes' attitude, in writings about only three men: Bonaparte, Nelson the sailor, and Toussaint" (273). At times, the portrait of Toussaint borrows from the landscapes in a quasi-romantic fashion to highlight the hero's singularity and tragic solitude: "Toussaint, standing alone on a neighborhood peak, watched the vessels" (288). The thrust of David Scott's meditation in *Conscripts of Modernity* is precisely the tension between these romantic elements in *The Black Jacobins* and James's self-proclaimed use of tragedy in the 1963 revision to emplot the story of Toussaint L'Ouverture and the Haitian Revolution. For Scott, romance envisages a horizon of potentially limitless freedom in which human beings determine their own destiny, while tragedy implacably evokes the past as a burden imposing contingencies on our choices. He laments, "tragedy may help us better than Romance to cope with so unyielding a postcolonial present as our own."[17] Scott's sensitive reading sheds light on the impact of James's 1963 revisions, which incorporated the passages about the *hamartia* and tragedy. And yet it seems to me that what receives short shrift in this discussion of genre is the Enlightenment itself.

Žižek speaks about the "obverse of the Enlightenment" in which the imperative to question received knowledge is undermined by the blind acceptance of social custom, a sine qua non of rational thought explicitly acknowledged by both Descartes and Kant. But if owning slaves is among these customs, then the machinery of Enlightenment reason quickly reaches a limit and freezes up, resulting in vacillations and hesitations—both Jamesian keywords. Nevertheless, the primordial, fundamental subject of Kant's thought—human beings, or *Menschheit*—is elaborated in such as way as to interpellate all cultural, reasoning beings, including by extrapolation *slaves themselves*, thereby negating or trumping the accepted social conventions that defined slaves as property rather than people (as well as the philosopher's own unfortunate and contradictory remarks about non-European ethnicities). Thus, I believe we can discuss Toussaint and the Haitian Revolution squarely within the complex body of thought and the historical moment that corresponded to it, the Enlightenment, which contains both of the tendencies that Scott locates in tragedy and romance, without making further forays into European traditions and genres.

Toussaint is first mentioned within the context of one of the most authoritative and oft-quoted texts from the Enlightenment, Abbé Raynal's *Philosophical and Political History of the Establishments and Commerce of the Europeans in the Two Indies*:

> "Everywhere people will bless the name of the hero who shall have reestablished the rights of the human race; everywhere will they raise trophies in his honour."
>
> Over and over again Toussaint read this passage: "A courageous chief only is wanted. Where is he?" A courageous chief was wanted. It is the tragedy of mass movements that they need and can only too rarely find adequate leadership. (25)

For Scott, Raynal holds slavery to be "contrary to humanity, reason and justice," and he describes Raynal's language as "an incitement," an "incendiary vision."[18] And yet for Michel-Rolph Trouillot, it was Diderot rather than Raynal who was the real author of the famous Spartacus passages. According to Trouillot, the most progressive aspect of the text is the reference to the "human race" as a single species, though he also points out that the terms "slavery" and "slaves" were charged with a rhetorical connotation: "'slavery' was at that time an easy metaphor, accessible to a large public who knew that the word stood for a number of evils except perhaps the evil of itself."[19]

For Susan Buck-Morss in her groundbreaking study, slavery was "the root metaphor of Western political philosophy, connoting everything that was evil about power relations," and this metaphor remains, even among modern-day historians and intellectuals, bizarrely detached from slavery as it was being practiced at the time.[20] For Sala-Molins, to recall our introductory comments, the inclusion of the black slave in the brotherhood of humanity was beyond the purview of the *philosophes*, though for Muthu and Nesbitt, the idea of a single human race, including people of non-European ethnicities, is consistent with Kant's use of the term *Menschheit*. Trouillot also questions the bequeathed truism, repeatedly asserted (by James and others), that Toussaint had read the Raynal/Diderot passages about the Black Spartacus. The origin of this fact or fiction can be traced to Cousin d'Avallon, a contemporary of the Haitian Revolution who published Toussaint's biography in 1802, in which he asserts, "Toussaint L'Ouverture was the most declared partisan of Raynal; this philosopher's work became for him a breviary, so to speak."[21] We will perhaps never know with certainty whether or not Toussaint read Raynal/Diderot, but the repeated assertion that he did so is in itself revealing since it posits a direct causal relationship between the Enlightenment and the Haitian Revolution. The implication is that Toussaint, and by extension the slaves in the Caribbean, were incapable of envisaging freedom without its conceptual elaboration on the other side of the Atlantic. Sala-Molins forcefully takes exception to this logic as does James himself when he declares, "slaves have always wanted to be free."[22]

We have seen how the duality of masses and leaders is an unmistakable hallmark of the Enlightenment. It is again reproduced in Raynal's quotation, but it is perhaps more noteworthy that James, in his commentary that follows the citation, represents Toussaint's reaction to this text as well as his own reinforcement of the leaders/masses split. James, unlike a more recent generation of Caribbean writers, attempts no revision of the duality. The question certainly bears asking how any historical account of a revolutionary epoch could be carried out without recourse to the leaders/masses dynamic. James, however, does not ask it. Rather than being considered as a mere aggregate of individuals, which, statistically and demographically speaking at least, is their only empirically verifiable status, the masses in James are homogenized into a single will or "spirit." This monolithic mass is then endowed with characteristics belonging to individuals only, such as intelligence, goodness, etc. Another dynamic of Toussaint's tragic flaw in the narrative is that the mass-subject constitutes the ideal standard against which merit is measured.

From the outset, Toussaint is described as a product of the Enlightenment, as someone not only endowed with the proper talents to lead the masses to emancipation, but also equipped with adequate education and exposure to the ideas necessary to comprehend contemporary thought and political economy. The reference to Raynal is still of significance here, not only because of the influence it (allegedly) exerted on him, but also because the mere fact of Toussaint's access to it reveals the attribute of *literacy*, which in many ways encapsulates all the differences separating him from the masses: "Having read and re-read the long volume by Abbé Raynal on the East and West Indies, he had a thorough grounding in the economics and politics, not only of San Domingo, but of all the great empires of Europe which were engaged in colonial expansion and trade" (91). Repeatedly throughout the text, James's tone reaches panegyrical heights when Toussaint's literacy is discussed (ironic, if we consider that in the 1971 lectures James admonishes his audience: "But I want you to remember that bunch of fellows who had been slaves, they hadn't been educated, they hadn't been corrupted by education").[23] In fact, it is in the realm of literacy that James classifies Toussaint squarely within the Enlightenment tradition. At one point, James cites at length a letter from Toussaint to the Revolutionary Directory that James calls "a milestone in his career." This remarkable document swears fidelity to France while at the same time making it clear that no attempt to reestablish slavery in the colony will be tolerated. James quotes Toussaint: "But if, to re-establish slavery in San Domingo, this was done, then I declare to you it would be to attempt the impossible: we have known how to face dangers to obtain our liberty, we shall know how to brave death to maintain it." But almost as remarkable as the eloquence of Toussaint's letter is the tenor of James's characterization of it:

> Pericles on Democracy, Paine on the Rights of Man, the Declaration of Independence, the Communist Manifesto, these are some of the political documents which, whatever the wisdom or weaknesses of their analysis, have moved men and will always move them. . . . But Pericles, Tom Paine, Jefferson, Marx and Engels, were men of a liberal education formed in the traditions of ethics, philosophy and history. Toussaint was a slave, not six years out of slavery. . . . Superficial people have read his career in terms of

> personal ambition. This letter is their answer. Personal ambition he had. But he accomplished what he did because, superbly gifted, he incarnated the determination of his people never, never to be slaves again. (197–98)

Toussaint's extraordinary accomplishments here take on a double register: not only was he "superbly gifted," an individual talent whose accomplishments were only more impressive in light of his background, but at the same time he retains a link to the masses from whom, thanks to his gifts, he stands out in sharp relief. James, in a characterization that he surely would have retracted in 1971, describes Toussaint as "leader of a backward and ignorant mass" (198). The figure of Toussaint in the narration *promises* to recast this leaders/masses deadlock into a dialectical relation, with Toussaint himself as the synthesis or third term, sublating the best qualities of both.

One of the most embedded and easily caricatured hypocrisies of the Enlightenment legacy is that its thinkers, despite declarations against slavery, at the same time shared racist criteria. James himself pointed out that their invectives against slavery were superficial and of doubtful sincerity, and so by aligning Toussaint with this tradition, he is portrayed as *more* enlightened than the *philosophes* themselves. Rather than a contradiction, James sets up this divergence as a plenitude, as a portrait of an enlightened leader who, precisely because of his background in slavery rather than in the European liberal tradition, promises an elusive bridge over the gap that amounts to the flaw or lapsus within the thought of the Enlightenment. Were there any doubt of Toussaint's circumscription within Enlightenment currents, James reiterates this ultimate valorization of him, as both a lettered *philosophe* and a man of the people:

> That was why in the hour of danger Toussaint, uninstructed as he was, could find the language and accent of Diderot, Rousseau and Raynal, of Mirabeau, Robespierre and Danton. And in one respect he excelled them all. For even these masters of the spoken and written word, owing to the class complications of their society, too often had to pause, to hesitate, to qualify. Toussaint could defend the freedom of the blacks without reservation. (198)

It is curious that the similarity that James finds between Toussaint and these representatives of the French Enlightenment resides in the question of *style*: "the language and accent." It would perhaps be too hasty to suggest that James emphasizes "style" over "content," and yet the language he uses to characterize Toussaint's texts certainly conjures up this age-old duality. If repetition amounts to textual proof, then the valorization of Toussaint grounded largely on stylistics is not entirely casual: "That was the style, the accent of Toussaint and his men. The British and the Spaniards could not defeat it" (155). This duality between "style, accent" and whatever would be its counterpart, substantive ideas or content, for instance, constitutes an offshoot of the structural contradictions of the Enlightenment itself. The pauses and hesitations of the *philosophes* are merely the translation of these contradictions into rhetorical or stylistic terms. That James refers to them as "*masters* of the spoken and written word" may or may not be an intentional play, but reading it as such is appropriate. Toussaint is depicted as having achieved this *mastery* while at the same time preserving an inextricable link to *slavery*, to the masses. James's commentary on the Constitution of Saint Domingue, published in July 1801 (on which I comment in more detail presently), also underlines the fact that Toussaint stood out in sharp relief from the masses while embodying the principles that would set them free: "The Constitution is Toussaint L'Ouverture from the first line to the last, and in it he enshrined his principles of government. Slavery was forever abolished. Every man, whatever his color, was admissible to all employments, and there was to exist no other distinction than that of virtues and talents, and no other superiority than that which the law gives in the exercise of a public function" (263). Within the context of this discussion, James's language in this quotation is remarkable. One would perhaps expect the use of the possessive form to characterize the relationship between the Constitution and Toussaint, as in "Toussaint L'Ouverture's." And yet a metonymy is employed to express this relationship: the "Constitution *is* Toussaint." Rather than the embodiment of a thought, a set of political principles, or even the result of a collaboration of a constitutional assembly, James characterizes the Constitution as the embodiment or result of Toussaint himself: "In it *he* enshrined *his* principles of government."

James portrays Toussaint as someone whose enlightenment has transcended the rules of the Enlightenment itself, the boundaries between *leaders* and *masses*. For James, it seems, these contradictions were not in fact at the heart of the Enlightenment, not part of its very structure, but rather something only anecdotally or circumstantially associated with it. And yet at this point in the narration, James had already begun to hesitate, or, rather, to depict Toussaint as hesitant. The Constitution is summarized as abolishing slavery and eliminating racial discrimination in all realms of public life, and yet, just sentences before, James had reported the following about the composition of the Constitutional Assembly: "For this purpose he summoned an assembly of six men, one from each province, consisting of rich whites and Mulattoes: there was not one black. As always now, he was thinking of the effect in France, and not of the effect on his own masses" (263). James's critique here is more or less explicit (the colon connotes deliberateness), though the ironic or contradictory connection between the racial makeup of the Constituent Assembly and the precepts against racial discrimination as stipulated in the Constitution is not spelled out or commented upon explicitly. He indicates that the demographic and racial makeup of the Assembly reflects Toussaint's concern for the impression created in France, and yet one of the main historical points of James's narration is that the mulattoes represented as much or more of a threat to revolutionary France than did the blacks. Throughout the narration, James has been assembling his portrait of Toussaint as the embodiment of the Enlightenment, to the point of resolving in him the Enlightenment's own internal contradictions (between center and periphery, leaders and masses). When the symptoms of these contradictions reemerge in Toussaint himself, James is left in the difficult position of having to justify them as either politics or the result of a tragic flaw.

Just as Toussaint's mastery of the enlightened *style* in writing betrays contradictions, the question of style itself extends beyond the realm of texts. The question was posed earlier as to whether Toussaint, regardless of the theoretical and practical difficulty of compartmentalizing the good from the bad in European civilization, in fact harbored this elusive desire of retaining only that which was beneficial from French civilization (such as agricultural development) while leaving behind the detrimental (such as corruption, greed, and exploitation). Did Toussaint covet only those aspects of French civilization that would contribute to the well-being of his nascent nation while eschewing the excesses? It seems that James's emphasis of Toussaint's mastery of style in writing also extends to other cultural areas:

> [Toussaint] was anxious to see the blacks acquire the social deportment of the better class whites with their Versailles manners. (246)
>
> But he still continued to favour the whites. Every white woman was entitled to come to all "circles." Only the wives of the highest black officials could come. A white woman was called Madame, the black woman was

> citizen. Losing sight of his mass support, taking it for granted, he sought only to conciliate the whites at home and abroad. (262)

James had asserted that what distinguished Toussaint from the *philosophes* was that the latter had to hesitate too often in their pronouncements, whereas in Toussaint the unmediated link or bridge to the masses themselves translated into fluency. The emergence of these pauses and hesitations in Toussaint therefore requires a cryptic qualification on the part of the author: "Toussaint showed himself to be one of those few men for whom power is a means to an end, the development of civilization, the betterment of his fellow-creatures. His very hesitations were a sign of the superior cast of his mind" (281). And yet, toward the end of the story, Toussaint's miscalculations, flaws, and hesitations become so abundant that James can no longer qualify them that easily. Not only did he have Moïse executed for conspiring against the whites, he above all failed to communicate his motivations to the masses: "But Toussaint, like Robespierre, destroyed his own Left-wing, and with it sealed his doom. The tragedy was that there was no need for it. . . . [B]etween Toussaint and his people there was no fundamental difference of outlook or of aim. Knowing the race question for the political and social question it was, he tried to deal with it in a purely political and social way. It was a grave error" (286). It can be assumed at this point that the narrator's use of the word "tragedy" is to be taken more rhetorically than rigorously. For Toussaint's neglect of the people seals his doom, and yet the Haitian Revolution was ultimately successful. Toussaint led his people to freedom but was not permitted to enter the promised land.[24] He instead accepted the invitation to rendezvous with General Leclerc only to be detained and imprisoned in France, duped by the same ploy to be used against the Spanish monarch Carlos IV almost exactly six years later.

Within one hundred pages of James's text, Toussaint goes from being incapable of erring, of seeming to "bear a charmed life" (250), to becoming a leader entirely out of touch with his people: "He was as daring and as tireless as ever, but his politics still lagged behind events" (321); "It was magnificent diplomacy but ruinous as a revolutionary policy. The slopes to treachery from the dizzying heights of revolutionary leadership are always so steep that leaders, however well-intentioned, can never build their fences too high" (325).

The story of Toussaint's demise is completed with his arrest soon thereafter. It is noteworthy that after his removal from the scene, James's account of the Haitian Revolution is not quite complete. Who is to fill the narrative void left by such a formidable protagonist? The masses themselves, of course, around whom there is a heightened discursive tension just after Toussaint's exit from the scene: "It is the curse of the masses" (338); "Once more the masses had shown greater political understanding than their leaders" (339); "The masses were fighting and dying as only revolutionary masses can" (346). And yet, consistent once again with the framework of leaders and masses, the focus of the narration shifts from the latter to the former, with Christophe and Dessalines—leaders of whom James is much less enamored—taking center stage. We shall gauge more precisely the nature of the relationship between James and Toussaint, and what the latter represents for the former, by comparing and contrasting the treatment Dessalines receives to that of Toussaint.

Unenlightened Autonomy

Toussaint for James undoubtedly represented, as we have shown, the embodiment of the best ideals of the Enlightenment. David Scott's *Conscripts of Modernity* bears the subtitle *The Tragedy of Colonial Enlightenment*, but his study favors the category of modernity over that of the Enlightenment and seems to conflate the two: "My point, in short, is simply this, that however many slaves preserved individual memories of nonmodern practices from their African homelands . . . the fact is that they were now obliged to conduct these remembered lives in conditions brought into being by the categories and institutions of the modern world."[25] It is not clear to me what is at stake in this emphasis on a widespread notion of institutional modernity, with its anti- or nonmodern tribal antithesis, and the depiction of African slaves, whether docile or rebellious, as passive "conscripts." This seems to me precisely the kind of binary trap prescribed by the logic of the Enlightenment. A counterexample or alternative to this approach might be found in Nick Nesbitt's discussion of the Chartre du Mandé, a 1222 oral declaration of the Mandé nation in what is today the Republic of Mali. The charter, according to Nesbitt, "founded a society based upon the universal and unqualified rights of all human beings to be free from enslavement."[26] The 1222 charter, contemporaneous with the Magna Carta (1215) and centuries before the *Declarations of the Rights of Man* (1789) or the eighteenth-century constitutions, proclaims, "Every human life is a life." Nesbitt hypothesizes that this proclamation of universal equality could have survived the Middle Passage and was known to Toussaint through the common Kreyol proverb (and title of Jean-Bertrand Aristide's autobiography) "Tout moun se moun." Though this account relies on speculation to a certain degree, since it is based on an oral document that did not leave written traces, it is certainly plausible enough to allow us at least to imagine a scenario in which African slaves were not mere passive enlistees in the game of modernity, but rather impacted and helped shape the unfolding of modern culture through a process that Fernando Ortiz calls transculturation, entailing not only an uprooting or acquisition of culture, but rather the "consequent creation of new cultural phenomena."[27]

While the C. L. R. James of 1963 or 1971 may have seen things differently, the author of *The Black Jacobins* in 1938 saw Toussaint as someone inextricably entangled in the web of European Enlightenment, in fact as someone who mastered the Enlightenment and achieved in rhetorical terms a fluency, as opposed to the hesitations of the *philosophes* themselves, which correlated to the chasm between Enlightenment theory and practice; philosophy and politics. It is worthwhile to reiterate a quote from Sala-Molins, who expresses effectively the machinery of these hesitations: "the slave trade is a crime, slavery is the crime of all crimes: let's do away with it! Do away with it? Wait a moment!"[28] We are led to believe that Toussaint will bridge this gap, overcome this hesitancy. And yet the most important precept of the Enlightenment—autonomy at all costs—demands not a bridge but rather a rupture, or, paradoxically, both. Borrowing momentarily from James's own literary framework, Toussaint's tragic flaw is not so much a specific miscalculation, not even the execution of Moïse, but rather a hesitation, an inability to choose between French civilization and Haitian independence, to *renounce* the former in favor of the latter. "The Black Revolution had passed him by" (321).

The necessity of rupture with authority, the Enlightenment's categorical imperative, is not merely a question of a psychological condition, an extended childhood or immaturity (as Kant would have it), but rather involves concrete material conditions resulting in privation once the break is complete. Stated otherwise, Kant places the onus of the rupture between master and slave squarely on the shoulders of the latter, when in fact it is clear that the master will go to great lengths to maintain the slave in a state of bondage. Toussaint knew that Saint Domingue society needed French technical know-how and capital to rebuild the island's agricultural infrastructure, which had been devastated by a war waged with scorched-earth tactics, and went to lengths to conciliate the French.

The very contradictions of Enlightenment are here condensed into a single historical moment that James captures with great timing and clarity. And yet almost immediately after outlining this situation, James elaborates his notion of the tragic, which characterizes Toussaint the individual rather than the historical choice he was forced to make. The contextualization of this "tragic individual" seems incongruous: "But in a deeper sense the life and death are not truly tragic. Prometheus, Hamlet, Lear, Phèdre, Ahab, assert what may be the permanent impulses of the human condition against the claims of organised society" (291). James begins by outlining Toussaint's historical dilemma, which illustrates precisely what the Enlightenment meant for the Caribbean. And yet this particular framework is almost immediately abandoned in favor of an analysis of Toussaint the individual, who is compared and contrasted with the tragic figures of Western literature—certainly a disconcerting analogy. James is no doubt correct in warning the reader that it would be an error to merely view Toussaint as an isolated figure in a remote West Indian island—and yet his remedy to this error, placing Toussaint squarely within the tradition of Western tragic figures, is also suspect. James's gesture does not at a stroke merely do away with the center/periphery dynamic, but rather his integrative comparison tends to put forth the center *as* the whole, thereby strengthening its pretensions to universality. Edward W. Said praises James, and specifically within the context of *The Black Jacobins*, for his capacity to critique Western imperialism while at the same time disassociating this critique from an appreciation of the West's "cultural achievements."[29] But Said overlooks that this disassociation between culture and politics is not only one of the principal dynamics lurking beneath the text of *The Black Jacobins*; in a sense, it describes the very structure of the "flaw" responsible for Toussaint's downfall. Toussaint is described as full of admiration for the aristocratic manners and gestures of a white Frenchman: "Struck by the carriage and bearing of a French officer, he said to those around him, 'My sons will be like that'" (246). Should we characterize this deferential attitude toward the French "carriage and bearing" as a reaction to imperialism or to cultural achievements?

James, in his use of an often cryptic or paradoxical language, makes explicit Toussaint's double-bind: that to be enlightened entails a renunciation of the Enlightenment, requires in fact a kind of barbarism. And yet James does not seem to embrace fully this dialectic, opting instead for a more literary and traditional sense of tragedy as his signifying model. Toussaint's final allegiance was to revolutionary France and thus to the

Enlightenment, and this, in James's eyes, is his saving grace, his "condemnation and his atonement."

James's reading of Dessalines, the Haitian leader who succeeded Toussaint, places into perspective Toussaint's dilemma and clarifies the author's affinities: "If Dessalines could see so clearly and simply, it was because the ties that bound this uneducated soldier to French civilisation were of the slenderest. He saw what was under his nose so well because he saw no further. Toussaint's failure was the failure of enlightenment, not of darkness" (288). Dessalines, then, serves as Toussaint's foil or antithesis and does not, as Said describes James, value Western cultural achievements.[30] Whereas James repeatedly emphasizes Toussaint's literacy and even canonizes him among the great writers of the Enlightenment, Dessalines is described as bearing the marks of the whip on his body, the scars amounting to a kind of epithet in lieu of literacy. Dessalines had no allegiance to the tenets of the French Revolution, was illiterate, and therefore, since his ties to "civilisation were of the slenderest," was able to muster the resolve necessary to declare independence while Toussaint vacillated: "[T]his old slave, with the marks of the whip below his general's uniform, was fast coming to the conclusion at which Toussaint still boggled. He would declare the island independent and finish with France" (301). Though in a celebrated Caribbean book George Lamming compares Toussaint to Caliban—"C. L. R. James shows us Caliban as Prospero had never known him: a slave who was a great soldier in battle, an incomparable administrator in public affairs, full of paradox but never without compassion, a humane leader of men"[31]—in my view, there is no question that in James's depiction, Dessalines is Caliban to Toussaint's Ariel.[32] And yet, paradoxically, his resolve to declare Haiti independent qualifies him to a certain extent as *more enlightened than Toussaint*, more eager to throw off the yoke of arbitrary and tyrannical authority. Dessalines merely embodies the same paradox as Toussaint, though now inverted: emancipation achieved through barbarous autonomy rather than civilized tutelage.

Dessalines also performs one of the most revolutionarily symbolic and enlightened gestures in the history of the struggle for independence in the Americas. Eager to differentiate the revolutionary army from the French enemy, Dessalines designs a new flag by removing the white from the French tricouleur. And yet this gesture also has its chilling historical counterpart. One of his first orders of business as emperor of the new nation is to exterminate the remaining whites in Haiti, a massacre that James goes to great lengths to explain, though not to justify. In fact, James places the cause of Haiti's suffering over the next two centuries squarely on this massacre:

> As it was Haiti suffered terribly from the resulting isolation. Whites were banished from Haiti for generations, and the unfortunate country, ruined economically, its population lacking in social culture, had its inevitable difficulties doubled by this massacre. That the new nation survived at all is forever to its credit for if the Haitians thought that imperialism was finished with them they were mistaken. (374)

"Its population lacking in social culture" sounds like a phrase that could have been uttered by Toussaint himself. If James asserts that Toussaint's failure was one of enlightenment, not of darkness, then we might surmise that the inverse formula is applicable to Dessalines, that is to say, that his *success* was of one of darkness and *not* of enlightenment. Toussaint (Ariel), as a result of being too enlightened, is doomed to unenlightenment, which by definition is barbarism itself. Dessalines (Caliban), overly barbaric (in James's view), is able to make a clean break with authority, and therefore achieves enlightenment. James, however, as I have pointed out, does not embrace this Caliban/Ariel dialectic. Rather, he reasserts in the 1963 appendix, "From Toussaint L'Ouverture to Fidel Castro":[33] "Toussaint could see no road for the Haitian economy but the sugar plantation. Dessalines was a barbarian" (393).

Michel-Rolph Trouillot's discussion of the Congo general Sans Souci reveals an interesting parallel. If I perceive a triangular arrangement, with James acting as a mediator between Toussaint and Dessalines, Trouillot perceives a similar structure in the attitude of the nineteenth-century Haitian historian Beabrun Ardouin, who defends the "civilized" Christophe against the "barbarian" Sans Souci, the fiercely independent general under Toussaint L'Ouverture. Sans Souci continued rebelling against the French after Leclerc's capture of Toussaint, while Christophe and Dessalines hesitated.[34] In both sets of triangular relationships, an Ariel/Caliban rapport emerges, with the historians (James and Ardouin) allying themselves with Ariel (Toussaint, Christophe) for the sake of "civilization" and against Caliban (Dessalines, Sans Souci), so-called practitioners of barbarism. At the very least, this parallel structure reveals that the values implied by a Ariel/Caliban characterization are not fixed but rather shifting in relationship to the nucleus of power.

The Enlightenment versus barbarism antinomy can be further elucidated through a comparative reading of Toussaint's and Dessalines' respective constitutions. Both constitutions forbid slavery in no uncertain terms, and Toussaint's powerful letter to the French directory, discussed above, leaves no ambiguity regarding the impossibility of restoring slavery in Saint Domingue. In the 1801 Constitution, Title 2, Article 3 declares: "There can be no slaves in this territory; servitude is abolished within it forever. All men who are born here live and die *free and French*."[35] Here freedom and French nationhood are linked both grammatically and existentially. No doubt Toussaint phrased it in such a way—to echo James's language—in order to reassure the French that he was not contemplating independence for Saint Domingue. Yet the textual contrast to the Haitian Declaration of Independence of 1804 commissioned by Dessalines is striking. The opening sentence reverses the common ideological association between civilization and barbarism that James reproduces in *The Black Jacobins*: "It is not enough to have expelled the barbarians who have bloodied our lands for two centuries; . . . We must, with one last act of national authority, forever ensure liberty's reign in the country of our birth."[36] Dessalines, by characterizing the new nation through the people's extended and multifaceted relationship to the land (both as birthplace and "ours for two centuries"), evokes a Calibanesque autochthony and recalls Kant's position against the Lockean imperialist alibi that only those who cultivate and exploit the land are entitled to claim ownership of it.[37]

Toussaint's Constitution declares, "The Catholic, Apostolic and Roman religion is the only one that is publicly professed,"[38] effectively prohibiting the practice of Vodou in the public sphere. Dessalines' Haitian Constitution of 1805 says the following about religion: "Article 50. The law does not recognize any dominant religion. Article 51. Freedom of worship is allowed." Toussaint explicitly prohibits divorce; Dessalines expressly permits it. Dessalines does not exclude whites from the national territory, a common misconception, but rather declares that "No white man, regardless of his nationality, may set foot in this territory *as a master or a landowner*,"[39] certainly a comprehensible interdiction after two hundred years of slavery and a fourteen-year war of independence against the erstwhile owners of land and slaves. More examples abound, but even a cursory comparative reading of the two constitutions reveals that Dessalines was certainly "enlightened" enough for us to question James's assertion ("Dessalines was a barbarian"), not only in the radical, dialectical sense of achieving autonomy and self-reliance through all possible means, including violence, but also in the more commonplace sense of allotting a maximum freedom to Haitians and ensuring national sovereignty through the rule of law.

Genre Trouble

James's text, though in essence a historical account of the Haitian Revolution, in fact employs a literary framework and structure—tragedy—to recount the events and place them in perspective. Starting from this observation, I have argued that this device produces a riveting account while at the same time creating the need to present the *hero* of this tragedy. The framework of this tragic hero, the superlative but flawed individual, betrays a host of contradictory criteria stemming from the structural dynamic of the Enlightenment, and bears out an implicit comparison with Carpentier, who not only dealt with so much of the same raw historical material as James, but who also fell into some of the same pitfalls, though for different reasons. I conclude this chapter by making this implicit comparison somewhat more explicit by addressing what seems to be the most incompatible element between them: the question of genre. For if James's problems stem from the literary framework employed in a historical study, then it is worth considering briefly how Carpentier fares framing his *fictional* account within historical guidelines.

James, we recall, compares Toussaint to the great tragic figures of European literature, such as Lear, Phèdre, etc. In the previous chapter, there was a commentary on a particular scene in Carpentier's *The Kingdom of This World*, where M. Lenormand de Mézy's wife gives a drunken performance of passages from *Phèdre* for a public comprised of the plantation's slaves, who take at face value the verses that speak of "unspeakable crimes" and "incest." The slaves in C. L. R. James's narration understand all too well, while Alejo Carpentier's slaves "understand nothing." Whereas James attempts to integrate the rebelling slaves of Saint Domingue into a worldview whose paradigms have been defined by the Enlightenment, Carpentier invests the entirety of his fictional or discursive machinery in the notion of incongruity, an investment that for similar, though inverted, reasons engenders contradictions. Though

Carpentier is renowned for his fiction and not so much for his historical or theoretical acumen,[40] he seems to come closer to framing more appropriately the historical dynamic by *opposing* Phèdre to the Afro-Caribbean world than does James the historian, who attempts to recuperate Toussaint within the tradition of the great Western tragic figures. Carpentier has intimated his method of incorporating historical material into novels: "[I]t seemed to me that Victor Hugues was an ideal character to write a novel, to focus a novel on him. Why ideal? Because I believe that historical characters, but not too historical, are the ideal ones for a novel. You can't write a great novel whose central character is called Napoleon Bonaparte."[41]

Toussaint occupies a halfway point between Victor Hugues and Bonaparte.[42] Though still relatively unknown outside of the Caribbean, James's intention is evidently to elevate the events of the Haitian Revolution to their rightful place in history: "What happened in San Domingo after Leclerc's death is one of those pages in history which every schoolboy should learn, and most certainly will learn, some day" (357). Thus another, somewhat less complex motive of James's literary rendering of the events of Saint Domingue: their popularization intended to achieve greater dissemination. And yet James's conviction and passion lie apparently not with the hero, but rather with these faceless masses, "the men, women and children who drove out the French" (257). They are referred to time and again, and yet we have seen the obstacles in place that impede the narrator's access to them, as well as James's intimations in his 1971 lectures, aligning himself with the masses of slaves and distancing himself from the individual leaders.[43]

In the case of Carpentier, these not-so-well-known historical figures populate his two famous novels that deal with the period of the French Revolution in the Caribbean, *The Kingdom of This World* and *Explosion in a Cathedral.* Henri Christophe, Pauline Leclerc, Victor Hugues, and others all play important roles in these novels and, one could say, in some ways serve the same didactical function as James's narration—the popular dissemination of information about little-known historical figures that impacted the Caribbean. And yet each of these historical figures in Carpentier's fictions shares center stage with purely fictional historical protagonists as well that serve as foils or antitheses to them. Ironically, these "other" characters, namely Ti Noël and Esteban, who operate under the shadow of the "authentic" characters, allow Carpentier a kind of entrée to precisely that which eludes James: a representation or account of the masses. Though Esteban and Ti Noël are empirically fictional "individuals" and thus disqualified as masses per se, their anonymous status and "passivity" qualify them as candidates within an imaginative realm for that "lost diary" that Lefebvre desires as a key to accessing the essence of the anonymous masses. The denouements of these two characters confirm their anonymous status as representatives of the masses: Ti Noël perishes in a hurricane and is never seen again; Esteban disappears into the mass of *madrileños* whose uprising against the Napoleonic occupiers gave rise to the events immortalized in Goya's paintings.

The irony of this rapport between James and Carpentier is that the former, while attempting to write a historical account of the Haitian Revolution, actually succeeds in conveying a literary portrait of Toussaint that is fleshed out with dialogue, description, extraordinary rhetorical flourishes, and psychological insights. The novelist Carpentier, on the other hand, by employing the technique of juxtaposition between known historical figures and fictive ones, succeeds in conveying the kind of historical portrait, a "feeling" for the insignificant individual who is merely part of the crowd that eludes James. In the final analysis, it may be that for Carpentier it is a question of the aestheticization of the Enlightenment. James's position is much more engaging, in the Sartrean sense. As Said correctly points out, "He saw the central pattern of politics and history in linear terms,"[44] whereas Carpentier's vision could be described as circular or spiraling. For James, more is at stake than aesthetics; the Enlightenment's promise of emancipation was not looked upon as something out of the past but rather as an ongoing process. Carpentier and James may at varying times reproduce or criticize the Enlightenment, but the one consistent factor that reappears in their writing is the emergence of a structural dynamic that is the result of the Caribbean acting as periphery to the enlightened center. This arrangement problematizes any attempt of these writers to simply take part in the "game" of the discourse of Enlightenment modernity, but it does not allow them to bow out of the game entirely either.

Part II

Chauvet, Condé, and the Postmodern Turn in the Caribbean Historical Imagination

3 Conflicted Epiphanies

Politicized Aesthetics in Marie Chauvet's *Dance on the Volcano*

L'art avait triomphé des tartuferies de la peau.

Jean Fouchard, *Le Théâtre à St-Domingue*

In a footnote in her formidable *Haiti, History and the Gods*, Joan Dayan says the following about the Haitian author Marie Chauvet (1919–1973, also known by her maiden name, Vieux-Chauvet): "Haiti's greatest writer has suffered the curse of near oblivion."[1] The dramatic history of the publishing of Chauvet's novels is itself almost worthy of a novelistic depiction. After Gallimard published *Amour, colère et folie* in 1968, a fictional triptych that contains thinly disguised allegorical criticisms of the Duvalier regime, Chauvet's husband seized most of the available copies and sequestered them for twelve years. Chauvet was subsequently exiled to New York, where she died in obscurity.[2] For decades, Chauvet's family in Port-au-Prince erected obstacles impeding the reprinting, distribution, and translation of her work. Dayan reports that "stories are told about a family still embarrassed by her unremitting analyses of lust and hypocrisy under the signs of romance and authenticity."[3] At the time of this writing, a translation of *Amour, colère et folie* (*Love, Anger, Madness*), undoubtedly Chauvet's most well-known work, is finally scheduled to be published by Modern Library, a full forty years after its initial publication. Ironically, the one work by Chauvet that has been readily available to the English-reading public, thanks to Salvator Attanasio's translation, is *La danse sur le volcan* (1957, *Dance on the Volcano*, 1959), which nevertheless has received very little critical commentary.[4] And compared to *Amour, colère et folie* and *Fonds des nègres*, novels in which violence and sexuality gather intensity with each page, *Dance on the Volcano*, though also a story of violence, since it recounts the explosive days leading up to the Haitian Revolution, in some ways hardly seems like a work by the same author. An observation by Ronnie Scharfman about *Amour, folie et colère* may provide us with a clue to determining what it is about *Dance on the Volcano* that distinguishes it from Chauvet's subsequent novels: "Marie Chauvet's discourse deconstructs oppressive power by exceeding it through the violence of the text."[5] *Dance on the Volcano* may be as much about violence as *Fond des nègres* and *Amour, colère et folie*, but these latter texts integrate violence into the fabric of their narration and exude it from within the narrative voice. One need only think of Claire's perverse and destructive fantasies about her brother-in-law Jean Luze or the climactic dream scene in *Amour* that culminates in her sacrificial murder. In contradistinction to this narrative, subjective violence that attempts to rival or exceed the realist, objective violence of the world depicted in *Amour*, the omniscient narrative voice of *Dance on the Volcano* struggles to maintain an incongruous equanimity in the face of seething racial and colonial hatred.

According to J. Michael Dash, "Maryse Condé may be the only major female novelist other than Chauvet to pursue the postmodern in Caribbean writing."[6] Though I engage the polyvalent implications of postmodernity in a Caribbean context in later chapters, for now I will let it suffice to characterize Caribbean postmodernity as a general attitude of wariness and suspicion toward the project of Enlightenment-informed modernity and the assumption that this project, the rudders of which are in the hands of the state, will lead to a horizon of social progress. Joan Dayan, too, though not addressing the question of postmodernity directly, states that Chauvet's *Fonds des nègres* entails a complete "reversal of the claims of progress or enlightenment."[7] What is striking about these points of view is that they seem almost utterly inapplicable to *Dance on the Volcano*, which was published only three years before *Fond des nègres*. Not only does the former novel take place in the eighteenth century, but the author earnestly engages the categories of the Enlightenment. In a movement that could be described as the inverse of Carpentier's novelistic evolution from *Ecue-Yamba-O* to *The Kingdom of This World*, Chauvet's internal conflicts and tensions regarding race, gender, and European heritage are on full display in *Dance on the Volcano*, a historical novel whose (dare I say) naïve narrative voice is in stark contrast to the scathing irony and disillusionment, Chauvet's "true voice," of *Amour, colère et folie*, set in the twentieth century. If Chauvet is strongly drawn to the figure of Minette in *Dance on the Volcano*, the light-skinned opera singer and theater performer who defied the barriers of race and gender in late-eighteenth-century Saint Domingue, in her later work, Joan Dayan asserts, "Chauvet knows that no claims to modernity or civilization can destroy the call of the past, the pull of blood."[8] In this chapter, I discuss how, in sharp distinction to Chauvet's later work, *Dance on the Volcano* is a novel that fits squarely into the modern tradition of engaging and critiquing the Enlightenment from "the inside," so to speak. Despite the fact that Chauvet's innovation is introducing a woman as an Enlightenment protagonist (though Maryse Condé, as I will show, uses gender in a more pointed fashion to disrupt Enlightenment paradigms), her protagonist reproduces Toussaint L'Ouverture's dilemma: the problematic disassociation of slavery and colonialism from the refined vestiges of French culture and civilization.

In the "Author's Note" to *Dance on the Volcano*, Chauvet makes a claim to historical authenticity: "This novel has been based on historical documentation. . . . The historical events portrayed here are authentic."[9] Alejo Carpentier makes a similar such assertion in the prologue to *The Kingdom of This World*.[10] While the Cuban author's claim to historical fidelity relies on the travelogues of the eighteenth century, Chauvet's historicity is rooted in a more recent text. The primary source for her novel, set in late-eighteenth-century Port-au-Prince, is Jean Fouchard's *Le Théâtre à St-Domingue*, from which Chauvet borrows the phrase echoed in the novel's title.[11] Fouchard's history of the theater in the eighteenth-century French colony reserves an entire chapter devoted to "Minette and Lise, two talented girls of color" who defied the institutions and prejudices of one of history's most violently racist societies, prerevolutionary Saint Domingue, to achieve fame and success as bel-canto singers and theater performers.

The fact that Moreau de Saint-Méry is a primary source for Fouchard, as he was for Carpentier and James, underscores the tight-knit intertextuality of historical writing in the modern Caribbean, even across languages and nationalities. And just as Carpentier "borrows" from the historical record to populate his fiction, so Chauvet relies on Fouchard's text to provide the shell of the protagonist and her family as well as their entourage. Almost all the important literary personae of the novel, such as the girls' music teacher, Mme Acquaire; Saint Martin, the director of the Port-au-Prince Comédie; Mesplès, the majority owner of the theater and a heartless moneylender;[12] and even Mozard, the local music critic, come from the pages of Fouchard's history. Chauvet's historical novel melodramaticizes Fouchard's account of the meteoric rise of the elder of the two sisters, Minette, whose mother is an ex-slave and whose father is the mother's white erstwhile master. In Fouchard's words: "Their mother was a mulatto. Their father, a planter for whom the girls were lucky enough not to bear the name that was branded on the mother's flesh, since, in exchange for the pleasures given to the libertine master, the mother had been freed."[13] Though Fouchard finds the name "Minette" full of "musical consonances," in Chauvet's novel the protagonist, lacking a surname, also rues her first (and only) name: "she was ashamed of her name: Minette! 'Kitten' it meant, a silly diminutive that shouted her social status aloud. It was banal, stupid, without dignity" (112). In a novel that owes so much to its historical counterpart, it is interesting to note this divergence between the historian who finds the name pleasant and the novelist who portrays her protagonist as finding shame in it. This subtle discrepancy might be one of the keys to deciphering the ideological impulse of Chauvet's novel. Despite the author's apparent commiseration and identification with her heroine, Minette, we can detect at the same time traces of a commentary on the *affranchi* class, free people of biracial descent in Saint Domingue, and their preoccupation with upward social mobility. The ambivalent attitude toward this class (with which I would venture to say that Chauvet, consciously or unconsciously, identifies),[14] which wavers between critique and defense, is the complex prism through which the novel's ideological content is refracted.

Overcoming legal and societal obstacles barring people of color access to the stage, Minette, by sheer force of her extraordinary talent and determination, and with the aid of liberal actors, gains access to the Comédie, where her voice and beauty seduce the public. Despite the opposition of entrenched reactionary elements, Minette achieves the equivalent of a kind of superstardom in late-eighteenth-century Port-au-Prince. Fouchard, in his chapter on the two sisters, quotes abundantly from the eighteenth-century colonial periodical *Affiches Américaines* to illustrate the "rave reviews" and public acclamation received by Mademoiselle Minette on the Saint Domingue stage: "But Minette was not finished with surprises and conquests. 1787 marked the high point of her career and it is in the apotheosis of her acclamations that she boldly sought out new, delicate roles full of nuances and difficulties. Minette at the age of twenty completely dominated the Port-au-Prince theater scene."[15] Through Chauvet's pen, Fouchard's history becomes a bildungsroman that fleshes out a portrait of Minette and her rise to fame. On her passage through adolescence to young adulthood, she acquires consciousness of the complexities of race politics in Saint Domingue, and though she is herself a light-skinned *affranchi* who overcomes with relative ease the prejudices of her epoch, she progressively empathizes (or, more appropriately, as I will show, sympathizes) with the plight of the black slaves. In the end, the story of Minette's artistic success, the development of her romance with the slave-owning *affranchi* Jean-François Lapointe, and the portrait of the life of the theater in late-eighteenth-century Saint Domingue recede to the background in the novel while center stage is increasingly occupied by the festering institution of slavery and the cauldron of racial and class conflicts in this French colony on the cusp of volcanic upheaval.

Fictionalizing History

It is almost as though, paralleling the explosive social conflicts in Saint Domingue, Chauvet struggles to control the content of her novel. The narrator seems to experience a certain fondness for portraying her protagonist singing French and Italian arias in the Comédie, surrounded by talented performers whose allegiance is to the theater alone and whose sole prejudice is against aesthetic bad taste. And yet, early in the novel, Minette experiences the first of a series of revelations that contribute to the growing realization that her notion of the aesthetic sublime cannot be divorced from the material realities of plantation slavery and colonialism: "The bleeding back of the slave alone had caused this welter of emotions with her. It seemed to Minette as if this spectacle had been deliberately staged in front of her house to remind her, should she ever forget it, of how the back of the slave looked after being lashed with a whip."[16] Just as Carpentier highlighted the theatrical component of Mackandal's execution, emphasizing the words "spectacle" and "seeing," Chauvet also indicates early in the novel that theater is a sinister metaphor or allegory for Saint Domingue's colonial society. The *lambis*, or conch shells, ringing out from the countryside foreboding slave rebellions and bloody reprisals disrupt the Eurocentric logic of theatrical performance and reception. Singing in the novel yields to the dance referred to in the title, the social upheaval leading to the Haitian Revolution, and to the volcano whose molten lava—the masses of black slaves descending from the hills and the reprisals by the landed gentry—destroys everything in its path, not only the institution of slavery itself but the refined vestiges of European culture. In the final one hundred pages of the novel. the principal thematic focus—Minette's rise to prominence in the theater milieu of Port-au-Prince—shifts to a more strictly historical account (with some novelistic liberties) of the early days of revolutionary Saint Domingue, the dates of which, thanks to historians such as C. L. R. James, Trouillot, and Fouchard, we can pinpoint historically. Some of these events include execution of the activists Ogé and Chavannes in

1790;[17] the sectarian fire that destroyed two-thirds of Port-au-Prince on November 22, 1791;[18] and Commissioner Sonthonax's abolition of slavery on August 29, 1793,[19] events for which Minette, in a role similar to Esteban's in Alejo Carpentier's *Explosion in a Cathedral*, acts more as a historical witness than novelistic protagonist.

While C. L. R. James's protagonists are Toussaint and Dessalines, and Carpentier's most famous historical protagonist is Victor Hugues, it is perhaps not surprising that important figures from the Haitian Revolution belonging to the *affranchi* class are represented in *Dance on the Volcano*. According to Myriam J. A. Chancy, the *affranchis* have historically been regarded with suspicion for their shifting allegiances in the complex unfolding of the Haitian Revolution.[20] Both Alexandre Pétion, ("Pitchoun" in the novel) and Louis-Jacques Beauvais appear in *Dance on the Volcano*.[21] Pétion and Beauvais equivocated in their loyalty to Toussaint L'Ouverture and sided with the French after Toussaint's capture. They definitively joined the revolutionary forces upon the arrival of Leclerc's replacement, General Rochambeau, known for his genocidal excesses.[22] Accordingly, Chauvet depicts Minette, who also belongs to this class, as someone who wavers between her love for European culture and her growing revulsion at the institution of slavery. The portrait of this social class, including especially that of the brutal slave-owning Jean-François Lapointe, Minette's love interest in the novel, reveals a degree of ideological heterogeneity among the *affranchis* that is often overlooked when ethnic and class categories are employed to decipher the complexities of the Haitian Revolution.[23]

In this brief plot summary I have outlined, it is already evident that Chauvet's novel, in its motifs, themes, and setting, falls squarely into and reinforces the transnational tradition of modern Caribbean historical writing inaugurated by C. L. R. James and Carpentier. As I pointed out, Chauvet, from the very outset, makes a claim to historical veracity, echoing Carpentier. But whereas in Carpentier's historical imagination the social conflicts of the late-eighteenth-century Caribbean play themselves out in binary fashion, white Europe against the black Afro-Caribbean, Chauvet (like James) incorporates the *affranchis*, who, though persecuted by the white colonists, were often themselves slave owners. The historically accurate insertion of this third social group into the narration renders the social conflicts portrayed so complex that it could be argued that Chauvet's bildungsroman suffers from a surfeit of class and ethnic antagonisms that at times eclipse the schematic clarity of novelistic exposition.

It is interesting to note that the three authors in question employ specific devices to link history with literary expression. In lieu of a "straightforward" historical account of the Haitian Revolution, C. L. R. James grafts a literary model—the *hamartia*, or tragic flaw—onto the narration of the rise and fall of Toussaint L'Ouverture. Alejo Carpentier, while claiming a brand of historical objectivity associated with "the marvelous-real" (wherein a quasi-magical revelation of the essence of American reality can emerge from minute recounting of the historical record itself) avails himself of the peculiarities of a specific historical moment (the late eighteenth century in the Caribbean) to play out what are, in fact, highly personal or psychological conflicts. Marie Chauvet's novel occupies a middle ground in this constellation. While the inclusion of the mulatto, or *affranchi*, class provides a historical verisimilitude that aligns her narration with that of James (who also provides a detailed account of the crucial role played by this class in Saint Domingue politics), like Carpentier, Chauvet's historical libido (to echo a term coined by Antonio Benítez-Rojo)—in this particular instance, the allegiances, class affiliations, and internal conflicts that emerge from the writing of historical fiction—reveals itself in the composition of the novel.

Dance on the Volcano opens in quintessentially Caribbean fashion. Roberto González Echevarría has suggested that more than any other particular motif or image, the Caribbean is especially characterized by boats.[24] Elaborating on this motif, I would suggest that more than the mere presence of maritime vessels themselves, the anticipated arrival of ships in a port or harbor is a particularly Caribbean literary device by which authors portray a cross-section of Caribbean society, class structure, and general demographic composition.[25] Chauvet's novel opens with the arrival by boat of the newly appointed governor in Port-au-Prince and the gathering multitude on the quays to welcome him (there are two other momentous port arrivals described in the novel, that of the Prince William, Duke of Lancaster—mentioned in Fouchard's history—as well as the revolutionary Commissioner Léger-Félicité Sonthonax). Of all the class, gender, ethnic, and racial rivalries described in the opening paragraphs, one particular antagonism is emphasized, that between white Creole or European women and their black or mulatto counterparts, both of whom are vying for the attention of the white men—soldiers or colonists—sweating profusely under their eighteenth-century wigs and velvet trousers. The narrator provides a historical fact: "A newly-promulgated law prohibited coloured women from wearing shoes, but the trinkets with which they had adorned their toes made them look even more unusual and desirable" (1).[26] And so in a novel in which social conflicts in fact explode into violence, it is interesting to note that the rivalry that inaugurates the narration is at once libidinal, racial, and aesthetic:

> On the other hand, only a totally dishonest observer could have failed to see that they [the black and mulatto *affranchi* women] were exquisite, coquettish and bewitching beings. When it came to making the most effective display of their well-formed breasts and the ample, flexible hips, these women could not be outdone. *The mixture of the two blood strains so radically different had produced prodigies of beauty.* (2, emphasis added)

Joan Dayan documents this contradictory cultural phenomenon in the eighteenth-century Caribbean, wherein white women emulated the dress and speech patterns of their mulatto rivals. Dayan mentions, and Carpentier portrays in detail, this curious tendency in Pauline Leclerc, Napoleon's sister, during her sojourn in the Caribbean.[27] In the quotation, Chauvet's narrator dramatizes this rivalry. The final sentence—about the mixture of two races producing "prodigies of beauty"—merits attention in an analysis of this novel since this judgment will later come into conflict with less flattering opinions regarding hybrid results in the realm of culture.

In Carpentier's *The Kingdom of This World*, the cultural intermingling of African and European cultures in the Caribbean resulted in an incommensurable mutual exclusion. The contemporary Puerto Rican novelist Edgardo Rodríguez Juliá (as I discuss in chapter 6) also represents the hybrid offspring of Europe and Africa as a monstrosity, a monstrous progeny. On the other hand, C. L. R. James sees the rise of Toussaint L'Ouverture in the struggle for Haitian independence, at least in part, as a continuation, a coming to fruition of Enlightenment ideals and the French Revolution in the Black Caribbean. Within this arrangement, therefore, we might group Chauvet with James as writers who view African and European hybridity in the Caribbean as potentially productive, and oppose them to writers such as Carpentier and Rodríguez Juliá who, while profiting from this arrangement for their creative inspiration, cast the duality as an ideological and historical antithesis.

So, if for Chauvet's narrator the result of the mixing of the races is beauty, not monstrosity, then it is worth interrogating the aesthetic criteria that inform such a judgment. Minette is described physically as sufficiently light-skinned to dupe both the troupe of actors and the Comédie's public. Her hair is described as "long tresses" and her nose as "finely shaped." We learn even more about the features of Minette's physiognomy through the description of her younger sister, Lise, who is depicted as even "more beautiful": her "hair was not so black, her eyes were less tightly drawn and her mouth not so sensual in expression as Minette's" (23). Minette's musical talent is discovered and developed by the Acquaires, established fixtures in the Saint Domingue Comédie. Partially as a moneymaking scheme and partially in genuine deference to Minette's talent for singing, the Acquaires organize a concert, a performance of *Isabelle and Gertrude* in which Minette will play the leading role of Isabelle. However, due to laws forbidding the performances of people "of color" in the theater, Minette's rehearsals are kept private, even from her fellow performers, until the moment of the performance (she is referred to as "la jeune personne"). The performance is a stunning success, and the director of the theater, François Saint-Martin, asks the Acquaires from what part of France hails Minette. When they respond that in fact that she is a local *affranchi*, or free person of color, Saint-Martin responds, "It's the first time in my life I was ever deceived by a 'mixed-blood'. . . . I always know" (52).

The point clearly is that Minette "looks white" and can pass as such. And yet the fact that she "is not" is a tension around which much of the novel turns. As C. L. R. James, always incisive, observes, "Behind all this elaborate tom-foolery of quarteron, sacatra and marabouw, was the one dominating fact of San Domingo society—fear of the slaves,"[28] a quote that is echoed in this chapter's epigraph by Fouchard: "Art had triumphed over the hypocrisies ["*tartuferies*"] of the skin." Because Minette retains a filial link to the slaves that is all but invisible in her physiognomy, her ascendancy to privilege in Saint Domingue is considered a dangerous precedent by some whites.[29] And yet the more interesting question in the novel is not how Minette is viewed by the upper echelons of Saint Domingue society, but rather how she situates herself within this society. Though she is increasingly appalled by the brutal treatment of slaves and even reaches a point where she declares unambiguously and on repeated occasions that she hates the whites, it might be said that her degree of identification with the plight of the slaves remains in the realm of commiseration—a visceral reaction against their suffering and persecution.

In order to describe what is troubling about Minette's epiphanies in favor of the black slaves and against the whites and slavery in general, it might be useful to borrow momentarily from a nearby context. The historian Michael Löwy describes the principal doctrine of Liberation Theology in Latin America (what he refers to as "Liberation Christianity") as "a preferential option for the poor." (In fact, this context is even closer to Chauvet than it may at first appear since Liberation Theology is a cornerstone of the political philosophy of the twice-deposed Haitian president Jean-Bertrand Aristide.)[30] Löwy goes on to write: "What's new about all this? Hasn't the Church always been charitably inclined towards the suffering of the poor? The important difference is that for Liberation Christianity, the poor are no longer perceived as mere objects--objects of aide, compassion, charity—but rather as subjects of their own history, as subjects of their own liberation."[31] Such a philosophy has strong echoes of the most progressive strains of Enlightenment thought in Kant, Condorcet, and others, as I discussed in the introduction. But though the Chauvet of *Dance on the Volcano* would certainly align herself with this Enlightenment view, this distinction between people as subjects of their own liberation or objects of compassion might be said to precisely characterize what is lacking in Minette's attitude toward the slaves. There is no question that she identifies with their travails. The reader is often reminded that Minette's mother, Jasmine, was a slave who has never undressed in front of her daughters so as to spare them the sight of the scars of the overseer's whip and the brand of the slave on her body. In one moving passage, Jasmine, just before Minette's engagement to sing at the Comédie, reveals the secrets of her skin to her horrified daughter:

> She ripped off her bodice and pointed to the brand on her right breast. Then she turned round and showed Minette her back streaked with scars.
>
> Minette tried to run away. Jasmine motioned her to be quiet, but she had to hold her daughter forcibly to keep her in the room.
>
> "You had to know this sometime. It was necessary, do you understand? . . . "You will be seeing white men, many of them. Never forget that your father was one of them and that he was my master." (33)

As in the case of James's description of Dessalines, the scars from whippings serve as rhetorical inscriptions that highlight through contradistinction another's literacy (either Toussaint's or Minette's), which is upheld as the one virtue above all others that holds the key to escaping slavery. The trauma of witnessing the signs of slavery on her mother's body produces a dual effect on Minette. On the one hand, it strengthens her empathy with the suffering of slaves along with her antipathy toward the inhumane treatment imposed upon them. But though it fosters a growing resentment toward the perpetrators and beneficiaries of slavery (namely the white colonists but also the slave-owning *affranchis*), this growing resentment has a disturbing dialectical counterpart, so to speak, that provides one of the novel's key tensions. Though Minette's vicarious suffering for the plight of the slaves is sincere since it is inscribed upon her mother's skin, the black slaves nevertheless represent for her, to use Minette's and the narrator's language, a generally degraded form of culture that has little to offer to someone with aspirations toward refinement. That is to say, following Löwy, cultural phenomena issuing from the lives of slaves, or even in general coming from "below," hold little interest for Minette, and they therefore remain for her "objects" of pity and compassion rather than subjects in their own right.

This tension in Chauvet's novel bears a strong resemblance to the problems faced by Toussaint L'Ouverture in *The Black Jacobins*; to such an extent, in fact, that we could even go so far as to posit Chauvet's Minette in a gender dialectic with James's Toussaint. In a novel that is so replete with historical references from the period, it is certainly curious that Toussaint is not mentioned a single time in Chauvet's novel, though Fouchard explicitly names him in his chapter on Minette and Lise.[32] And it is noteworthy that, historically speaking, Chauvet's narration ends precisely at the moment at which, according to James, "Toussaint begins to emerge as the man of the future."[33]

Both Minette and Toussaint are described as transcending their humble origins (slavery) thanks to their extraordinary individual talents. Even the tenor of C. L. R. James's apotheosis of Toussaint as a supremely gifted individual who stands apart from the masses of slaves is uncannily echoed in Chauvet's verbal portrait of Minette: "Everything that Minette said and did was to be accepted without contradiction. If she had been able to rise so high, it was because she had been born with the luck that raised her above her kind" (127). And just as James describes Toussaint as someone who mastered the game of the Enlightenment by retaining a link to slavery and thereby overcoming hesitancies, so Chauvet characterizes Minette as someone who "chooses to sing in the language of the Other, better than the Other," as Lucienne J. Serrano expresses it.[34] But if James and Chauvet describe their protagonists as transcending their origins, where are their individual talents leading them? According to James, Toussaint attempted to retain all that was good and productive in French civilization without attributing any "moral superiority" to it. Minette in *Dance on the Volcano* has a similar power of compartmentalization. She despises slavery and racial prejudice yet aspires to practically every other facet of French civilization. Though Minette experiences a series of epiphanies in the novel that lead her to an outright hatred for white people, she never goes so far to question the possible connections between European high culture and the material reality of slave labor and the slave trade. Her passion for the beauty of the French language, European opera and theater is, in her mind, a feeling unrelated to her hatred for the whites. The penchant for seeking such a causal connection between base and superstructure belongs, of course, to the realm of Marxist thought, present in differing degrees in Carpentier and James, and apparently to a lesser one in Chauvet. The latter's protagonist, echoing Toussaint in some respects, suffers from a metonymic blindness that refuses to see that the cherished artifacts of high European culture are products of the same source that produced the institution of slavery.

The novel is replete with instances in which both Minette and the narrator prefer the French language to Haitian Creole. Very early in the novel, when Minette is about twelve years old, a stranger knocks on the door of their little house on rue Traversière. It is Joseph Ogé, who is described as "dark skinned, with an air of delicacy and refinement about him," who spoke "flawless French with just a trace of the drawl peculiar to Creoles" (11). Joseph Ogé is the brother of the historical Vincent Ogé, who along with Chavannes was executed for demanding full rights of citizens for people of color—an episode that is described in detail in both C. L. R. James's and Chauvet's accounts. Joseph, who becomes Minette's tutor and political conscience in the novel, is the first of an array of nonwhite characters who are described as possessing "excellent" or "impeccable" French. At one point, employing a metaphor that oddly reverses the real relationship of violence between master and slave, the narrator describes a slave as speaking "a French that was impeccable except for the maiming of the r's" (106). Moreover Joseph's pedagogical curriculum for Minette and her sister, Lise, includes "Racine, Corneille, Molière and Jean-Jacques Rousseau" (11), again echoing James's litany of intellectual influences on Toussaint, such as Abbé Raynal, an author that Joseph introduces to Minette as well (65).

The point is not to criticize either Chauvet or James for valorizing a European canon of texts at the expense of whatever might be imagined as an Afrocentric pedagogical program in the late eighteenth century.

(Nevertheless, it is probably Carpentier, in his depiction of Ti Noël, and, as I will show, Maryse Condé who go furthest in imagining just what such an education might be like.) Chauvet appropriately emphasizes that teaching slaves to read was a severely punishable violation of the law in Saint Domingue, a fact that merely highlights the potential liberatory power of literacy among slaves. Cousin d'Avallon, who wrote one of the earliest biographies of Toussaint, declares, "Reading and writing are, among the negroes, the nec plus ultra of human knowledge."[35] And yet there are in the novel specific instances of what we might call, for want of a more precise term, Afro-Caribbean cultural production of the period; that is to say, specific productive or creative aspects of the cultural life of slaves apart from their quotidian travails. Carolyn Fick documents dances of African origin such as the *calenda* and "lascivious" *chica* that were practiced by the slaves in Saint Domingue, as well as the broad manifestations of Vodou as both a religious practice and a ceremonial dance.[36] In what we could call a discernible motif in Caribbean writing about the late eighteenth century, the counterpart to the operas, arias, minuets, and general European musical culture in the novel are the instances of African drumming and use of the *lambis*, or idiophonic conch shells, by the runaway slaves. The otherwise obscure fact that drums and *lambis* communicate precise linguistic messages, usually detailing plans for slave rebellions and escapes, is practically common knowledge among readers of Caribbean literature, given the frequency with which this theme appears therein. For Carpentier, the very differences of form, function, and reception between European and African musical and theatrical performance in the Caribbean amount to a matrix of creative expression. And the chasm between the two weltanschauungs amounts to a polar split, a marvelous example from *The Kingdom of This World* being the recitation by Monsieur Lenormand de Mézy's drunken wife of verses from Racine's *Phèdre* for a bewildered group of the plantation's slaves forcibly gathered for the event.

In a curious example of Caribbean intertextuality, it is amusing to imagine that Chauvet (perhaps) makes a reference to this Carpenterian episode in *Dance on the Volcano*. In addition to the required texts by Jean-Jacques Rousseau, from whom Minette "came to know of the attitude of a white man of independent spirit who was enamored of liberty and who demanded it for others" (24), Minette also studies with her mentor Joseph a text by Racine, *Athalie*, "in which Minette made her first acquaintance with the classic art of tragedy, with its sonorous and well-wrought verses and their harmonious and rhythmic phrasing" (24).

To the delight of her mother, Jasmine, who bears the secret scars of slavery on her back, Minette embraces wholeheartedly the aesthetics and the philosophy of the French tradition. The narrator points out, "Jasmine listened ecstatically, and she, who had so carefully hidden her past from her daughters, went so far as to tell her that at one time she had known a young woman who, like Minette, recited beautiful verses before a large audience" (24). Since no other details are revealed about this mysterious recitation, can we assume that Jasmine was among the slaves hearing Mme de Mézy recite verses from *Phèdre* in the episode Carpentier describes? Whether or not this scene was intended as an intertextual homage to Carpentier, the more significant conclusion to draw from it is the idea or motif of Racine and what this seventeenth-century French dramaturge represents for the modern Caribbean historical imagination. For Carpentier, Phèdre's confession of the crime of incest represents utter and reciprocal incomprehensibility of classical theatrical representation, which is oriented toward the past, for the Afro-Caribbean worldview. In Chauvet, the reaction of both Minette and especially her mother, the ex-slave, to Racine's verses reveals that classical French theater represents a degree of culture toward which one must strive. As though to complete this circle of Racinian intertextuality, in the theatrical version of James's *The Black Jacobins*, after the character of Dessalines has confessed his complicity in Toussaint's capture, the character of Marie-Jeanne, at Dessalines' request, quotes a long passage from *Iphigénie*, a work that is also mentioned in Chauvet's novel. Dessalines responds, after hearing the verses: "Well that suits them in France. In France they write plays. But listen, listen. That is San Domingo. We can't write plays about Voodoo!" [37] One can only assume that James's historical vision (at least in 1939), in opposition to "the barbarian" Dessalines, would indeed incorporate Racine and even Mozart, whose music accompanies the drama at one point, into an integrative and dialectical view of the world.

But if the Carpentier of *Ecue-Yamba-O* looks askance upon European musical and theatrical representation while concomitantly valorizing Afro-Caribbean culture for the immediacy with which it engages and affects contemporaneous events, Chauvet's novel apparently does not share this point of view. Even if the sound of the *lambis* portends an imminent slave revolt leading to a horizon of freedom, *lambis* and drums are virtually without exception in the text referred to with pejorative qualifiers: "disquieting messages they tapped out on their drums and blew on their *lambis*" (13); "So it was when one morning a terrible rumbling of drums was heard from the nearby hills, accompanied by the raucous, lugubrious and sinister sound of the *lambis*" (143). If the two extremes of the cultural poles are represented by French opera, verse, and theater, on the one hand, and by the *lambis* and drumming pertaining to the rebelling slaves, on the other, there are nonetheless instances of a cultural middle ground in the novel. If the Comédie represents classic works such as Monsigny's *La belle Aresène* and Racine's *Iphigénie*, there are in the novel references to so-called "native plays"—popular works by local composers and playwrights that depict daily life in the colony, with titles such as *Arlequin mulâtresse protégé par Makandal* that make obvious reference to Afro-Caribbean sources. Minette's sister, Lise, even achieves stardom in her own right by performing these native plays. And yet time and again in the novel (and in Fouchard's history), Minette categorically refuses to perform them:

> These gestures and phrases in Creole had a disagreeable effect on her. For her the theatre was Racine, Corneille, Molière, and she could not understand how people could waste their talents singing vulgar airs in patois. Minette considered the performance of such simple ephemeral plays *as a degradation of talent*. (67, emphasis added)

> But Minette would have no part of any of it. She defied Mesplès and refused to accept a rôle in *Julien et Zila*, a Creole translation of *Blaise et Babet*. She would not appear in badly-written, vulgar plays, in rôles that were tragic although their authors professed to write comedy. Minette was ashamed to speak Creole in public, even on the stage. Was it not the language of African Negroes, and therefore a *symbol of degradation*? (259, emphasis added)

While it would be inaccurate to describe these "local" or "native" plays as a product of slave culture, there is no doubt that they were closer to popular culture than the canon of seventeenth-century French drama of which Minette is so fond. Whether or not Minette's intransigent position against the local plays was considered by the author as a vital component for the novel's unfolding, it is something that Jean Fouchard describes in some detail:

> In order to please the good lady, Minette agreed to play the role of Toton, even if this burlesque vaudeville was far afield from her personal taste. She

> resigned herself to collaborating towards the success of this opera. The style was less disturbing to her than the vulgarity of the Saint-Domingue patois. She never agreed to speak Creole. *In her eyes it represented a degradation.* (323, emphasis added)

Also, from Fouchard:

> With what disdain does she speak of "those ephemeral productions that *degrade* the lyrical stage and are but local."[38]

In both the historical record and the fictional account, it is clear that any cultural manifestation that represents or issues from below is tantamount to degradation. And yet Minette's mother was one of these "degraded" beings and bears the reminders on her skin. Moreover, Jean-François Lapointe, Minette's lover, is a mulatto slave owner who treats his slaves as brutally as any white colonist. If Minette's major epiphany in the novel is her commiseration with the plight of the slaves and her hatred for the whites, these lingering contradictions amount to the novel's major internal conflict, especially if we recall the opening passages about how the mixture of two races had created "prodigies of beauty." The contradiction manifests itself as a false distinction between the sublime beauty resulting from the "genetic" or "racial" blending on the one hand and, on the other, a corresponding cultural hybridity—the patois or Creole language despised by Minette—which is viewed as a monstrosity or a degradation. Though in the novel's denouement there is something akin to a resolution between another of the novel's major tensions, between art and politics, the beauty/degradation schism is never quite overcome.

Politicizing Fiction

So far we have gauged Minette's attitudes toward cultural production through her views of, in vertical ascension, the *lambis* and drums performed by runaway slaves, "local" or "native" theatrical pieces that incorporate Creole, the "correct" use of the French language, and the canonical works of European opera and theater that alone qualify as art for Minette. Therefore it is interesting to peruse the portrait of another character of black descent, in this case a slave, with talents comparable to those of Minette. At one point in the novel, Minette visits a plantation in the countryside, where she is attended to by a young slave named Simon: "Opening her valise, she took out a fresh dress which she laid across a chair. She lifted her head, hearing the sound of a violin. Someone was playing, exquisitely, the aria from *La Belle Arsène* that she had sung for Lapointe only the other day. The violinist was the young slave, Simon!" (182). Simon was taught to play the violin by his master, Monsieur Saint-Ar, who represents a partisan of the "civilizing mission" of slavery. And yet this mythic representation of a different kind of slavery, rural, less brutal, and more nurturing than the practices that Minette had observed before, is belied by a contiguous scene in which another of M. Saint-Ar's slaves gets his hand caught in the mill. M. Saint-Ar admonishes the maimed slave in front of his guests: "Do you think the work can be done properly if I employ old people and invalids? . . . Come, take him away and see to it that he is taken care of." The other colonists see in M. Saint-Ar's attitude a paragon of indulgence and kindness toward the slaves. And yet the juxtaposition between Simon, the violinist-slave and the mill-worker slave with the amputated arm—a Caribbean motif with clear textual resonances in Carpentier and the historical Mackandal—is revealing. The mill accident reveals that for M. Saint-Ar, despite the façade of nurturing and indulgence toward the slaves, they in fact represent dehumanized fungible capital for him just as they do for the most brutal and "unenlightened" plantation slave owner. Simon's violin, then, represents an illusory culture superstructure that is an empty edifice erected upon a real material base. To drive this point home, just as the sugar mill worker is rendered redundant by the accident, so too Simon the violinist suffers from an occupational hazard:

> The violin-playing continued. In fact Simon played without interruption for the three-hour-long dinner. . . . Huge drops of sweat dripped down his black face and his mouth was so pale it looked white.
>
> "What's the matter with him?" Minette asked.
>
> "He's fainted. It always happens whenever he plays for a long time."
>
> Simon was regaining consciousness. He stretched his trembling hands before his eyes and rubbed his finger-tips with a grimace of pain.
>
> "My damn cramp again," he sighed. (190)

Despite Simon's relatively comfortable existence, his tendency to get cramps while playing the violin marks him as just as redundant as the one-armed mill slave. Later in the novel, Minette is back in Port-au-Prince and unknowingly comes upon a slave auction. Up for sale is none other than Simon himself: "For sale, a Negro violinist!" (263).

> Simon looked down at his hands. Oh, his cursed hands were the cause of all this. Of late his attacks of the cramps had become frequent. His left hand would begin to bend inward, stiffening his wrist and then his entire arm. And at such moments Simon felt as though even his heart stiffened and stopped beating. How sad to leave the house where he was born, where he was called "*mon petit*" and patted on the shoulder! Who was this new master who wanted to buy him? Where would he take him? What would he do with him? (265)

Though Simon is a slave and Minette is not, and though she has achieved stardom on the stage of the Port-au-Prince Comédie while he is sold to his second master, the point is implicitly made that Simon to a certain extent represents a mirror image of Minette. Textual support of such a reflection might be indicated by the fact that the air Simon performs on the violin comes from Minette's preferred opera, *La belle Arsène*. Though Minette does not explicitly acknowledge this epiphany, it could be said that at least on an unconscious level she comes to understand the fact that talent and achievement in the realm of European art and music is not sufficient to elevate a subject from the degradation of slavery.

Though Minette never acknowledges that the situation of the slave Simon bears a resemblance to her own, the cumulative effect of epiphanic phenomena results, directly or indirectly, in a change of attitude in Minette regarding theatrical performance and politics. Toward the novel's final chapters, Minette is preparing for yet another performance in the Port-au-Prince Comédie. It is one that is engulfed in the political events that would eventually lead up to the days of Toussaint L'Ouverture and the Haitian Revolution: "The army of the *affranchis*, now 1500 strong, entered Port-au-Prince. It was wildly acclaimed by crowds of coloured people. With ringing shouts of 'Long live the Confederates!', under proudly fluttering flags, and to the beat of victorious drums, the armies of Beauvais and Lambert paraded through the city and lined up for inspection on the Place de l'Intendance" (301). This is the backdrop against which Minette performs her role—a fragile peace treaty between the whites and *affranchi* class in which the former begrudgingly and in bad faith accorded full rights of citizens to the latter. On the eve of her performance, however, it is learned that the whites, having acquired the agreement of the *affranchis* to deport three hundred rebellious slaves to the outskirts of Port-au-Prince, defied the agreement and provoked the *affranchis* by decapitating the three hundred slaves. Yet again, Minette is faced with her hatred for the whites. In a key moment that structurally parallels Ti Noël's revelation in *The Kingdom of This World*, Minette comes to a particular realization about her hatred for the whites: "It was a hatred that was not limited to the colonists but included all the Whites in the world" (306). While Ti Noël's revelation against the tyranny of kings transcends race, Minette's epiphany explicitly refers to it. One wonders if her hatred for whites now includes the erstwhile admired Rousseau and Racine. After her final performance in the Comédie, more racial violence breaks out. Minette sings above the noise of the crowd a fragment of a sermon by Bossuet, one of the novel's key pre-Enlightenment references: "Christians, let us meditate on those whose power seems to be all around us. Let us think of the final hour which will entomb their greatness" (308). This final performance by Minette in the novel marks the completion of her transformation from talented performer to engaged citizen. As though to comment upon the conversion, chapter 34, the novel's penultimate, begins with a description of a day that "dawned clear and beautiful—the feast day of St. Cecilia"—November 22. Though the text does not say so explicitly, Saint Cecilia is the patron of musicians and artists, and is therefore an ironic or paradoxical setting to Minette's renunciation of art in favor of politics: "The fire spread from house to house. But instead of trying to put it out, the Whites began to hunt down *affranchis*, to kill them. All those who had not followed Beauvais's troops in time were killed: men, women and children. . . . Terrified of the arrival of the hate-maddened Whites, many persons of colour abandoned their homes and tried to flee the city. Women on their knees implored St. Cecilia for help" (310).

Thanks to Fouchard, we can confirm that the tragic day was, in fact, November 22 (Saint Cecilia's Day), 1791. Citing figures that are echoed in Chauvet's novel, Fouchard claims that "five hundred houses and stores disappeared in the flames. . . . The Comédie of Port-au-Prince disappeared in the flames that November 22 of 1791. . . . Minette and Lise probably lost their lives during those tragic days."[39] Chauvet slightly alters Fouchard's version. In the fighting and burning of Port-au-Prince on November 22, Minette witnesses her family murdered by white soldiers, and she herself receives a fatal wound—but her demise is not complete before the arrival of the Revolutionary Commissioner Léger-Félicité Sonthonax. Although Sonthonax made his declaration abolishing slavery in Saint Domingue in August 1793, almost two years after Minette receives her fatal stab wound in the novel, the anachronism is necessary for the novelistic denouement, in which Minette dies knowing that the slaves have been freed.

What is most striking about Chauvet's novel is not necessarily its artistic achievement, which in my view is surpassed by her later, more embittered trilogy *Amour, colère et folie*. This last work goes much further in its violent questioning of the assumptions of enlightened modernity, represented not only by the French brother-in-law Jean Luze—whose name embodies him as an ambassador of the French Enlightenment—but also, and ironically so, by the narrator Claire, whose dark complexion and the alienation it occasions offer rhetorical contrast to her given name. Questions of intense sexual repression, lingering racism, privileges of class and skin color, and the ongoing ravages of neocolonial exploitation combine to form an explosive volcano in *Amour* as well, and Chauvet's singular achievement in that novel is to demonstrate how these forces of oppression coalesce in the dark recesses of Claire's narrative psyche. Claire's disturbing and haunting dream, in which she prostrates herself before the imago of the loathed and brutal local commander Calédu, his imposing phallus prominent, is the climax of a narration that one can only be read, apparently, as a repudiation of the values of enlightened modernity about which Chauvet still seemed ambivalent in *Dance on the Volcano*.

Nevertheless, despite this interpretation of Chauvet's mature work as a renunciation of the principles and possibilities that seemed so attainable in *Dance on the Volcano*, another reading is possible. *Amour, colère et folie* certainly lends itself to be interpreted as a grotesque expression of the irrational, a traumatic voyage into a heart of darkness, as Ronnie Scharfman puts it. But such an expression might also be viewed as an allegorical reaction to the forces, themselves irrational, of extreme political and social repression, in an evocation of Goya's dictum that the dream of reason produces monsters, also articulated within a realm of severe political repression. In the denouement of *Amour*, Claire achieves a provisional political, sexual and psychological liberation by assassinating the sadistic Calédu with a knife that was a gift from her French brother-in-law, Jean Luze. As Ronnie Scharfman writes: "To stab herself in bed with the dagger, metonymy for Jean Luze and the symbol of Caledu's murderous nightmare phallus, would condense suicide, rape, orgasm, and hymen. But by killing Caledu, Claire frees herself from all of these self-destructive convergences."[40] Chauvet responds to the oppression of the Duvalier regime and the Tonton Macoutes with a negatively dialectical allegory that internalizes the external forces of tyranny. The hermeneutical horizon of this allegorical expression, witnessed in Claire's final liberating gesture, is freedom.

If Chauvet's earlier novel *Dance on the Volcano* effectively incorporates and echoes many of the tropes, themes, motifs, and even intertextual references to other Caribbean works of a historical nature preceding it, namely James's *The Black Jacobins* and Carpentier's *The Kingdom of This World*, it also confirms the tradition or subgenre of historical writing about the eighteenth century in the Caribbean and is also on the cusp of a new decade, the 1960s, that will inaugurate a reaction and alternative vision to this way of viewing Caribbean history and modernity. By introducing questions of gender into the eighteenth-century setting, Chauvet plants the seed for a disruption of the Enlightenment macronarratives so dear to James and Carpentier and nurtures this potential in *Amour, colère et folie*. A more recent generation of Caribbean writers, starting with Chauvet's fellow Francophone writer Maryse Condé, will seize upon this potential disruption to challenge the modern reproduction of Enlightenment historicity in the Caribbean.

4 Alliances and Enmities in Maryse Condé's Historical Imagination

For me Tituba is not a historical novel. Tituba is the opposite of a historical novel. I was not interested at all in what her real life could have been. I had few precise documents. . . . I hesitated between irony and a desire to be serious. The result is that she is a sort of a mock-epic character. When she was leading the fight of the maroons, it was a parody somehow.

Maryse Condé, afterword to *I, Tituba, Black Witch of Salem*

MARIE CHAUVET'S *récit Amour* concludes with the oneiric and sacrificial assassination of the sadistic local commander Calédu, who embodies for the protagonist, Claire Clamont, the oppressive legacies of racism and patriarchy. And yet for Maryse Condé, commenting on this symbolically charged denouement, "the well-known link between executioner and victim is apparent, even if the conclusion is reversed, even if the conclusion is not a triumph since, in the end, nothing has changed. The death of Calédu would not be enough to stop the march of history."[1] And so for Condé, it makes little difference whether Calédu murders Claire (the false foreshadowing in Claire's climactic dream) or, as it turns out, Claire kills Calédu; oppression in Haiti marches on. In a critique with Jamesian overtones, Condé wishes that Chauvet "had gone further in dissecting for our benefit the sterility of the machinery of power that is set in motion. She doesn't do so, opting instead for brief notations on the growing misery of the peasant class."[2] And yet this subtle critique of Chauvet might be read in contradiction to another of Condé's critical pronouncements:

"Myth," writes Édouard Glissant in *Caribbean Discourse*, "is the first of a still-naïve historical consciousness, and the raw material for the project of a literature."

No, retort the women writers in their own individual way. We have to rid ourselves of myths. They are binding, confining and paralyzing.[3]

Claire's symbolic act of killing Calédu might be read precisely as what Condé describes (and prescribes), a liberation from the phallocentric and pigmentary myths that certainly oppress Chauvet's protagonist and, by metonymic extension, Haitian and Caribbean women. And yet, at the same time, Condé gently reproaches Chauvet for dwelling too long in this subjective realm of myth, for not providing a more objective account of the historical conditions that have permitted the unfolding of the structures and institutions propagating oppression. Condé's own historical fiction might be said to strive to strike a balance between these two realms, myth and historicity.

But then again, Chauvet's *Dance on the Volcano* does to an extent dwell in the realm of history while eliding myth. At one point in Chauvet's historical novel, the protagonist, Minette, makes the acquaintance of Zoé, a free black who is working for the Saint Domingue underground resistance, so to speak, forming illegal alliances whose common aim is to free the slaves of the French colony. Zoé is one of the first characters in the novel to speak to Minette explicitly of the injustice and brutality of slavery. Thanks to Zoé, Minette experiences one of her first revelations in the novel: "Everything was unjust—the laws, the order of things, the entire pattern of social prejudice" (87). Moreover, Zoé points out to Minette: "My parents were slaves in Martinique. It is a country that very much resembles St-Domingue as far as suffering and injustices are concerned" (87). Zoé's childhood on a French island in the Caribbean, along with Condé's own critical remarks about Chauvet, provide us with a constellatory segue to the Guadeloupean Condé, who sets the action of one of her most famous novels, *I, Tituba, Black Witch of Salem*, in Barbados and New England. In this mock historical autobiography, one of the victims of the Salem witch trials narrates an account of her youth in Barbados, her travails with Samuel Parris and the Puritans in New England, and her return to Barbados to join the ranks of a maroon society. As in Chauvet's novel, *Tituba* is also a mock bildungsroman about a Caribbean woman whose own existence is the result of an interracial rape. Condé's novel begins with an account of this violation: "Abena, my mother, was raped by an English sailor on the deck *Christ the King* on day in the year 16** while the ship was sailing for Barbados. I was born from this act of aggression. From this act of hatred and contempt."[4] In Chauvet's novel, the rape of Minette's mother by her white master engenders the protagonist and fosters in her the dual psychological effect of solidarity and revulsion regarding slavery; this engendering act in *Tituba* is at once allegory and metonymy: the rape allegorizes the brutal birth of people of African descent into the Americas; the fact that it occurs on a slave ship called *Christ the King* signifies that the heinous act is metonymically part and parcel of imperious Christendom, and that Christianity's "civilizing mission" was an accomplice to the crime of the transatlantic slave trade. It is noteworthy that after Tituba's travails in New England and her liaison with the Jew Benjamin Cohen D'Azevedo, who finally frees her, the ship upon which she returns to Barbados is the less denominational *Bless the Lord.* Part of the ideological and discursive aim of Condé's novel is to posit a Caribbean spirituality as a non-Occidental alternative to puritanical and imperialist Christendom.

Chauvet's and Condé's novels are both historical coming-of-age stories about gifted Caribbean women who are fatally impacted by the institution of slavery. Despite their many points of comparison, the distinctions between them, which, I hope to show, entail primarily a generational weltanschauung, are also noteworthy. The inclusion of Condé's historical novel among the other texts in this study is merited not only by the fact that Condé is clearly participating in the tradition of modern Caribbean historical writing inaugurated by C. L. R. James and Alejo Carpentier, and continued by Marie Chauvet; Condé's novel *does* partake, consciously or unconsciously, in a dialogue with these earlier texts, and yet at the same time there is present in *Tituba* a parodying element, signaled by Condé herself (as quoted in the epigraph), that partially provides a demarcation line between the earlier generation and the more recent. In Condé's novel *Traversée de la mangrove* (*Crossing the Mangrove*), Condé invents the character of Lucien Évariste, an aspiring Guadeloupean writer who, with ironic nostalgia, emulates "Alejo Carpentier and Lezama Lima" as artists who evoke the mythology and orality of Caribbean history.[5] This specific evocation of Carpentier in a parodic vein confirms, at least in part, Condé's implicit dialogue with the Cuban writer regarding the representation and value of history for an evolving Caribbean subjectivity.

Another source of Condé's parodic tone is the repetition of "stock" scenes from the Caribbean literary tradition. In an interview with Ann Armstrong Scarboro that appears in the afterword of *I, Tituba*, Condé herself points out, apropos of the feminist elements: "The question of grandmothers telling stories and thus teaching their granddaughters how to become writers is one of the biggest clichés of black female writing. . . . I know that in any female epic, some elements must be present, and I deliberately included some of them" (211–12). A similar phenomenon occurs in Condé's novel regarding the Caribbean tradition: the parodic or pastiche element is not so much a result of an explicit attitudinal irony toward the past or toward tradition; rather, the sheer repetition of certain stock scenes or tropes inevitably tends to empty them of their evocative power and to create a de facto irony. The images of Mackandal's amputation and subsequent public execution are powerful allegories of dismemberment, death, and resurgence in Carpentier (and echoed in Chauvet). The historical lynching of Victor Ogé, mentioned in James and dramatized in Chauvet, is another forceful episode. And yet, when such scenes are repeated in Condé's novel, or with even more radical intent in Reinaldo Arenas's treatment of the Mexican revolutionary Fray Servando Teresa de Mier, the emotive effect is somewhat diffused and defused. Therefore, the inclusion of Condé in this study permits an elaboration on what could be described as a generational demarcation, a graduation from a form of Caribbean modernity to a posterior articulation, a postmodernity. J. Michael Dash, to reiterate an aforementioned quote, also considers Condé a postmodern writer: "Maryse Condé may be the only major female novelist other than Chauvet to pursue the postmodern in Caribbean writing."[6] Though Dash perhaps justifiably (but, in my view, arguably) refers to Chauvet's later novel, *Amour, colère et folie* as postmodern, I view her earlier novel about the Haitian Revolution as unquestionably belonging to a modern vein in Caribbean literature.[7] I use the term "postmodern" to refer to Condé's *Tituba* in a specific sense: since the target of its parodic verve is precisely the ethos of Caribbean historical writing of an earlier generation (including Chauvet and Carpentier), Condé's texts are postmodern because they amount to a parody, commentary, or pastiche of these earlier texts.

Condé is conscious of the fact that her Caribbean predecessors grappled with the Enlightenment historicity, and she therefore ineluctably writes in response to that tradition. Even if *Tituba* is not specifically a text about the eighteenth century in the Caribbean, her short three-act dramatic text *In the Time of the Revolution* (whose original title in Creole is *An tan revolisyon* and which was performed in Guadeloupe in 1989)[8] certainly is, and reveals that Condé's historical approach already entails an engagement with or perhaps a rebuttal to the rules of historical self-consciousness that thinkers as diverse as Georg Lukács and C. L. R. James attribute to the Enlightenment. Speaking of the literature of the Hispanic Caribbean, Roberto González Echevarría asserts that it begins "in the transition from the eighteenth to the nineteenth centuries. . . . Modern literature begins in the Hispanic Caribbean when its inhabitants begin to write with an awareness of their own historicity, with the consciousness of being a part of the world historical forces."[9] Lukács observes, "Now if experiences such as these are linked with the knowledge that similar upheavals are taking place all over the world, this must enormously strengthen the feeling first that there is such a thing as history, second that it is an uninterrupted process of changes and finally that it has a direct effect upon the life of every individual."[10] These "rules" of Enlightenment historicity come into play in Condé's historical imagination, though the Guadeloupean novelist at times acknowledges the late-eighteenth-century shift in historical consciousness while questioning the applicability of this sweeping paradigm for people living in the Caribbean. In his *Voicing Memory*, Nick Nesbitt states, "In this sense, positivist Antillean historicism, for all its efficiency, fails to live up to its own criteria insofar as its search for truth terminates in a totality of seemingly true facts that fail to represent the exploded nature of the Antillean experience." Nesbitt then goes on to cite a revealing quotation from Condé, "To know one's past, to dominate it, to know its reality without making of it an object of backwards-looking veneration, is one of the conditions of freedom."[11] Condé's attitude toward the Caribbean past can be said to both align her with and distinguish her from her predecessors, including Chauvet, along with her contemporaries. To "dominate" historical discourse is not a question of mastering its minutiae in the hope that a marvelous revelation will emerge from it (à la Carpentier), nor of deciphering how the rules of Enlightenment historicity have played out in the unfolding of Caribbean modernity. Rather, for Condé, the mastery of the past is a question of adopting a sovereign, irreverent, and at times cavalier attitude toward Enlightenment historicity (including chronology, temporal cause and effect, and the idea of a world historical consciousness emerging in the eighteenth century) and thereby defusing its overdetermining power. Édouard Glissant also articulates another expression of this vision of Caribbean history that is at odds with Lukács's view of a convergent, single history: "The implosion of Caribbean history (of the converging histories of our peoples) relieves us of the linear, hierarchical vision of a single History that would run its unique course."[12] Condé's *In the Time of Revolution* might be said to enact Glissant's pronouncement; by dramatizing key revolutionary moments in France and the Caribbean in the late eighteenth century, we might be led to believe that for Condé, as for Carpentier and James, these events unite the people in France, Saint Domingue, and Guadeloupe in 1789, 1794, and 1802 as converging into a singular torrential flow of world history. And yet Condé's aim is clearly to challenge this common view.

Shifting among the events in these years, Condé reviews the terrain covered by Chauvet, Carpentier, and James. For the latter two, Toussaint L'Ouverture and Victor Hugues are historical protagonists. They also appear in Condé's play and embody a comparable problematic: the failed exportation to the Francophone Caribbean of a failed European Revolution. As the play's narrator, "the Storyteller," informs us:

> Revolution is like a woman: you do whatever you want with her. Soldiers of fortune sodomize her, poets read her poetry, the middle class makes her cough up the cash. In the kingdom of France, revolution aborted the baby that had turned its womb into a mountain of justice. All that remains is a stinking pile of coagulated blood lying in the gutter. (465)

Meanwhile, we are reminded, "For us in Guadeloupe" not much has changed. And so, like Carpentier, Condé seems to be of the opinion that the French Revolution, in the final instance, had little impact on Caribbean civilization. Condé goes a step further in the radicalness of this judgment, however, in asserting the categorical failure of the French Revolution in the first place. Thus, in her skepticism regarding the accepted view of the paradigm shifts in historical consciousness in both Europe and the Caribbean, Condé provides a glimpse of at least one characteristic of the postmodern or post-Carpenterian Caribbean historical imagination. If Carpentier hesitates between views of history as either dialectically evolving or repetitively cyclical, then one constant in Condé's historical imagination is the fundamental doubt concerning notions of progress and the promises of freedom attainable either through revolution or political representation. *In the Time of the Revolution* dramatizes an array of historical figures from the Francophone Caribbean, such as Toussaint, Victor Hugues, Dessalines, Louis Delgrès, and others who articulate a hopeful or heroic historical prognosis for the Antilles. And yet whether it is a question of Victor Hugues abolishing slavery in Guadeloupe or Toussaint declaring the institution null and void in Saint Domingue, Condé's narrator in the drama, "the Storyteller," repeatedly casts a skeptical gaze back on these historical developments. After Hugues's pronouncement, the Guadeloupean ex-slaves are conscripted into the French army to fight the British; Toussaint announces: "Work is a virtue. Anyone caught wandering and idle will be arrested and punished by the law" (472). Meanwhile, the slaves and ex-slaves themselves maintain their transhistorical demand for freedom—"Libètè!"—which is never granted in full. Not surprisingly, another aspect of this skeptical operation is the desacralization of heretofore revered Caribbean figures. Even Toussaint L'Ouverture is not spared the Storyteller's disdain. After his character in the play reinstates a kind of de facto slavery, in which "All overseers, drivers and farmers who do not scrupulously fulfill the duties that farming imposes on them will be arrested and punished with the same severity as soldiers who fail to meet theirs," (473), the Storyteller proclaims:

> So it goes, so it goes! As for me, I found Toussaint Louverture a little frightening, in spite of all the respect to which he is entitled. You didn't? Didn't he remind you of anyone? No? Good! Too bad! Too bad for me; I'm kind of oversensitive when it comes to freedom! (473)

Louis Delgrès, a Martinique-born officer, was one of the leaders of the rebellion against the French in Guadeloupe in 1802. Cornered without retreat, Delgrès achieved martyr status in Guadeloupe when in a kamikaze gesture he blew himself up along with hundreds of French and rebel soldiers. Delgrès issued a proclamation echoing Toussaint's letter to the French directory, which declared the preferability of death to the return to slavery.[13] Condé's irony takes aim at this proclamation:

> Citizens, I'm going to read you a proclamation by the commander of Basse-Terre, Delgrès. [*He reads very badly.*] May the whole universe hear this last protest of innocence and despair. In the finest days of a century that will be forever celebrated for the victory of philosophy and enlightenment. (484)

The audience listening to the proclamation understands little and declares that the proclamation is in "White man's French." Thus at a stroke Condé desacralizes the memory of Delgrès and links his proclamation to the Enlightenment, which is viewed as mostly irrelevant and inapplicable. As Nesbitt states it, "Each time a character risks glorifying or celebrating the autotelic agency of Ignace or Delgrès as autonomous agents of history, skeptical comments from a more sober character undermine this gesture."[14] This expression of skepticism is a good indication of the direction that Condé takes the Caribbean historical imagination in a posterior moment to James and Carpentier. If these prior authors participated in the long tradition of denouncing the hypocrisy of European philosophers who decried slavery while maintaining vested interests in its continuation, then Condé takes this critique a step further by also casting a suspicious regard on the pronouncements by the revered Caribbean champions of freedom such as Toussaint and Delgrès.

Condé's Storyteller, who in fact is more of a historical commentator than narrator, adds an interesting dimension to the Enlightenment as it is viewed in the modern Caribbean historical imagination. His nickname is "Zephyr," a reference to the Guadeloupean spirit that goes about the island telling tales.[15] And yet in Condé's play, the Storyteller-narrator is endowed with a temporal, and not merely spatial, mobility. The Storyteller enjoys a historical vantage point that allows him to question or cast judgment on historical events and their agents. And yet, significantly, this figure around whom the drama (and allegorically, history itself) coheres is not the historian or the philosopher, but rather "the Storyteller," whose name evokes the act of narration as the supreme activity for interpreting Caribbean reality, historical or otherwise. The Storyteller's transhistorical mobility permits the liberal employment of historical anachronisms, which is also a constant in Condé's historical imagination. I will discuss in greater detail the use and significance of these anachronisms in *Tituba*, but it is already interesting to see, in *In the Time of the Revolution,* the use of anachronisms that essentially announce how little things have changed since the onset of so-called historical consciousness in the Caribbean and that serve to question notions of social advancement and historical progress. Three such anachronisms in *In the Time of the Revolution* are worth mentioning: "What would old Toussaint think if he came back to life and saw his country up for auction, handed over to the rage of the Tonton Macoutes, his people bleeding from the eternal wounds of injustice and hunger?" (466). In the section of the text subtitled "1802," the Storyteller intones: "And then in my time, we didn't dream about poetry, literature, all that meaningless stuff. We dreamed about freedom. Not like you who dreams about BMWs or VCRs or vacations to Caracas!" (478). In this section of the text, there is a contrapuntal distinction between the resistance to the reinstatement of slavery in Saint Domingue and its successful reestablishment by General Richepanse in Guadeloupe. The Storyteller comments: "What do you want me to say? That I've invented a happy ending like in American movies? This time will be like all the others. Death, which never has its fill, will have a belly full; and those who love freedom will end up in mass graves" (486). Tonton Macoutes, BMWs, VCRs and Hollywood movies anachronistically signal that the Storyteller's real historical vantage point is the contemporary (present) moment. But these contemporary references are not meant to indicate the direction or denouement toward which the spirit of history is leading; rather, they indicate mere accoutrements in a synchronic view of time in which the cohesive element is the never-ending thirst, never quenched, for human freedom: "For us in Guadeloupe, not much has changed" (465).

Condé's *In the Time of the Revolution* significantly demonstrates her participation in the modern Caribbean historical imagination of James, Carpentier, and Chauvet. The play reiterates some of the tropes of her Caribbean predecessors, namely the Carpenterian paradox of, on the one hand, the impact of the French Revolution on the Caribbean, and, on the other, the persistence of a worldview for which the upheavals of the late eighteenth century were a mere part of a continuum of oppression. But if this text clearly participates in the modern Caribbean tradition of literary interpretation of the events that rocked the archipelago at the end of the eighteenth century, it is perhaps even more interesting to look closely at another of Condé's historical texts, *Tituba*, which takes place in the seventeenth century and therefore dramatizes a pre-Enlightenment moment in Caribbean and American history. By creating a mock autobiography of Tituba, Condé allows herself a forum to elaborate a Caribbean reality that already anticipated many of the hallmarks of European Enlightenment.

Condé warns the reader, "Do not take Tituba *too* seriously, please" (212). One of the sacrosanct conventions of the modern Caribbean historical imagination is rigorous historical authenticity and documentation. Both Carpentier and Chauvet make explicit claims to historical accuracy as an overture to their respective novels, and the rigor of James's archival work is clear both in the body of his text and in the bibliography. And yet this foundation is one of the first targets of Condé's parody. As Nesbitt observes: "Condé, like Césaire before her, has repeatedly asserted a stubborn refusal to erase the particularity of French Antillean subjective appearance within an abstract scholarly discourse. She consistently strives to overcome the petrification of historical experience as archival fossil."[16] As I discuss in later chapters, this irreverent and defiant approach to historical accuracy and orthodoxy is a hallmark of Caribbean postmodernity.

There is abundant prima facie evidence to demonstrate an explicit intertextuality between Condé's novel and prior twentieth-century historical writing from the Caribbean, and, though critics have not tended to point out these similarities explicitly, Carpentier's *The Kingdom of This World* seems particularly alluded to. If Ti Noël, the protagonist of Carpentier's novel, is a slave, so is Condé's Tituba, and her movements away from the land of her birth and "over the seas," only to return to her native Barbados at the end of the novel, partially mirror Ti Noël's displacement to Santiago de Cuba once the Haitian Revolution is under way and his return to Haiti many years later. If Ti Noël in his later years comes back to the site of the ruins of Monsieur Lenormand de Mézy's plantation, now in ruins, so Tituba revisits the house of her former nemesis and master, Susanna Endicott. If Ti Noël and Mackandal are inspired by the wise old Maman Loi in Carpentier, with her secret knowledge of the powers of plants and herbs, Tituba likewise is educated by Mama Yaya, who also lives in the woods and "cultivated to a fine art the ability to communicate with the invisible" (9). If Ti Noël in *The Kingdom of This World* experiences a revelation that elevates his consciousness from the hatred of whites to the hatred of tyranny in general, so Tituba early in her narration channels her resentment toward white men: "My mother had been raped by a white man. She had been hanged because of a white man. . . . My adoptive father had committed suicide because of a white man. Despite all that, I was considering living among white men again, in their midst, under their domination" (19).

Tituba's alliances and enmities in the novel take on a schematic pattern. In the novel there emerge numerous alliances with women, black (Mary Black) or white (Hester Prynne), against men (Samuel Parris); and occasional alliances with blacks of either sex (Yao, her adoptive father, and John Indian) against whites (Susanna Endicott). The pattern that emerges is that either race *or* gender necessarily plays a factor in the formation of alliances or enmities, but that either element necessarily amounts to an insurmountable obstacle to human solidarity. That is to say, Tituba can never cross the divide of *both* gender *and* race. The figure of the white man, then, amounts to an enmity of an oppositional purity. This categorical opposition to white people, we recall, also characterized Ti Noël's resentment in *The Kingdom of This World* and Minette's epiphanies regarding slavery in Chauvet's *Dance on the Volcano*. And yet, toward the end of Carpentier's novel, this opposition was dialectisized by the old man's revelation, recalling an irreverent sailor's song from his youth and reflecting on his more recent hardships under the yoke of Christophe, Haiti's black emperor, that in fact tyrants of all races are the true adversary. Does Tituba's apparently unbreakable deadlock with the white man also await a dialectical synthesis or resolution in the novel?

After Tituba is accused of being a witch in the Salem debacle, the narration quotes the historical Tituba's deposition in the infamous trials, which in a footnote is attributed to the Essex County Archives (104). And so, in a sense, the author's interruption of her own narrative with a footnote to proclaim historical accuracy is squarely consistent with a similar discursive practice in both Carpentier and Chauvet. (As we shall see in chapter 6, the Puerto Rican author Edgardo Rodríguez Juliá will explode this authenticizing gesture with a series of footnotes leading us on a labyrinthine trail of apocryphal historical documentation.) Moreover, Tituba laments that her role in the historical events will be minimized to a mere sentence attesting to her presence at the trials:

> I felt that I would only be mentioned in passing in these Salem witchcraft trials about which so much would be written later, trials that would arouse the curiosity and pity of generations to come as the greatest testimony of a superstitious and barbaric age. There would be mention here and there of "a slave originating from the West Indies and probably practicing 'hoodoo.'" There would be no mention of my age or my personality. (110)

This complaint about historical underrepresentation is another link to earlier Caribbean historical writing. C. L. R. James elevates the rank of historical significance of Toussaint L'Ouverture to among the most transcendent historical personages of the Age of Revolution and predicts that one day the name of the great Haitian founding father will be known to schoolchildren the world over; Carpentier exploits the largely unknown nature of Victor Hugues's heroic and nefarious exploits in the Caribbean; Chauvet relies on Jean Fouchard's history of Saint Domingue theater to highlight the stellar ascent of a young girl of mixed racial heritage in a brutally racist society. Even Condé's play *In the Time of the Revolution* could be said to serve a similar heuristic role in the popular dissemination of information about the key figures and events in Caribbean history. In *Tituba*, Condé's practice is comparable to those of her predecessors, with an important difference: her protagonist's biography is a blank page except for the few lines of her deposition and the fact that "for the record" she was a slave of West Indian descent possibly practicing Vodou. As Pascale Bécel, in a brief but insightful article, states it, "Condé's re-invention of Tituba's story similarly implies a form of recovery of the past which is open to change and becoming."[17] Tituba's complaint is, "Why was I going to be ignored?" (149). This minimal biography is the point of departure for Condé to provide an imagined forward-and-backward (before and after the Salem witch trials) trajectory, all the while highlighting a wealth of anachronistic details that emphasize rather than efface the ludic.

In his reading of Carpentier's *Explosion in a Cathedral*, Roberto González Echevarría points out Carpentier's modern approach to history in his narration: "The common strategy in the historical novel is to bypass the problem and narrate as if the text were contemporaneous with the action of the novel. [This is also Chauvet's approach in *Dance on the Volcano*.] But Carpentier has not allowed himself such an easy way out of the dilemma. He obviously narrates history from a perspective that is already the future of that history. Historical narrative is, of necessity, always in the future: at the moment in which history and its outcome are one."[18] In Carpentier's novel, this "posterior" perspective is signaled by anachronisms: Marx's nineteenth-century "specter," for example, is unequivocally alluded to in this narration of the eighteenth century. It may be argued that such anachronisms in general violate the so-called historical integrity of the narration and therefore open up the possibility of a ludic historical meditation, wherein chronology and diachrony, perhaps the most fundamental laws of temporality, are bracketed. But, in fact, quite a different operation is taking place. Rather than creating an aperture of historical possibility, Carpentier's anachronisms—the inclusion of details that only someone from the eighteenth century's future could have known about—actually result in a closure of possible interpretation. It is an understanding of history where the past is bound to evolve as we in the past's "future" know it did, where the past's denouement has already been determined and cannot be otherwise. Carpentier represents history's protagonists as hesitating on the precipice of momentous decisions—one thinks of Victor Hugues's move to reinstate slavery in *Explosion in a Cathedral*—but the drama of those moments is foreshortened and the irony heightened since we are most likely already aware of their denouement. The resulting historical vision is therefore more appropriately described as telic rather than ludic.[19]

Though Chauvet's and Condé's historical novels both have their point of departure in historical characters about whom little is known, the latter text's ludic wink to contemporary, present-day thought and language distinguishes her from the Caribbean historical imagination of a prior generation. I have already mentioned that in *In the Time of the Revolution*, which in other respects has so much in common with James and Carpentier, Condé employs a synchronic view of history that treats present-day references not as teleology but rather as temporal debris. In *Titu-*

ba, the protagonist's imprisonment and alliance with Hester Prynne, the protagonist of Nathanial Hawthorne's nineteenth-century novel, is one of the best-known anachronisms. There are more instances in the novel's language that reveal a particularly contemporary way of thinking and references, for example, "How many more stonings? Holocausts?" (136); "I hope that generations to come will live under a welfare state that will truly provide for the well-being of its citizens" (118); and, in a reference to Billie Holliday's song, "All around me the trees were bristling with strange fruit" (172).

These issues of historical (in)accuracy in *Tituba* tie in with the question of alliances and enmities. If, in fact, Tituba is locked in an unmediated opposition with the figure of the white man, though there can be alliances formed with either black men or white women, the character of the Jew Benjamin Cohen d'Azevedo seems to be a mediating figure that possibly allows Tituba to break the deadlock. After Tituba's role in the witch trials and incarceration, she is purchased by Cohen d'Azevedo, a Sephardic Jew of Portuguese-Dutch descent. Condé provides a sympathetic view of this Jewish character, despite an unflattering and somewhat clichéd physical description (hunchbacked, "eggplant colored"). In a compelling essay, Nathalie Debrauwere-Miller provides an interpretation of the range of allegorical implications of Cohen d'Azevedo and Tituba's alliance. Though it is true that the Jew's physical portrait in the novel is tinged with some anti-Semitic commonplaces, such as the ruddy complexion and hunchback posture, not to mention his profession as a wealthy merchant, these clichés are in counterpoint to the commonplaces attributed to Tituba herself as a black woman with heightened sexual prowess.[20] Even in Tituba's afterlife, she speaks of her unabated sexual desire: "I myself have loved men too much and shall continue to do so" (78). These two unlikely lovers, Cohen and Tituba, the diabolical red and the black—both colors have traditional satanic associations in Christianity—embody the negative stereotypes that characterize Jews and blacks in the West, and their sexual and ideological alliance and departure from New England to carry on their respective diasporas amount to a transformation of their traditionally circumscribed identities. Frantz Fanon asserts the following distinction between the Jew and the black: "The Jew can be unknown in his Jewishness. He is not wholly what he is. . . . His actions, his behavior are the final determinant. He is basically a white man, and apart from some debatable characteristics, he can go unnoticed."[21]

The Jew for Fanon, then, is essentially a variation on the theme of whiteness; following this logic, Tituba's association and alliance with Cohen d'Azevedo should or could therefore represent a mediation toward breaking the black/white divide that characterizes much of the novel. But Condé apparently rejects this point of view, and not surprisingly, given her dispute with Fanon regarding his harsh judgment, also in *Black Skin, White Masks*, of Mayotte Capécia's *Je suis martiniquaise* (1948): "Mayotte loves a white man to whom she submits in everything. He is her lord. She asks nothing, demands nothing, except a bit of whiteness in her life."[22] Condé responds passionately and convincingly to Fanon in defense of Capécia's novel: "Contrary to what Frantz Fanon thinks and says, *Je suis martiniquaise* is a precious written testimony, the only one that we possess, of the mentality of a West Indian girl in those days, of the impossibility for her to build up an aesthetics which would enable her to come to terms with the color of her skin."[23] Just as Carpentier serves as a modernist figure against which a younger generation of Hispanic Caribbean writers attempt to articulate an alternative historical vision, so it is plausible that in a Francophone context Fanon figures as an understood interlocutor in Condé's portrait of Tituba. Moreover, Fanon is explicitly and anachronistically evoked in *Tituba*, as Pascale Bécel perspicaciously remarks,[24] when John Indian declares, "They'll say your skin is black, but you're wearing a white mask over it" (32), a remark whose irony is heightened when we realize that John Indian is the malleable opportunist who molds himself to white expectations.

If, for Fanon, Jews are white and black women desire *lactification*, or "whitening," then Condé's protagonist rejects both claims: Tituba is diametrically opposed to white men and Cohen d'Azevedo is Jewish, not white, since he is also unequivocally portrayed as a victim of white Protestantism embodied in the figure of the Puritan Samuel Parris. In the novel, a group of Puritans gather outside the house where Cohen d'Azevedo's family and Tituba live. "Did we leave England for this? To see Jews and niggers multiply in our midst?" (132). They proceed to burn down the home, killing all nine of the children. In the novelist's view, at least, it would be difficult therefore to see Cohen d'Azevedo as an extension or variation of whiteness, and the oppositional arrangement remains in place. As Tituba asks Metahebel, Cohen d'Azevedo's daughter, "isn't it time the victims changed sides?" (126).

It might be argued, then, that this desired reversal, of the victims and victimizers changing sides (significantly, we recall, this is how Condé characterized the denouement of Marie Chauvet's *Amour*, when Claire's and Calédu's roles as executioner and victim are interchangeable) is further proof that Condé does not view historical unfolding in dialectical terms. Her statement to Ann Armstrong Scarboro, in the afterword of *I, Tituba*, that her depiction of late seventeenth-century Puritan society in New England is in fact a thinly veiled commentary on present-day race relations in the United States, would seem to bear out this judgment: "I wanted to imply that in terms of narrow-mindedness, hypocrisy and racism, little has changed since the days of the Puritans" (203). Though it would be a stretch to suggest that Condé entirely rejects a view of historical "progress," it could be said that the discourse of *Tituba* harbors suspicions regarding this dialectic as it has been traditionally articulated in the Caribbean by figures such as James, Fanon, or Césaire. This suspicion, indifference, or outright rejection of the dialectical view of historical progress is a hallmark of the postmodern Caribbean historical imagination.

The discursive climax of Tituba's association with Cohen d'Azevedo is the dialogue that summarizes their rivalry of persecution: the Jew lists a chronicle of discrimination suffered by his people with dates, placenames, and the nature of the persecution, to which Tituba can only respond:

> "And what about us? Do you know how many of us have been bled from the coast of Africa?"
>
> But he went on. "In 1298 the Jews of Rottingen were put to the sword and the wave of murders spread to Bavaria and Austria. In 1336 our blood was shed from the Rhine to Bohemia and Moravia."
>
> He outdid me every time. (127)

The point of this exchange, it is safe to say, is not that the persecution of the Jews "outdoes" the plight of Africans and African Americans during slavery. If the Jew "outdoes" Tituba—"il me battait a tous les coups," in the original French—then the blows, or *coups*, are in fact the dates by which the Jew orders, retains, and recites a specific history—a power that has been lost to Tituba (despite the fact that, technically, Cohen d'Azevedo should perhaps recite these dates according to the Hebrew calendar rather than the Gregorian one). This inequality between them—the power of historical recall and continuity on the one hand versus historical rupture on the other—hearkens back to Tituba's complaint regarding her underrepresentation in the chronicles of the Salem witch trials. Despite the bonds that unite Tituba and Cohen d'Azevedo, clearly highlighted in the novel, the ludic reinvention of the historical self, such an important characteristic of Condé's novel and postmodern Caribbean literature in general, is in stark contrast to the Jewish consciousness of extended historical continuity.[25]

Dialectics of the Invisible

The literary reinvention of the Caribbean woman whose subjectivity is not entirely overdetermined by historical forces is only part of the discursive agenda in this novel. Despite the knowledge that Tituba acquires through experience and experimentation with nature under the tutelage of Mama Yaya in the woods of Barbados, it is clear that this brand of knowledge is viewed as a kind of Enlightenment *avant la lettre* in opposition to the Puritanical worldview in place in the American colonies at the time of narration.

These opposing worldviews can be assessed according to their respective attitudes toward the visible and the invisible. If, for Carpentier, music is the measuring stick by which diametrically opposing experiences of temporality can be gauged, for Condé, attitudes toward the visible, the invisible, and the generally empirical help to flesh out the Afro-Caribbean worldview. Early on in the novel, while still in Barbados, Tituba encounters Mama Yaya, who "taught me about herbs. Those for inducing sleep. Those for healing wounds and ulcers. Those for loosening the tongues of thieves. Those that calm epileptics and plunge them into blissful rest. Those that put words of hope on the lips of the angry, the desperate and the suicidal" (9). During her period of tutelage under Mama Yaya, Tituba's understanding of the medicinal powers of plants and herbs anticipates everything from truth serum to antidepressants in an approach that is better described as medicinal than magical. And yet this empirical view is coupled with a hybrid attitude toward the "invisible" that is seemingly at odds with Enlightenment norms but that at the same time allegorizes a horizon beyond the social norm of slavery and colonialism. "This ability to communicate with the invisible world, to keep constant links with the dead, to care for others and heal" (17) is what the Puritans and the planters in the Caribbean condense under the reductive rubric of witchcraft.

After Maman Loi's demise, Tituba abandons her solitary yet free existence in the woods and willfully submits to slavery under Susanna Endicott in order to live reunited with her lover, John Indian. Interestingly, one of the most painful aspects of slavery is that Tituba is treated as "invisible." As Susanna Endicott speaks disparagingly about Tituba with her friends, Tituba notes: "They were talking about me and yet ignoring me. They were striking me off the map of human beings. I was a nonbeing. Invisible. More invisible than the unseen, who at least have powers that everyone fears. Tituba only existed insofar as these women let her exist" (24). This fear or resentment of invisibility foreshadows the extension of the metaphor toward history: Tituba's resents the short shrift she receives in the historical record of the Salem trials. For Tituba, then, the invisibility to which she is relegated by the "West" (a category that here comprises the European colonists in the Caribbean as well as the Puritans in New England) is the equivalent of an ontological annihilation, an irrelevance.

Tituba avenges her mistreatment by using her powers to provoke Susanna Endicott's illness. When Doctor Fox is called to diagnose her illness, he brandishes a volume entitled *Wonders of the Invisible World*. The doctor is searching for the outward signs of satanic possession: the kind of positivistic reasoning he employs and the relationship between visible manifestations and cause and effect seem to evoke a way of thinking that is on the cusp of Enlightenment thought: "I have found neither red nor blue spots similar to a flea bite. And still less painless marks that when stuck with a pin do not bleed. I can therefore make no positive conclusion" (31). Though the assumption that the cause of illness is satanic is hardly evocative of the Enlightenment, the method employed of determining conclusions based on observable phenomena contains the seed of a way of thinking that a century later, emptied of its metaphysical content, will become standard methodology.

Nevertheless, when Tituba finds herself in the midst of the New England puritanical hysteria, a doctor is once again called in to diagnose the apparent effects of witchcraft on two girls, Betsy and Abigail. After a complete auscultation, the doctor announces his diagnosis, which is striking in its chiasmatic relationship with Doctor Fox's pronouncement in Barbados: "I can see no disorder of the spleen or the liver nor congestion of the bile or overheating of the blood. In a word, I can see no physical cause. I must therefore conclude that the evil hand of Satan is upon them" (81). As though to complete the parallel with the former Barbadian physician, who was armed with a bound volume on the invisible world, the New England doctor arrived with "a number of leather-bound books, which he opened at carefully numbered pages" (81). But unlike his Caribbean counterpart, who can arrive at no positive conclusion due to a lack of observable causes, the New England physician's thought processes operate in an inverse fashion: instead of avoiding a positive conclusion due to insufficient causes, the Puritan, through negative reasoning, arrives at a positive diagnosis based precisely on a void of observable causes. Rarely has an anti-Enlightenment attitude been portrayed with such succinctness. Unlike C. L. R. James, then, who views the Enlightenment in the Caribbean as attaining a level of completeness in the Haitian Revolution that outshone the betrayed ideals of the French Revolution, and, unlike Carpentier, who playfully pits the Caribbean in diametrical opposition to the Enlightenment, Condé embodies in Tituba a hybrid worldview of the legacy of the Enlightenment in the Caribbean: on the one hand, the practices of medicine, the knowledge of the natural world, and the ideas of social welfare resonate with certain goals and methodologies of European rationalism and Enlightenment; on the other hand, Tituba also practices a spirituality, including communication and communion with the departed, that is at odds with enlightened materialism. Perhaps most importantly, Tituba is portrayed as having arrived at these capabilities and attributes without any exposure to Western ideas or civilization. Therefore, unlike the common characterization of Toussaint L'Ouverture as someone who absorbed ideas of modern freedom from reading Raynal, Tituba's ideas that resemble those of enlightened modernity have not so much a resulted from the latter as they have emerged in parallel or anticipatory fashion to them.

In the final analysis, it seems undeniable that the edifice of Condé's ludic or parodic project of inventing an autobiography of Tituba is at least partially built upon Carpentier's foundation. If, for the Cuban author, the crux of the opposition between the West and the Afro-Caribbean world can be found in respective conceptions of temporality, memory, and representation, then much the same can be said of *Tituba*. In the novel's epilogue, Tituba, speaking from the afterlife, remarks, "My people will keep my memory in their hearts and have no need for the written word." It is worth recalling that in *Traversée de la mangrove*, Condé fashions the aspiring writer Lucien Évariste, who strives to emulate Alejo Carpentier as a Caribbean author who incorporates orality into his literature. This preference for an oral tradition over writing resonates with Carpentier's vision of the Caribbean, where the transparency of Western modes of transcription, musical or otherwise, unanchor the sign from its specific experience, calling into question the value and transmissibility of historical experience.

But even if Condé evokes Carpentier with a degree of irony or parody, the two Caribbean authors share the belief in the singular role of literature and narration in revealing the nature of Caribbean historical or temporal reality. In this sense, both Carpentier and Condé privilege the storyteller (rather than the historian) as the organizing principle of the Caribbean past and its value for an evolving subjectivity. The contextually distant but eminently relevant example of Walter Benjamin's "The Storyteller" comes to mind. For Benjamin, the art of storytelling was already a vanishing human legacy by the early twentieth century due to the modern advent of information technologies and the degradation of human experience. In a celebrated phrase, "It is as if something that seemed inalienable to us, the securest among our possessions, were taken from us: the ability to exchange experiences."[26] Though Benjamin is not speaking specifically about historical discourse, it is noteworthy that Condé's own Storyteller from *In the Time of Revolution* serves a similar function, as a "voice" that constellates phenomena over time into a meaningful pattern and does so in joyful defiance of the rules that determine the historian's discipline.

Several characteristics set Condé's *Tituba* apart from Carpentier's fictional project, though: the first is the suspicion she harbors of the dialectical view of history as articulated primarily by her male forebears. For Condé, at least in *Tituba*, as well as for the Storyteller in *In the Time of the Revolution*, masters remain masters and slaves remain slaves; the relationship may be reversed, or a reversal may be longed for, but the fundamental framework persists. She also displays a ludic approach to history that entails an irreverent disregard for historical and chronological accuracy, though ample and erudite historical allusions certainly inform the fiction. These characteristics could be said to pertain generally to the postmodern expression of the Caribbean historical imagination. Condé, however, introduces a factor that neither her postmodern Spanish-speaking contemporaries Reinaldo Arenas and Edgardo Rodríguez Juliá, nor certainly any of the writers of a previous generation take into account: the concept of gender as a critical perspective for questioning the assumed limits subjectivity. In her essay "Order, Disorder, Freedom, and the West Indian Writer," Condé makes it clear that patriarchal ideological underpinnings characterize the understanding of the Caribbean of both a prior (Fanon, Glissant) and more recent (Confiant, Chamoiseau, and Bernabé) generation of Caribbean writers and theorists.[27] It might even be said that this emphasis on gender sets Condé apart from her Francophone predecessor Marie Chauvet, whose portrait of Minette in *Dance on the Volcano* rescues from historical oblivion a remarkable woman of color from eighteenth-century Saint Domingue, but also acquiesces to rather than defies the traditional notions of gender and its intersections with history, politics, and art.[28] Condé's revindication of Tituba, not as witch, but as an underrepresented subject of history, inserts gender into and consequently alters the machinery of the Caribbean historical imagination.

Part III

The Center and the Periphery Cannot Hold

5 Cuban Cogito

Reinaldo Arenas and the Negative Historical Imagination

I am like a prisoner who is enjoying an imaginary freedom while asleep; as he begins to suspect that he is asleep, he dreads being woken up, and goes along with the pleasant illusion as long as he can.

René Descartes, "Meditations on First Philosophy"

The world is independent of my will. . . . Even if all that we were to wish for were to happen, still this would only be a favor granted by fate, so to speak: for there is no logical connection between the will and the world, which would guarantee it, and the supposed physical connection itself is surely not something we could will.

Ludwig Wittgenstein, *Tractatus logico-philosophicus*

Grito, luego, existo.

Reinaldo Arenas, *Antes que anochezca*

Wittgenstein's proposition, as stated in the epigraph—that there is no causality between the will and the world—might be taken generally as an anti-Enlightenment position. The Enlightenment held that the will can to some extent determine the world, that the latter is largely a question and result of the former. What is required is a conscious decision to declare one's own autonomy, to throw off the yoke of extraneous authority, whether that authority consists of an oppressive political system, a comforting system of religious beliefs, or even a doctor's prescription for a healthy diet. For Kant, the enlightened individual need not look beyond his own intelligence for these prescriptive guidelines.

Enlightenment proclaims the sovereignty of the will, that the world is subject to it, or that at least a proper (or improper) application of the will can determine the world to a degree. For Diderot, the determining factor in politics is not this or that form of government, but rather whether or not a monarchy or democracy is subservient to a sovereign "general will."[1] For Adorno and Horkheimer, the Enlightenment in fact begins with the imposition of humanity's will over nature, the conversion of the world into a tool for man's will. And yet mastery over this aspect of the world is also the seed of the Enlightenment's *failure*: "Myth turns into enlightenment, and nature into mere objectivity. Men pay for the increase of their power with alienation from that over which they exercise their power. Enlightenment behaves toward things as a dictator toward men. He knows them only insofar as he can manipulate them."[2] The mere postulating of a causal dynamic between the will and the world indicates some kind of hypostatized rupture between the two entities. Myth is understood not only as an originary dynamic that the Enlightenment aimed to tear down, in which the will was subordinate to the world, but also as a lost plenitude, a "time" when the will was subordinate to the world because it formed part of it. Upon asserting sovereignty over the world, the will stood apart from it. Following Adorno and Horkheimer, this rupture or separation does not in itself constitute the Enlightenment's failure. Rather, if the relationship between the will and the world has been recast as a subject/object dynamic, then the Enlightenment's failure resides in its neglect to take account of this very dynamic: "The point is rather that *the Enlightenment must consider itself*, if men are not to be wholly betrayed. . . . Ruthlessly, in despite of itself the Enlightenment has extinguished any trace of its own self-consciousness. The only kind of thinking that is sufficiently hard to shatter myths is ultimately self-destructive."[3]

One might argue that Latin America and the Caribbean have never had the luxury of eclipsing their own self-consciousness regarding the Enlightenment—this might be viewed as a paradoxical benefit of modernity's ambivalent legacy here. But if Carpentier and James represent a modern generation of Caribbean writers who participate, from Europe's "periphery," in Adorno and Horkheimer's call for self-reflexivity, a reevaluation of the Enlightenment's legacy, then a more recent generation of writers, including Reinaldo Arenas and Edgardo Rodríguez Juliá in addition to Maryse Condé, write in response to this elevated historical purpose in a mode resembling parody or pastiche. Aníbal González discerns the existence of a tradition of novels from the 1960s and 1970s "in which the legacy of Carpentier's historical fiction is reevaluated."[4] Though González focuses his reading on Rodríguez Juliá, a specific text by the Cuban author Reinaldo Arenas (1943–1990), *El mundo alucinante* (*The Ill-fated Peregrinations of Fray Servando*, published in 1969, but, according to Arenas, written in 1965),[5] which I analyze in this chapter, is another of the key texts that he mentions explicitly as forming part of this "tradition."

In chapter 4, we saw that Maryse Condé's historical imagination dialogues with a prior generation of Caribbean writers while marking a departure from its understanding of Enlightenment historicity. Condé engages the historical material that preoccupied James, Carpentier, and Chauvet, but regards with suspicion the commonplace concerning the so-called advent of historical consciousness that befell the Caribbean in the late eighteenth century. Condé's skeptical attitude regarding dialectical historicism heralds an even more radical view toward historical representation in the two writers I discuss in this section. Arenas and Rodríguez Juliá radicalize Condé's skepticism not only by questioning the traditional notion of progress inherent to Enlightenment historicity (even if such progress is not guaranteed, the *philosophes* agree about humanity's potential for achieving it); these writers from the Hispanic Caribbean also employ an array of experimental literary techniques with which they call into question the very rudimentary possibility of historical representation in the first place, assailing the edifice of so-called historical objectivity (and the ideologies that stem from it) on the ground floor of language and subjectivity.

El mundo alucinante is on many levels a contestatory response to the particular tradition of Latin American and Caribbean historical representation of which Alejo Carpentier could be considered the maximum figure. While this antagonistic relationship between Carpentier and Arenas has been noted by critics,[6] I focus here on a Cartesian notion of subjectivity as a conceptual tool to help articulate the divide that separates the practices of fictional and historical representation of the two Cuban authors. For if in prior chapters I have been using Kant's essay as the cornerstone of Enlightenment thought both in Europe and the Americas, then Descartes' cogito may be considered its epistemological precursor. Cartesian principles, apart from playing a surprisingly predominant role in Arenas's text (as I will show), are also an expression of the tenor of Arenas's response to Carpentier. Just as Condé chose seventeenth-century Puritanism in the Americas to articulate, through contrast, her vision of an Afro-Caribbean civilization that in some respects anticipated the tenets of the Enlightenment, Arenas rejects the grandiloquence of Carpentier's historical imagination by positing first and foremost a more rudimentary and preliminary interrogation regarding problems of subjectivity that arise from historical representation and narration in general.

The Resentment of Influence

If we attempt to imagine the cultural milieu in which Arenas wrote his first novels in Cuba in the early 1960s, there can be little doubt that the predominant approach to the literary representation of history was defined by the historical novels of Alejo Carpentier. *The Kingdom of This World* was already considered a classic of Latin American letters by the 1960s, and when Carpentier published *Explosion in a Cathedral* in 1962, the novel must have seemed to have an almost prescient simultaneity with the Cuban Revolution itself.[7] Arenas himself referred to Carpentier, with his novel about the French Revolution viewed from the Caribbean, as the "literary idol of the time."[8] The tour de force represented by *Explosion in a Cathedral* must have attributed to Carpentier a preponderance as an authorial figure regarding the correct literary method for representing history. In a revealing quotation, Arenas himself has specifically commented on Carpentier's methods of historical representation:

> In Carpentier's novels, there arrives a moment in which each time the characters move . . . it is necessary to connote the steps that they take, the period of the carpet upon which they trod, the cloth with which they cover their head, the furniture upon which they at last sit; that is to say, it is necessary to exhaust the context so faithfully that there is a moment, for example, in *Explosion in a Cathedral*, in which the character of Sofía practically cannot move with all the junk [*utilería*] with which Carpentier has encumbered her.[9]

In this polemical passage, Arenas, in a discourse that bears similarities to poststructuralist tenets, apparently objects to the very idea of a historical "context" accessible, reconstitutible, through writing and representation, and especially to the gesture of "exhausting" it. Furthermore, in a prologue to his own historical novel written in 1980, Arenas asserts; "That is one reason I have always distrusted the 'historical,' those 'minutiae,' the 'precise data' or 'fact.' Because what, finally, is History? A file full of more or less chronologically ordered manila folders?"[10] Fifteen years after writing *El mundo alucinante*, Arenas's views on what he sees as the fallacious notion of rigor and accuracy in historical representation still seem to refer to Carpentier as an understood interlocutor. Such a point of view amounts to a gauntlet thrown down against the logic of Carpentier's historical fiction, theorized in the prologue to *The Kingdom of This World*, in which the revelatory or "marvelous" can emerge from a rigorous reconstruction of the historical record in the Americas. The ironic opposition to this method will in some ways define Arenas's own countermethod of historical representation.

Though Arenas's response to Carpentier's method is complex and multifaceted, one observation we can make is that Arenas intuits a paralysis resulting from it: the *utilería*, an assemblage of tools or theatrical props with which Carpentier crowds his narration, limits the freedom of movement of the protagonists. This paralysis will be in contradistinction to the boundless mobility in Arenas's portrait of his own historical protagonist, the Mexican revolutionary José Servando Teresa de Mier Noriega y Guerra (1763–1827), whose life span straddled the transition from the late eighteenth to the early nineteenth century. The very fact that Arenas would choose to write a historical novel—in the 1960s and on the heels of *Explosion in a Cathedral*—about this particular period in Latin American history is an invitation to compare his approach to that of Carpentier. And yet Arenas's project is not an attempt to reconstruct the Enlightenment through the life of Fray Servando. There is no doubt that *El mundo alucinante* does contain references to and commentaries about the Enlightenment, but part of the discursive stance of the novel is that there can be by now little to add to this debate. One common point of view, that the principles of the Enlightenment came to fruition in Latin American figures such as Fray Servando and Simón Rodríguez, whose presence in Europe only highlighted the Enlightenment's failure or atrophy in its continent of origin,[11] is one that would seem derivative of the kind of modernist historical interpretation already performed by Carpentier and James.[12] Susana Rotker, in her fine introduction to a translation of Fray Servando's *Memoirs*, states it in the following manner: "In the *Memoirs*, for example, the ones who are the Others, observed from the more or less anthropological angle that the accounts of imperial travelers are inclined to adopt, are the Europeans."[13] Though we might imagine that such an arrangement, this reverse portrait of an unenlightened Europe observed and analyzed by an enlightened American traveler, might have had enormous appeal for the historical imaginations of such writers as Carpentier and James, this paradigmatic Enlightenment encounter between ideological Others does not appear to be the motivating factor in Arenas's discourse. In fact, it is *against* this modern expression of the Caribbean historical imagination that Arenas seems eager to stake a claim.

It might be argued that whereas Mier's *Memoirs* are replete with a somewhat quirky Enlightenment "content" (which especially includes a denunciation of European ignorance regarding the American colonies and irrational social organization, or "barbarism," in Europe),[14] Arenas in fact systematically empties or disregards this content in favor of a portrait, in both America and Europe, of that which is in urgent need of being supplanted by the Enlightenment. Inquisitional bonfires in Mexico, murderous bands of criminals and thieves in Spain and Italy, decadence and corruption in France, and, of course, Fray Servando's rat- and bedbug-infested prison cells contribute to this reverse portrait of a so-called enlightened West. Also notable in this regard is the sheer quantity of deaths and murders in the novel, sometimes related with a disturbing realism that is at other times tempered by a generally burlesque or carnival air. The cult or dance of death, a recurrent motif in Arenas's narration (in *El mundo alùcinante* and especially in the astounding story "Adios a Mamá"), is in stark opposition to enlightened discourse. Arenas captures in emblematic or allegorical compactness his view of the Spanish *Ilustración* in a description of Jovellanos—who himself embodies (in Goya's famous portrait and historically) Iberian Enlightenment—and Godoy, the Machiavellian paramour of the queen María Luisa: "I watched Jovellanos bow to Godoy and then kneel and lower his head to kiss the tips of that beast's shoe. At that Godoy tapped him three times on the nape of his neck so that I had thought he would kill him. I ran out of that place without even speaking to Jovellanos of my difficulty" (91). Jovellanos, one of the most prominent proponents of the Spanish Enlightenment, genuflects before Godoy who, embodying political power and blind ambition, almost resembles a figure out of the pages of a Latin American novel. Arenas's Fray Servando is *opposed* to almost all the social and political phenomena he observes in the "world," but, unlike Simón Rodríguez, for whom wide-sweeping educational reform (inspired by Rousseau's *Émile*) is the only solution to these blights, Arenas's Servando offers no alternative program, does not even propose to clear a space for scientific inquiry, and favors instead what Jameson calls the Enlightenment's "demolition program."[15] Part of the allegory or emblem of Jovellanos kissing the feet of Godoy includes Fray Servando fleeing from the scene in an attitude of escape that represents one of the predominant motifs of the novel.

The surprising quantity of criticism written on *El mundo alucinante* has focused primarily on two aspects: the novel as a political allegory[16] of life in postrevolutionary Cuba and an intertextual engagement with the *Memorias* of Fray Servando[17] and Valle Arizpe's *Fray Servando* with which Arenas establishes a kind of dialogue or counterpoint. This predominant motif of escape leads critics to discern an allegorical reference to Castro's Cuba. Fray Servando represented for Arenas, as he declared in an interview with Perla Rozencvaig, "the revolutionary who fights for a revolution, who participates in it and later, when the revolution becomes a dogmatic system, must flee and is moreover persecuted by it."[18] And there can be little doubt that part of Arenas's ideological program in portraying history in a fashion resembling the grotesque is to express skepticism similar to Condé's regarding the possibility of historical progress. Obviously such a view would be in extreme contrast to the prevailing view of history in Cuba in the 1960s, at a time in which the revolutionary regime saw itself as the vanguard of historical unfolding. But the allegorical content of the novel also extends to a view of Enlightenment historicity in general.

The novel, then, is viewed either as a political allegory referring to Castro's regime or as a historical and textual commentary on Fray Servando's *Memoirs*. These apparently opposing interpretations—is the novel about the present or the past?—coalesce in the personage of Carpentier himself, who no doubt embodied for Arenas both these tendencies: an authority figure of the revolutionary regime's official cultural apparatus as well as a particular approach to historical representation.

Arenas's "mundo," to recall our preliminary remarks about Wittgenstein, refers not only to the world of Fray Servando, to his tribulations and peregrinations, and not even to the epoch to which he belonged, but also and especially to the world of the historical imagination itself. If the title of the novel recalls Wittgenstein's proposition that there is no link between the will and the world, Arenas's novel could be read precisely as a dramatization of this axiom, and Arenas asserts and revindicates a radical rupture between the historical imagination and history "itself," the historical object. Though the novel's title at first glance seems unremarkable enough, the modifier "alucinante" captures especially well the ambiguity and multiple valences of the questioned subject. We might be tempted to translate the adjective literally as "hallucinating," but whereas in English that might nonsensically (though perhaps significantly) mean "the hallucinating world," the Spanish voice functions more like "exciting" in English, as that which *provokes* excitation or hallucinations. Even if we limit our interpretation to the latter case, the suggestion of multiple hallucinating subjects remains: Fray Servando, Arenas, the narrative voice(s), the reader, the historian, an age. This multiple subjectivity resonates particularly well when we take into account the most memorable technical innovation in Arenas's novel: the interplay among the various subject pronouns in the narrative voice. Though I shall presently analyze portions of the text with greater scrutiny, let it suffice for the moment to look at the celebrated opening sentences of the novel, which capture sufficiently not only this technique in operation but its hermeneutic import as well:

> We're coming from the stand of the palm trees. We're not coming from the stand of palm trees. Me and the two Josefas, we're coming from the stand of palm trees. All by myself I'm coming from the stand of palm trees. (3)

Regarding the two Josefas, the historical Mier, in fact, had two sisters who shared the name Josefa. Arenas clearly privileged these sisters to the exclusion of Fray Servando's numerous other siblings precisely because of the blurred subjectivity suggested by the duplicated name.[19] Critics have tended to argue that the constant oscillation of subject pronouns in the narration either renders the narrating subject null and void,[20] or that this play and tension among multiple narrative points of view and pronominal registers results in a subjective aperture. One specific tension in the novel is the opposition between an archaic, formal language and a more contemporary argotic voice.[21] This stylistic trait—the ironic juxtaposition between formal, historical language and contemporary slang—can be considered a hallmark of the postmodern Caribbean historical imagination. We have already seen how Condé blends anachronistically historical references with contemporary ones. The Puerto Rican author Edgardo Rodríguez Juliá, as I will show, pushes this tendency to an extreme by inserting the language of contemporary drug culture into his historical discourse.

In my view, the numerous subjective oscillations and contradictions in the narrative voice add up not only to a negation, but also to a very specific kind of Cartesian negativity, in which the historical self—both the authorial voice who organizes the historical meditation as well as the historical protagonist itself—engages in an oscillating play of self-effacement and self-affirmation. If Arenas, as I have been arguing, is writing *against* Carpentier in *El mundo alucinante*, then "Cartesian" is an appropriate adjective to describe the kind of authority represented by Carpentier for Arenas. In a commentary about his novel whose title (in Spanish) puns on Descartes' most well-known work, Carpentier declared, "*Reasons of State* [*El recurso del método*, 1974] is *The Dis-*

course of Method in reverse, because I believe that *Latin America is the least Cartesian continent imaginable.*"[22] Most commentators interpret this declaration at face value, focusing on the saga of the Latin American dictator in *Reasons of State*, and, by extension, the deployment of tyrannical political power in the region, as the expression of a kind of irrational, anti-Cartesian spirit.

The general equating of "Cartesian" with "reason" is certainly a commonplace. One critic of Carpentier's novel asserts that "to say Descartes is the equivalent of affirming the fundamentality of reason as a criterion of truth and the source of knowledge."[23] However, the name of Descartes is also and perhaps even more appropriately associated with his most memorable legacy, the attendant cogito, which, as Derrida argues in his classic debate with Foucault, is not particularly linked to reason. For Derrida, the cogito is not a bulwark of reason; it is neutral, a degree zero, a dividing line between madness and reason. Even the mad, those who by definition lack reason, can enjoy or experience the cogito. "Whether I am mad or not, *Cogito, sum.*"[24] And so the name of Descartes is not only necessarily the equivalent of reason, but rather of the cogito; and though the cogito does not guarantee reason, it does in fact guarantee something else, even to those lacking reason: *a generally indivisible subjectivity.* We may, then, turn Carpentier's formulation against himself, and suggest that in terms of his own authorial subjectivity, of his own persona as a historical narrator (and certainly when compared to Arenas), Carpentier is in a sense the *most* Cartesian figure imaginable! His representation of history may be fragmented, cyclical, and liturgical, with a spiraling opposition between circularity and linearity, but there is hardly ever any doubt in Carpentier's narration about the preponderant authority, the subjective sovereignty of the narrator himself. Carpentier's authorial persona (especially in his historical novels) is Cartesian not because it represents and projects "reason," but rather because at every turn it seems to proclaim implacably, "I exist." In fact, this seems to be the case no matter how structurally fragmented Carpentier's texts appear. If we look back at *Reasons of State* in the light of Carpentier's reflections about it, it is clear that it was conceived as a kind of anti-Cartesian allegory. And yet the text's "deep structure"—a textual composition in which key events recur in patterns of seven chapters, a cycle that, according to González Echevarría, corresponds to the liturgical pattern of Lent followed by Carnival—reveals a Cartesian spirit at work.[25] Arithmetic patterns are one of Descartes' privileged criteria through which he confirms not only his own existence but that of the world as well; Carpentier repeatedly avails himself of these same arithmetic or intervallic patterns as a principal signifying structure in his works' composition.

In his riveting autobiography *Antes que anochezca* (*Before Night Falls*), Arenas narrates the persecution he suffered in Cuba during his childhood, adolescence, and early adulthood. When he finally escapes to Miami in the 1980 Mariel boat lift, he encounters a new series of adversities and persecutions to endure—notably the ostracism of the North American and European academic Left when it learned of Arenas's anti-Castro fervor. This leads him to exclaim, "Grito, luego, existo" (I scream therefore I am), a veritable pronouncement of his view on Cartesian subjectivity. The undisguised reference to the cogito replaces cogitation with a primal expression of rebellion, resistance, or revolt (and recalls a similar pronouncement by Albert Camus: "Je me révolte, donc nous sommes"). Arenas's scream, which echoes splendidly the grammar and syntax of Descartes' original Latin formulation, attributes a primacy to the scream that would ideally precede being. And yet, in the grammar of the pronouncement ("grito"), a cogito is already present and undermines the attempt to elude the subjectivity that is the sine qua non of narration and thought. Almost uncannily, in the same paragraph in which Arenas makes his anti-Cartesian pronouncement, he again mentions Alejo Carpentier in an antithetical mode. Some pages later in the same chapter Arenas lambastes another writer in almost precisely the same way he characterizes Carpentier: "Carlos Fuentes expressed himself in a perfect English and appeared to be a man who had no doubts whatsoever, not even metaphysical ones. He was, for me, the most remote thing to what could be compared to a true writer. . . . He was an encyclopedia."[26] The references to the *Encyclopédie* and the absence of doubt have a strong resonance within the context of this discussion, and evoke not only the Enlightenment but the kind of Cartesian mentality and knowledge diametrically opposed to the brand of expression embodied in Arenas's scream.

The Cartesian cogito acts as a dividing line between madness and reason and, I am suggesting, between Arenas and Carpentier. According to it, everything in the world is subject and vulnerable to my doubting its existence: my body, this paper, for example, may be figments of my imagination or images produced by dreams. Everything is vulnerable to the nihilistic sweep of doubt, with one crucial exception: existence itself. For the very act of doubting confirms that I at least exist since I could not doubt without first existing. Arenas's novel abounds with such quasi-Cartesian paradoxes: "But I am certain that the best thing is not the best. For the best would have been that I had not been. That I had been nothing. . . . But then how had I ever known that that was best? How should I have ever known that?" (89). Only by existing could the narrator have known that nonexistence was the preferable option. Arenas's panoply of narrative techniques, such as the constant alternating of subject pronouns employed by the narrative voice, the oscillation of temporal perspectives, and the outright narrative contradictions, are in the service of a *failed attempt* to cancel out this "I," the subject or writing ego. This procedure is doomed because the implementation of these techniques runs the risk of betraying a cogito behind the scenes as it were, since, as Arenas is no doubt aware, it requires nothing less than a conscious act of an integral self in order to express this same self as a disintegrated entity. In other words, the cogito, though perhaps originally conceived and certainly evoked commonly as a bulwark and safeguard against the threat of self-effacement and annihilation, unwittingly takes effect even if self-effacement is what is desired.

It is not merely in fact that Carpentier is "Cartesian" while Arenas is not; rather, the cogito for both writers acts as a subjective point of departure. Carpentier occupies a positive space made possible by the psychological process in which, all radical doubt dispelled, the narrator is now free to assert his authorial sovereignty. Arenas, on the other hand, opts to dwell in a negative Cartesian terrain, the phase in which radical doubt reigns supreme and that is populated by the psychic demons such as Descartes' own evil geniuses and deceiving gods. Arenas's text is negative insofar as, though doomed to failure, it is in fact a prolonged expression of an attempt to cancel out (or multiply) this emergent "I" of narration, historical or otherwise.[27] Arenas's failure to escape the cogito is already explicitly proclaimed in the prologue, where he declares apostrophically to Fray Servando, "You and I are the same person." This attempt to bridge the gulf between himself and his historical object and thereby efface himself is mirrored by the story itself, by Fray Servando's constantly thwarted attempts in the novel to *escape* from both his prisons and his world.

Escape, in a sense, functions as Fray Servando's cogito, since it is the ineluctable feature of his existence. At one point in the novel, after Fray Servando has been condemned by the Inquisition for his sermon discussing the pre-Hispanic Guadeloupean tradition in Mexico and identifying Saint Thomas with Quetzalcoatl, he is exiled to Spain. In chapter 14, "Which recounts the Friar's visit to the gardens of the King," one of the novel's most prodigious, Fray Servando seeks out Spanish monarch Carlos IV in an attempt to appeal the judgment against him. After passing through an allegorical tour of the king's gardens, Fray Servando's Virgilian guide reveals himself to be the king himself. At this moment, Fray Servando entreaties the king's protection against the inquisitor Leon, and the sovereign responds, "'Why do you wish to change that which most precisely has made you what you are?' he said. 'I do not think you so simple as to believe that there is any way to liberate you. The act of seeking that liberation—is that not delivering yourself up to an imprisonment a hundred times worse?'" (100). This passage bears the stamp or echo of Carpentier's *The Kingdom of This World*, when, in the final passages, it is suggested that Ti Noël's lifelong struggle for freedom is in fact doomed to futility, and that oppression and injustice will return as cyclically as the seasonal hurricane that sweeps over the island of Hispaniola as the novel closes. In Carpentier's vision, we recall, man's greatness lies precisely in his wish to better himself, whether or not that particular desire is ever realized. This Carpenterian echo in Arenas's novel is a point of departure for articulating a postmodern negativity of the variety that Aníbal González suggests when he discerns a generation of writers whose conceptualization of history is in some form—whether pastiche or parody—a response to Carpentier's edifice of historical representation.

Juan José Barrientos points out that the description of one of the characters in *El mundo alucinante* is actually a caricature of Carpentier himself. The character is described as "armed" with compasses, rulers, and other measuring apparatuses, and as obsessed with the architectural details of Mexico's Palacio Nacional.[28] I would add that in addition to caricaturing the figure of Carpentier the author, these descriptions also have another highly significant and specific textual resonance. In *The Kingdom of This World*, Ti Noël's revelation, his "supreme instant of lucidity," takes place immediately following the appearance of the *agrimensores*, or land surveyors, "measuring everything and writing things in their gray books with thick carpenter's pencils."[29] In retrospect, it seems almost surprisingly clear that the techniques of these land surveyors—which involve activities such as measuring, calibrating, calculating and writing—are analogous to the practices of historical representation in Carpentier's fiction. It is even plausible that the juxtaposition of their appearance with Ti Noël's revelation is intended as a self-conscious joke, a narrative "wink" to the reader on the part of Carpentier, especially if we consider the specific language, echoing the author's surname, referring to the land surveyor's "carpenter pencils" ("lápices de carpintero"). Man's happiness, according to Ti Noël's revelation, resides not only in bettering himself, but also, in a language that strongly resonates with Kant's definition of Enlightenment, in the self-imposition of works or tasks (*"imponerse Tareas"*). These Tasks, by juxtaposition in the text, would seem to refer more to the kind of activity performed by the *agrimensores*, or land surveyors, or by Carpentier's archaeological activity of meticulously reconstructing the chronology of little-known Caribbean histories, all the while attempting to place in relief the "marvelous" that emerges from this chronology. In an early essay about Arenas's novel, Eduardo G. González quotes a key passage from Foucault's *History of Madness* that is also relevant to this discussion: "*Where there is an oeuvre, there is no madness*: and yet madness is contemporaneous with the oeuvre, as it is the harbinger of the time of its truth."[30] Oeuvre, work, tasks—this is the degree zero Arenas's novel strikes up against, beyond which he tries to imagine a negative subjectivity untethered to a cogito.

Paralysis and Mobility

The mind/body dualism is one of the most recognizable legacies of Cartesian thought. If, as I have suggested, Arenas attempts (and fails) to dwell in a Cartesian negative terrain, it is interesting to note the importance of the body as a factor in this negativity. The body and the unreliability of the information supplied by the senses play a crucial role in the psychological processes leading up to Descartes' cogito. And so it follows that whereas the narrators in Carpentier's historical fiction, especially in *The Kingdom of This World* and *Explosion in a Cathedral*, enjoy a disembodied omniscience, a noteworthy aspect of Arenas's negativity is the status of and emphasis on Fray Servando's body.

In Descartes' meditations, the first level of doubt negates the body's senses as a reliable indicator of information stemming from the world; this is because in dreams we mistakenly *think* we perceive things as clearly as we do in waking life. And yet even within that error some certitudes persist, such as an understanding of corporeal nature in general. In the second, more radical level of doubt, the hypothesis is put forth that perhaps we are controlled by an evil god, who not only makes us doubt the existence of the body, but who would also have us question whether self-evident notions, such as the fact that two plus three equal five, are not in fact another of his malicious ruses. Yet one fundamental certitude is impervious to the power of this evil god (and to the sensory deception in dreams): the fact that a disembodied "I" exists.

Perhaps the most powerful description in Arenas's novel focuses on Fray Servando's body after he has been imprisoned yet again in Los Toribios. He has already escaped numerous times from prison; therefore his jailers now devise a technique of shackling the friar in such a way as to double in bondage the very figure of his body itself. In an ornate and rather baroque arrangement, every part of Fray Servando's body (including nose hair and eyelashes) is encircled in a variety of chains of different strengths, thicknesses, and lengths. Part of the function of this extended description of Fray Servando's shackles is to convert the body into an inert central mass:

> So that this chain prevented the friar from talking or breathing through his nose—nor of course did he any longer smell. . . . So that it was extremely difficult for the prisoner to perform any of his bodily functions, though fortunately these were rendered pretty thoroughly unnecessary by the almost total lack of nourishment meted to the friar. . . . Miniscule, infinitesimal chains prisoned the friar's eyelashes, eyebrows and even, leaving no possibility of signal or escape, the hairs of the nostrils of his nose. The friar could no longer even blink. (158)

The intention of this bizarre iron vestment is to efface the body through paralysis and invisibility—and perhaps this amounts to yet another parodic commentary on the "*utilería*" with which, according to Arenas, Carpentier "paralyzes" his characters. The neutralizing of Fray Servando's body is directed toward the very essence of his narrative being: the unending cycle of imprisonment and escape. Contrary to this seemingly lifeless human body housed in the network of shackles, the corpus of chains itself seems to take on a kind of lifelike autonomy of its own, or perhaps it incorporates itself as part of Fray Servando's body. The iron enclosure is described as though it possessed the corporal integrity and vitality that Fray Servando now lacks. The vast network of chains is described with a quasi-organic language: it is formed of "metallic braids" that are the subjects of a whole host of active verbs; one chain is described as having an "appendix." Fray Servando's body is subsumed by this new metallic body, so much so that he "looked like some gigantic spider caught upside down in its own web and oozing some dully glowing viscid syrup" (159).

The irony of this situation, especially given the proximity to the episode where Servando flees the concupiscent Orlando, is that, despite the most horrific images of captivity imaginable, with an architectural precision reminiscent of Sade's orgies or Piranesi's prisons, Fray Servando finds this imprisonment quite tolerable: "Fray Servando had had much experience in adapting to prisons. This one was hard, then, but hardly impossible" (159). But perhaps in the novel's most effective bathos, Fray Servando's body, once encumbered with this formidable exoskeleton, finally begins to react like a recognizable body. He is able to adapt to his new "surroundings," to this new body, and use his metallic shell to perceive heat and other sensations: "He learned to take in air through the network of chains, and learned to suck into himself the filthy noisome water dashed at him through the metal mesh that hid his face. . . . And with the years, penned up in that terrible cage, he would even at last have learned to see—through the chains and through the roof—to see the sky, the sun" (159). The prominence of the verb *aprender*, to learn, in this passage suggests that Servando's imprisonment in Los Toribios is a kind of primary or inaugurating bodily experience. It is as though he never possessed a body before the imposition of this metallic one. When we consider the precedents in the novel of Fray Servando as essentially a desired but nondesiring entity, as a figure for whom sexual advances are for all intents and purposes indistinguishable from persecution itself, it is remarkable that his own sexual desire manifests itself only when his body has been metamorphosed into this iron monstrosity: "And from the constant friction of these links, the friar's imprisoned member was in a constant state of excitement, which caused him great mortification" (158). Dare I say that this "miembro prisionero," this imprisoned member, acts as synecdoche for Fray Servando himself, who, as King Carlos IV in his gardens suggests, only comes fully into being, only finds the full measure of himself (to echo Carpentier's language), while imprisoned.

In what could be described as a Cartesian (or perhaps Sartrean) moment in the imprisonment in Los Toribios, the narrator declares that despite the accoutrements of total incarceration, "the friar's thought was free" (160). Descartes observes, "I am like a prisoner who is enjoying an imaginary freedom while asleep; as he begins to suspect that he is asleep, he dreads being woken up, and goes along with the pleasant illusion as long as he can."[31] The temporality of Fray Servando's world is already indistinguishable from the oneiric or hallucinatory state of the sleeper. Thus the existential situation embodied by Fray Servando differs from the Cartesian figure because the latter can at least imagine an escape or alternative, whereas Fray Servando, despite the numerous historical alternatives that are testified to, is always trapped in his particular situation that gives rise to the repeated motif—that there is no escape.

The negatively dialectical play in which what is desired—nonexistence—would cancel out the subject and conditions of desiring and therefore render the entire process null and void is expressed in a variety of ways. One chapter opens with series of lyrical meditations in the first person: "The best thing would have been not to say what I said. But what do I do now? The best thing would have been not to be born" (89). The use of the grammatical perfect here is a reminiscent of a similar use of grammatical tense in Descartes. The implementation of the cogito creates a kind of perpetual present that nullifies the interplay of forgetting and recollection that constitutes the essence of our empirical experience of temporality. Temporality—and much less history itself—is not Descartes' primary concern, though at times he does hint at the fact that temporal considerations must eventually come into play: "Let whoever can do so deceive me, he will never bring about that I am nothing, so long as I continue to think that I am something; or make it true at some future time that I have never existed, since it is now true that I exist."[32] Whether we consider the cogito to be a reassuring foundation upon which to build knowledge and assert the will, or a neutral degree zero that separates madness from reason, Descartes' revealing use of a perfect tense to describe the temporality of the cogito is in fact unsettling for the nascent subject. It guarantees no continuity of existence and in fact unequivocally suggests the possibility that though I may indubitably exist in the present, the same assertion cannot be made concerning the future. Thus this temporalizing gesture, robed in the perfect tense and yet robbed of a future proper, is in fact anti- or atemporal. It indicates neither a future existence nor even a memory in the future of having existed. Arenas's cited meditation, by employing the imperfect of the subjunctive, considers alternate or "parallel" realities that must inevitably borrow from spatial or linear categories to characterize them. Alicia Borinsky refers to the novel as a "movement that does not lead anywhere in a straight line but diffuses in multiple directions."[33] Emir Rodríguez-Monegal borrows Borges's metaphor of "the garden of forking paths" to describe a narration in which several historical alternatives are "chosen" simultaneously and suggests that this is the appropriate one to characterize time in *El mundo alucinante* and is furthermore Arenas's "tacit model."[34] And while there is no doubt that the novel avails itself of these multiple possibilities, there is an important difference with the Borgesian model that Rodríguez-Monegal describes: these multiple alternatives do not, in fact, occur simultaneously. After a detailed description of his visit to the walled city of Pamplona, the narrator in the following chapter refers to the Navarran city as one "I have never had the pleasure to visit, though there are many who deny that" (114). This contradiction is essentially temporal, in that one historical account *subsequently* negates a prior one, a structure that precludes simultaneity. Simultaneity of historical alternatives would necessitate a radically divided or disintegrated subjectivity, when in fact Fray Servando's being is characterized by a persistently concerted cogito.

Fissured Edifices

Fray Servando's tour of the king's gardens is reminiscent of Dante's tour of hell accompanied by Virgil, and no doubt the scenes beheld by Fray Servando are infused with a certain allegorical import as well. But there is also a certain Cartesian aspect to those outlandish descriptions. Descartes describes the images perceived in dreams as having a similar status to paintings, which contain certain identifiable elements:

> For even when painters try to create sirens and satyrs with the most extraordinary bodies, they cannot give them natures which are new in all respects; they simply jumble up the limbs of different animals. Or if perhaps they manage to think up something so new that nothing remotely similar has ever been seen before—something which is therefore completely fictitious and unreal—at least the colours used in the composition must be real.[35]

At least some of the images described in the king's gardens employ both of these picturesque techniques of jumbling identifiable parts into new combinations as well as of creating images that are even more original. In these allegorical gardens, Fray Servando witnesses "women who attempted to transfer their sex to their foreheads" (99), "a woman who tried to give birth through her mouth," and "a man who had poked his eye out and tried to place it on his back" (97). What stands out in these images so reminiscent of Bosch's allegories[36]—and, we could go so far as to say, in all the images described in the gardens—is that each one represents a failed attempt. The words *pretendían*, *trataba,* and *quería* all indicate that this radical reorganization of corporeal nature is far from a fait accompli and actually represents a kind of vanity or ineluctable failure. Seen thus, it is possible that the grotesque quality of these attempts at "betterment" in the king's gardens is further evidence of parodic streak in Arenas. For whether or not the figures in the garden represent an attempt at betterment, they do in fact embody—and this is the connection with Carpentier's metaphysics of "man" in *El reino de este mundo*—an impossible or continuously foiled desire. For now, however, I would like to pursue this interpretation by considering another of the characters in the garden, not the women and men who, in Boschian manner, try to rearrange the architecture of their own bodies, but a figure who, even more radically, is reminiscent of the Cartesian painter who tries to invent "something so new that nothing remotely similar has been seen before." The corresponding figure in Arenas's narration is not a painter, but rather a poet who has devoted his life to composing a brilliant poem. Fray Servando's description of this awesome poem and its effect on the reader seems to have more than a little in common with Carpentier's method of representing history and the "marvelous" effect that emerges from such a representation: "As he read, his words became transformed into an echoing deep magic which more than made me drunk, they transported me, and it was like a wondrous monument in which every stone occupied its precise and necessary place without having even the most miniscule crack or fissure" (97).

I have already discussed at length the importance of the notion of *rajadura*—crack, chasm, or split—in Carpentier, a psychologico-narrative shortcoming in *Ecue-Yamba-O* that was later sublimated into a historical condition in *The Kingdom of This World*. The crack in Carpentier's narrative edifice (or monument) is something to be covered over, hidden, or sublimated. Arenas, in a responsive gesture, specularizes or thematizes the chasm, especially between subject (of desire, history, narration,) and object. If the description of the first part of the poem as a perfectly balanced and symmetrical monument somehow refers to Carpentier's reconstruction of history (and the description of Christophe's citadel seems particularly alluded to), the poem's open-ended conclusion is Arenas's response to this monumentalizing gesture. Not only is the poet incapable of finding the appropriate final word to complete the poem, he attempts to invent neologisms in a desperate attempt to furnish the final block or keystone that will provide support and closure to the monument: "And I saw the poet again, who now had exhausted his vocabulary and was trying to combine syllables at random, though as anyone could see these had no meaning. I could hear him as he wandered off into the undergrowth about the alley, murmuring: 'Heternosto,' 'tonetis,' 'alans'" (99).

Referring back once again to the Cartesian painter, this memorable passage from Arenas can be described as either a jumble of recognizable elements (like the figures who attempt to rearrange their body parts) or perhaps as an attempt to dream up something entirely new and unrecognizable. Deciding between the two, as in Descartes, is not of great importance since the Cartesian painter must in either case avail himself of one unequivocally recognizable element: color (or paint). In the case of Arenas and the virtuosic poet in the king's gardens, the unmistakably identifiable element in the poet's neologisms (as well as the other figures in the garden) is *failure*, not only in an anecdotal sense, but in a specific way that is perhaps the key to interpreting the allegorical import of this chapter and the novel itself. The poet's failure to provide the missing word, the final stone to complete the monument, is in fact a commentary on the subject itself, which, always contained within the cogito, can never transcend entirely its situational particularity in order to produce or become the perfect monument, the perfect object; or, in other words, to ever move entirely beyond the subject-object divide. The first of the poet's neologisms, in fact, "heternosto," suggests such a condition and can be loosely interpreted as "our otherness" or "our fragmentation." The open space in the poem, the monument's vacant stone, signifies this subjective crack, an opening that Arenas, unlike Carpentier—who attempts a variety of techniques to conceal or integrate it—will uphold as the very condition of narration and signification.

Whereas Carpentier projects the marvelous as an objective phenomenon arising from a kind of literal revelation, Arenas exposes the fraudulent nature of this supposed objectivity by opposing to it the *alucinante*, the hallucinating or hallucinatory effect of a subject unfettered by either time or space, but which by definition is always restrained by the cogito, by the very conditions of subjectivity. For Arenas, the cogito is not a starting point from which to erect the edifice or monument of representation, but rather a limit or barrier that, while permitting the enunciation of an "I am" thereby precludes any possibility of being another or being otherwise. Arenas proclaims in the epistolary introduction, addressed to Fray Servando, "you and I are the same person."[37] The grammatical subject of that enunciation precludes and belies the predicate. *El mundo alucinante* in fact is an extended meditation on the failure or falsity of this proposition, that Arenas and Servando are the same person, and the dazzling variety of narrative techniques employed to attempt to achieve this union between the two is the very evidence indicating its impossibility.

6 Heightened Perceptions

Rodríguez Juliá and the Mechanics of Temporality

> The further the facts, the more history petrifies into myth. Thus, as we grow older as a race, we grow aware that history is written, that it is a kind of literature without morality, that in its actuaries the ego of the race is indissoluble and that everything depends on whether we write this fiction through the memory of the hero or of victim.
>
> Derek Walcott, *What the Twilight Says*

> Historicity is neither a representation of the past nor a representation of the future: it can first and foremost be defined as a perception of the present as history.
>
> Fredric Jameson, "Nostalgia for the Present"

IN HIS ESSAY "Puerto Rico y el Caribe: Historia de una marginalidad" (Puerto Rico and the Caribbean: History of a Marginality), Edgardo Rodríguez Juliá describes a Caribbean cultural condition that is characterized primarily by a feeling of loss and incompleteness:

> If Fanon showed us the reality of colonial Manichaeism, the great Caribbean writers and artists converge in speaking to us about *modorra*, that *taedium vitae* or sleepy lethargy so characteristic of these sad tropics. It is a colonial condition in which the soul is as though suspended, vacillating between a flat, half-baked society with a precarious past and an uncertain future, and a nostalgia for a tradition that is neither entirely foreign nor entirely one's own.[1]

If this feeling of incompleteness is described as a malaise that constitutes part of this Caribbean condition, at the same time Rodríguez Juliá documents a host of Caribbean writers and artists who in one form or another bear witness to it. This abundance of proper names and references—both historical and fictional—is one of the hallmarks of his writing. In a discursive strategy that could be called a topos of Caribbean postmodernity, he avails himself of this seemingly negative quality—this *modorra*, or soporific sense of reality—and upholds it as a possible if tenuous and ironic foundation of Caribbean identity. (By embracing these negative qualities as criteria for discerning a Caribbean identity, Silvio Torres Saillant, commenting on V. S. Naipaul's pessimistic view of Caribbean culture, employs a similar strategy: "One need only concede that tension, hesitation, ambivalence, even the desire to escape, stem naturally from the archipelago's traumatic history. One can easily recognize the common compulsions lurking behind seemingly antithetical voices.")[2] What partially justifies this embrace of rejection, of this paradoxical "not belonging" to the Caribbean as an identitarian criterion of pertinence, is its sheer recurrence as a motif among the Caribbean's writers and artists. In addition to Fanon, Francisco Oller (a nineteenth-century Puerto Rican painter), Palés Matos, Derek Walcott, V. S. Naipaul, José Lezama Lima, C. L. R. James, Eric Williams, and others form a seemingly complete litany of names that attest to the incompleteness of this Caribbean ethos.

For Rodríguez Juliá, the most palpable manifestations of an identifiable Caribbean reality occupy a spatial dimension. He refers to the Caribbean as a *heterotopía*, a multitudinous space whose common link is the cultural artifact. In addition to spaces such as those inhabited by the canvases of Francisco Oller, "his landscapes and still-lives," Caribbean architecture and cuisine also constitute privileged manifestations in a horizontal realm to which the essayist can point as though to say, this is, or was, the Caribbean:

> The rural Puerto Rican house, with its raised level or *soberao* supported by narrow columns or *zocos*, is a balcony-less version of the Trinidadian *case*.
>
> The *carrucho*, which is eaten today in Puerto Rico with a satiety that is threatening the existence of the queen conch in our waters, is the Haitian *lambi*, practically the national dish of that country.[3]

These cultural artifacts establish the points of contact among the islands of the Caribbean, contributing for Rodríguez Juliá to a de facto cultural "Antillean Confederacy." And yet, despite the wealth of spatial manifestations that attest to the cultural unity of the Caribbean, temporality, in one form or another, seems to conspire against this unity. Rodríguez

Juliá speaks of part of Puerto Rico's past, which is referred to as "the time of the Spaniards," a phrase whose temporality has a double register: on the one hand, it describes a dispossession of what the author calls part of "*nuestro tiempo*" (our time), which was appropriated by Spanish colonialism. The second temporal register is an important aspect of the Caribbean condition Rodríguez Juliá is attempting to describe. He points out that the phrase "the time of the Spaniards" was often heard in the 1950s and has since fallen into disuse. Thus the evocation of this expression refers to a doubly removed past, both to a distant colonialism as well as to the 1950s, when the expression was commonly used. This dual temporal remove strikes a double-edged blow against a positive Caribbean identity for which the author longs. That verifiable common space for Caribbean architecture, art, and cuisine suffers not only from a "precarious past"—colonialism, rendering ownership claims stemming from origins obscure—but also receives a coup de grace from the present: the "*porvenir incierto*," or uncertain future of which Rodríguez Juliá speaks is the fragile memory of the contemporary moment, an effect, no doubt, of a kind of second neocolonialism, or globalization—Rodríguez Juliá himself calls it a "colonial condition." The nostalgia for these spaces that are disappearing from the present generation's memory is one of the essay's most striking features:

> I grew up in one of those wide galleries; on the street level, coffee was stored. . . . *If I told this to my son it would be like speaking to him of distant country.* It seems to me that few young Puerto Ricans know what an *ausubo* shelf is; and yet they all know what MTV is and where Orlando is located. Our spaces are beginning to resemble this city in Florida more than Santo Domingo.[4]

In the Caribbean—and Rodríguez Juliá makes it clear that he is speaking of the "Puertoricanization of the Caribbean" and not, he laments, vice-versa—time conspires against space, and it is out of this conspiracy that *modorra*, a symptom of an existential paralysis or historical estrangement, is born. He says of the Caribbean: "We share a space, but do we share a historical project? This spatial-temporal dynamic is emblematic of Rodríguez Juliá's writing. Speaking to his son about *that time* would be like speaking about a *distant country*. That subtle allegorical slippage—one thinks of Walter Benjamin's charting his own past as though it were a map—characterizes to some extent the method of Rodríguez Juliá's historical fiction. In what could be referred to as a postmodern motif, questions of historicity translate into detailed exploration of imaginative spaces. Reinaldo Arenas also translated what he saw as historical paralysis in Carpentier into a spectacular spatial mobility. In the case of Rodriguez Juliá, what remains to be determined is the meaning with which he invests these allegorical spaces.

Dystopias

Reinaldo Arenas's historical novel constituted a response to Carpentier's foundations of historical representation by challenging the assumptions and ideologies that underwrote Carpentier's techniques of representing the past. If, for Nick Nesbitt, Maryse Condé "refuses a mimetic historiography" in which "the historical text serves as the supposedly transparent imitation of an external objective world,"[5] then for Arenas, the historian's "rigorous" leap of faith over the subject/object divide renders historicity (as Fredric Jameson defines it in the chapter epigraph) indistinguishable from fiction and the past from the present. Rodríguez Juliá's writing about Puerto Rico during the time corresponding to the Enlightenment achieves a similar effect of rendering transparent the pretensions of historical writing. But for the Puerto Rican novelist, it is more a question of the inexhaustibility of textual indices than an existential condition per se. Though this view of history as an endless chain of textual references bears similarities to general poststructuralist views of historical discourse, the specifically Caribbean character of Rodríguez Juliá's fiction is rooted in the dual colonial scission separating the Caribbean present from its past, in a postmodern moment that he calls "the Puertoricanization of the Caribbean."

In one of the most profound critical commentaries on Rodríguez Juliá's body of work, which, in addition to the two historical novels discussed here, includes important "chronicles" on twentieth-century Puerto Rican culture, such as *El entierro de Cortijo* (*Cortijo's Wake*) and *Una noche con Iris Chacón* (A Night with Iris Chacon), Rubén González reflects: "The literature of Rodríguez Juliá, its ethical dimension, regales us with the possibility of rendering intelligible that which at times has been ignored and incomprehensible: history—our mutilated past, as Arcadio Díaz would put it—and the phenomenon that we call Puerto Rican culture, feminism and machismo put to the test: landscapes and tradition that, in Caribbean fashion, vanish; our continued devotion to the 'good life' [*bienestar*] that each day strives more and more to resemble the mirage of Orlando, Florida."[6] With these words, González appears to be reflecting on Rodríguez Juliá's essay discussed here, an essay that seems to me a helpful primer for embarking on his historical fiction about the Enlightenment period in Puerto Rico, both the formidable tome *La noche oscura del Niño Avilés* (The Dark Night of the Child Avilés, 1984) and the more condensed *La renuncia del héroe Baltasar* (1974, *The Renunciation*). Both works represent a highly imaginative version of the eighteenth century in Puerto Rico, and therefore belong to a specific modern lineage whose founders are Alejo Carpentier and C. L. R. James. The so-called "historical" events of these phantasmagoric historical novels are the author's imaginative response or reaction to the historical dual divide—Spanish colonialism and contemporary "globalization"—between the historical subject and the object of his writing. Rodríguez Juliá's intent is not so much to rescue the past for an absent-minded present. Rather, historical oblivion—taken as a Puerto Rican or Caribbean a priori—creates a radically imaginative space where anything was possible since everything can be forgotten. In this chapter, I first discuss how Rodríguez Juliá allegorizes and satirizes the advent of so-called Enlightenment modernity in *La noche oscura del Niño Avilés*. I will then turn my attention to *The Renunciation* in order to show that if Carpentier was the implicit interlocutor of Arenas's historical novel, Rodriguez Juliá's text constellates well with C. L. R. James's view of history and dialectics in *The Black Jacobins*.

In *Niño Avilés*, Rodríguez Juliá "rescues" an apocryphal past and fashions a faux epic of the founding of a maroon colony in the swamps near San Juan that he calls Nueva Venecia, which, not unlike aspects of Caribbean history he discusses in his essay, is doubly absent, supposedly suppressed by the colonial authorities as well as remembered and again forgotten by subsequent generations. Rodríguez Juliá underlines this absence by pointing out that many (fictional) historians—both contemporaneous to the events in question and subsequent ones as well—were already denouncing the founding of Nueva Venecia as an apocryphal event.

In chapter 4, I pointed out that, unlike the use of historical anachronisms in Carpentier's historical fiction, wherein modern references and vocabulary are signposts indicating the past's teleological trajectory to the present, Maryse Condé's use of anachronisms opens up a ludic conception of history in which the paucity of the historical record leads to a playful indeterminacy. For Condé, the Caribbean image of the mangrove, present in the title of one of her most well-known works of fiction, is a rhizomic symbol of this multitudinous indeterminacy in the intersections of history and identity. It is appropriate to recall this distinction between Carpentier and Condé in their historical fiction, since the latter's approach is further radicalized in Rodríguez Juliá's novel. The meaning of Condé's and Rodríguez Juliá's anachronisms reveal perhaps more than any other single feature that a different generation than Carpentier's is at work. As was mentioned previously, Aníbal González points out that *Niño Avilés* belongs to a tradition of novels from the 1960s and 1970s (though Rodríguez Juliá's novel was published in 1984, it was written in the previous decade) that critiqued Carpentier's legacy of historical fiction.[7] Rodríguez Juliá himself explicitly acknowledges his debt to Carpentier, from whom he learned "the possibilities of a critical history."[8] If a positive *telos* determines the historicity of *Explosion in a Cathedral*, then in Rodríguez Juliá's novel temporality and historical processes are more obscure. They tentatively may be located at the intersection of the two negative realms he discusses in his essay: a past that never entirely was and the oblivion of the present moment. Out of this uchronia, Rodríguez Juliá forges a dystopia.

Rodríguez Juliá's narration of this eighteenth-century epic also contains a wealth of anachronisms, but their effect is not to confirm a telos of inevitable historical unfolding. The language of contemporary popular culture, for example—"date un pase," (take a [drug] hit); "les voló los sesos" (he blew their brains out)—are obvious linguistic anachronisms in a narration taking place in the eighteenth century.[9] These and other anachronisms in Rodriguez Juliá's text, such as the hodgepodge of proper names that apparently refer to people belonging to other epochs, contribute to a notion of history that does not necessarily lead in direct fashion to the present. Rather, they tend to contribute to a portrait of the past that is indistinguishable from the present, in which the mechanics of temporality tend to obfuscate the linear march of time rather than to elucidate it.

Aníbal González, Antonio Benítez-Rojo, and Eric Camayd-Freixas all point out in their studies of the novel that historians, not literary critics, were the first to react to the novel, and according to González, "with a certain degree of scandal."[10] Much of the critical labor involved in interpreting the novel has dealt with its sources—both literary and historical. Aníbal González broke critical ground when he pointed out that both Fray Iñigo Abbad's *Historia geográfica, civil y política de la isla de San Juan Bautista de Puerto Rico* (Geographic, Civil and Natural History of the Island of Saint John the Baptist of Puerto Rico, 1784) and Fernando

Ortiz's *Historia de una pelea cubana contra los demonios* (History of a Cuban Fight against the Demons, 1959) were major sources for *Niño Avilés*, observations that were later taken up in greater detail by other critics. Benítez-Rojo reads the novel as one that "moves up against" Abbad's eighteenth-century *Historia*.[11] Camayd-Freixas does the lion's share of "sourcing." In addition to an extended reading of the connection between *Niño Avilés* and Sigüenza y Góngora's false chronicle *Infortunios de Alonso Ramírez*, Camayd-Freixas also takes it upon himself to suggest possible historical counterpoints for most, if not all, of the novel's proper names.[12] Identifying these myriad sources for *Niño Avilés* not only has the benefit of grounding within specific traditions what can be a disorienting literary experience, but it can also, as Benítez-Rojo's reading demonstrates, shed light back on these older texts. He shows not only that there is a "desire" of fiction to become history in *Niño Avilés* but that in the novel's historical, "positive" counterpart, Abbad y Lasierra's *Historia*, there is the corresponding inversion—history's desire to become fiction—embodied in the enlightened historian's tendency to abandon his neoclassical "didacticism" and lapse into novelistic language. For Benítez-Rojo, this tendency represents history's "libido."[13]

And yet the identification of these sources may have a falsely reassuring effect. For part of the parodic operation of *Niño Avilés* not only targets these older traditions of the colonial chronicles and the picaresque, but also calls into question the very operation by which an older text exercises influence on a more recent one. Literary tradition and influence are, in the final analysis, historical processes; if, for Rodríguez Juliá, Caribbean reality suffers from a double historic excision—an improper or foreign-owned past and a forgetful present—then the machinery of tradition and influences malfunctions, like the image in Nicolás Guillén's poem "La rueda dentada" of a broken gear-wheel that does not bite or catch.

The prologue to *Niño Avilés* contains in condensed fashion the complexity of the lengthy novel itself and parodies the idea of a historical continuity based on textual perseverance. In order to decipher this prologue, it is necessary to work through the plethora of proper names that populate it. Its narrator, and presumably the "organizer" of the selected chronicles that narrate the novel's proceedings, is Alejandro Cadalso, who signs and dates the prologue October 9, 1946, which, as Camayd-Freixas notes, is Rodríguez Juliá's date of birth.[14] Cadalso begins the prologue by citing Rafael González Campos, the first of a string of fictional chroniclers. This first pseudochronicler from the eighteenth century sings the praises of the lacustrine city in the swamps around San Juan, comparing its beauty to that of Venice, "pearl of the Adriatic," yet also warns of its "perverse charms."[15] How did we come across this eighteenth-century contemporaneous account of La Nueva Venecia? Because, we are told, "González Campos's chronicle belongs to a collection of documents discovered by the archivist Don José Pedreira Murillo in 1913" (xi). And so González Campos's ur-account of the lacustrine city was bequeathed to the narrator secondhand, filtered through the consciousness of an early-twentieth-century historian. The archivist Pedreira Murillo made the connection between González Campos's description and a triptych he recalled having seen hanging in the Municipal Archive of San Juan painted by Silvestre Andino, "the brilliant nephew of José Campeche."[16] (Campeche, of course, is not only a real painter—"the first Puerto Rican painter," as the footnote tells us—but his *real* portrait, *El Nino Juan Pantaleón Avilés de Luna Alvarado*, is the genesis and pictorial inspiration of the novel.)

This painted triptych portrayed strange landscapes full of canals, islands, and buildings whose architecture resembled beehives. But the triptych and the chronicles have more than a casual connection. The narrator informs us that the documents are in fact detailed descriptions of the miniatures: "While the word complements the image, deciphering visions and animating landscapes, Andino's paint brush has attempted to recount the myth of the cursed city" (xi).

This ekphrastic relationship between image and writing suggests that we have moved beyond the realm of event and into a kind of hypertextuality where each text supposedly attesting to (or debunking) the historical veracity of Nueva Venecia ultimately leads only to another text. In a linguistic arrangement that is reminiscent of Severo Sarduy's description of the neobaroque, this daisy chain of indices results in a promiscuous propagation of the signifier and spectacular deferment of the signified, like fragments of a broken vessel that can no longer add up to any totality—totality in this case amounting to an incontrovertible historical account of the existence of Nueva Venecia.

The narrator mentions that some historians concede no historical value to the Pedreira collection: "We are dealing, according to them, with an apocryphal history" (xi). The remainder of the prologue deals with the debate among historians as to the authenticity of the documents we are about to read. Some historians, such as Tomás Castelló Pérez Moris, believe that the entire story of Nueva Venecia is a fantasia composed around the painted triptych. One historian, Gustavo Castro, pointed out in 1932 what will be for the narrator an important factor in establishing the authenticity of the documents. He notes that Pedreira Murillo discovered the collection "among the ruins of a very strange tower situated on the San José estuary. He was led to this site by a resident of the place known as Pedro the Lame. The singular dwelling, even in its ruinous state, resembled the beehives mentioned by the different chroniclers of the collection and painted by Andino Campeche" (xii). Through a spiraling series of erasures, Nueva Venecia has been condemned to oblivion, "repressed by the collective memory," as the narrator tell us; and we also learn that its physical ruins, those bizarre beehive-like towers, "were bombarded during the Yankee siege of 1898" (xii). Allegorically, if we recall the discussion of Rodríguez Juliá's essay, the bombardment signifies the modern "Yankee" erasure of a distant Puerto Rican past. Contributing to this erasure, "all of the documents relating to Nueva Venecia were burned in 1820." Except, of course, that sheath of documents discovered by Pedreira Murillo. It appears that the narrator has made yet another astounding archival discovery: that Don Ramón García Quevedo, adjunct secretary of the Obisbal archive, saved these documents from the Inquisitional auto-da-fé in 1820, and himself navigated through the marshes around San Juan to leave them in the tower, where they were found by Pedreira Murillo a century later.

In this prologue, text, image, and historical referent or signified (the city of Nueva Venecia) form a complex web of cross-referentiality. An organic connection is suggested between historical sign (the folio of documents) and referent (the tower where they were found), but no sooner is this mythic connection suggested than it is debunked: the detractors of the chronicles insist not only that García Quevedo penned the chronicles himself, but that he constructed the tower to house them as well. Let us review the dates and events that constitute the narrator's prologue:

Cadalso's prologue	1946
González Campos's account	Eighteenth century
Pedreira Murillo archival discovery	1903
Silvestre Andino's triptych	1800?
Pérez Moris, modern detractor	1932
Yankee bombardment	1898
Inquisitional burning of documents	1820
Ramón Mellado commenting on the triptych	1840

The back-and-forth movement of historical markers, from the twentieth century to the eighteenth, up to an earlier moment in the twentieth that hearkens back to the nineteenth, without any fixed center of reference, imitate a spiral—a geometrical form that is suggested architecturally by the beehivelike towers of Nueva Venecia. The spiral, as a symbol of historical method, suggests the impossibility of even imagining a historical referent separate from the accounts attesting to it. Historicity is now serpentine, or a spiral: a modern historian refers to an eighteenth-century event that is attested to by a sheath of documents that had been discovered by an early-twentieth-century historian. These, in turn, bear a resemblance to an eighteenth-century triptych. Both sources were rescued from the Inquisitional auto-da-fé in 1820.

The impossibility of fixing the existence of Nueva Venecia historically gives way to a complex web of speculation that obeys no particular laws of chronology. The date that accompanies Alejandro Cadalso's signature at the end of the prologue, which coincides with Rodríguez Juliá's date of birth, is falsely reassuring, and no doubt amounts to a kind of practical joke at the reader's (or critic's) expense. It would be tempting to infer that the narrator, Cadalso, is some kind of alter-ego for Rodríguez Juliá. But Rodríguez Juliá, the author of the book, did not yet exist *as such* on October 9, 1946. As Fredric Jameson points out and as Rodríguez Juliá is certainly aware, attaching any hermeneutical importance to this autobiographical importation is "illicit" because "it presumes that the present (still then a future) was already there when the events of this past took place."[17] This coincidence between Rodríguez Juliá's birth date and the date signed by Alejandro Cadalso to the prologue is reminiscent of a similar textual importation in Carpentier since in *Explosion in a Cathedral* Esteban shares the same birthday, December 26, with Carpentier.[18] Esteban's and Carpentier's common birthday establishes a kind of "identification" or projection on the part of the author for his fictitious character who witnessed and documented some of the most momentous events and texts of the late eighteenth century in the Caribbean. In the case of Rodríguez Juliá, however, the author's date of birth coincides only with the fictitious birth of a text, Cadalso's prologue, and reinforces the sense of referential indeterminacy.

If Rodríguez Juliá's birth date is tantamount to a practical joke at the expense of readers and critics since it supplies the illusion of anchoring a fictional text in the "real" world outside the text, there is further evidence of parody in *Niño Avilés*. It would seem that some of the most powerful mythic, historic, and literary archetypes of the Caribbean reappear in this novel but now under the rubric of repetition rather than revelation. In Carpentier's *Explosion in a Cathedral*, Esteban's contemplation of the spiraled conch shell is a privileged moment in which the nature of American reality and temporality are revealed. And yet, when this same figure of the spiral appears repeatedly in *Niño Avilés*—at times, it seems, on each page—with each repetition it is further emptied of its transcendent signification, its revelatory power. The same could be said about the presence of African percussion and the call of the conch shells in the novel, which were already a hallmark in the novels of both Carpentier and Marie Chauvet. As I pointed out in the prior chapter on Maryse Condé, the repetition of stock scenes from Caribbean literary history inevitably bestows an irony, a banalization upon them. And yet, given the generic intermingling in the Caribbean, where myth, history, and literature borrow from each other, it is not easy to say exactly what Rodríguez Juliá is parodying, or to identify the target of his irony. If his narration parodies Carpentier and the dominant motifs of the modern Caribbean historical imagination, then this gesture would in turn require a kind of normative subjectivity, an alternate grounding from which something is ridiculed. As Linda Hutcheon points out in *A Theory of Parody*: "In this more traditional kind of parody, recognizable noble turns of phrase will be applied to inappropriate subjects. . . . As in literature or painting, this kind of parody is frequently conservative in impulse, exaggerating stylistic idiosyncrasies."[19] This description of the conservative impulse in most (but certainly not all, as Hutcheon goes on to explain) expressions of parody is arguably applicable to Reinaldo Arenas's parody of Carpentier in *El mundo alucinante*. The same might be said about Condé as well, who explicitly identifies the parodic streak in her own historical novel. Even though, on the one hand, Condé envisages a hybrid Caribbean subjectivity that inserts gender as a factor determining the state of the subject, she also pinpoints aspects of feminist writing as precisely that which is being parodied in *Tituba*, thus obscuring the ideological impetus of her historical novel.

If, for Arenas, the persistence of the cogito renders fiction a viable alternative to the historical version of events, then for Rodríguez Juliá textuality blurs the distinction between fiction and history. The Nobel laureate Derek Walcott observes (in an epigraph to this chapter) that in the New World and, one assumes, especially in the Caribbean, "history is a kind of literature without morality."[20] This seems to be precisely the kind of convergence upon which Rodríguez is founding his fictional project. It would seem that for Rodríguez Juliá, all historicity—a category that encompasses literature—is a suspect operation, and literary critics' attempts to locate historical references and sources in the text as keys to deciphering it would not be immune from this judgment. Indeed, perhaps the most disconcerting disjunction between official historiography and Rodríguez Juliá's extended and detailed descriptions of eighteenth-century slave rebellions is that, except for a few isolated and brief insurrections, as Eduardo San José Vásquez points out, no major slave rebellion was ever recorded in Puerto Rico in the eighteenth century.[21] And yet, at the same time, observes Rubén González, the military battles and black uprisings in San Juan described in Rodríguez Juliá's novels, though they never took place, bear a remarkable resemblance to those from other Caribbean settings, such as Haiti or the Dominican Republic.[22] Perhaps Rodríguez Juliá's historical imagination is the expression of an allegorical desire to reverse what the author sees as the unfortunate trend of the "Puertoricanization of the Caribbean." But if this is the case, *La noche oscura del Niño Avilés* thwarts our attempts to "always historicize." What, then, remains?

Allegories of Modernity

Jean Franco, addressing Jameson's polemical notion of the national allegory in Third World literature, rejects the categories of allegory and the postmodern on the grounds that both concepts fail to account for Spanish America's unfinished engagement with modernity: "Yet just as national allegory fails to describe adequately the simultaneous dissolution of the idea of the nation and the continuous persistence of national concerns, so postmodernism cannot adequately describe those texts that use pastiche and citation not simply as style but as correlatives of the continent's uneasy and unfinished relationship to modernity."[23] And yet this incomplete engagement with modernity and nationhood in Latin America and the Caribbean, as well as the lingering effects of colonialism and globalization that Rodríguez Juliá discusses in his essay, can be seen as precisely that which supplies the cultural specificity with which these regions articulate a postmodern national allegory. Moreover (as I discuss in the conclusion), this "Third World" articulation of the postmodern reinforces and reminds us of postmodernity's inherent connotation as an extension or sequel of modernity. Despite Franco's caveats, allegory seems to me the appropriate genre to describe Rodríguez Juliá's narration. The abstract reference toward which the allegory indexes is the incomplete and ambivalent emergence of modernity in Puerto Rico and the Caribbean.

Many critics have speculated that the action of the novel takes place in the eighteenth century because this was the epoch in which a Puerto Rican national consciousness emerged. Rubén Ríos Ávila observes that "Rodríguez Juliá's voyage to the eighteenth century has as its ethical mission the search for genealogical origin of the national ethos."[24] Erik Camayd-Freixas also points out that "Juliá chooses the late 18th century setting because it is the foundational moment of Puerto Rico's (official) historical identity."[25] Aníbal González suggests that the novel is "a great allegory about the history of Puerto Rican culture."[26] In my view, the setting of the action in the eighteenth century serves a double function in this regard. As Paul de Man has pointed out in his well-known study, the notion of allegory "appears as dryly rational and dogmatic in its reference to a meaning that it does not itself constitute. . . . Allegory appears as the product of the age of Enlightenment and is vulnerable to the reproach of excessive rationality."[27] While no one familiar with *Niño Avilés* would accuse the novel of "excessive rationality," part of the irony of its program, as Antonio Benítez-Rojo has shown, is the subversion of these Enlightenment modes, such as Abbad y Lasierra's eighteenth-century study of Puerto Rico. The originality of *Niño Avilés*, its cutting edge, is the irreverence with which it portrays this period. All of the traditional signposts are discarded or distorted beyond recognition. Some of these signposts would include the implementation of social reform with the state tending to supplant the church as an organizing center; scientific experimentation as a basis of knowledge displacing former modes of beliefs that are now labeled "superstition"; the development of technology in order to heighten perception and increase productivity. These elements are all present in Rodríguez Juliá's narration, but they are no longer infused with the underlying notion of social progress that is an essential element, in one form or another, in the narrations of Carpentier and James and with which Maryse Condé takes issue. In what is, in fact, a very Foucauldian operation, Rodríguez Juliá posits these emblems of enlightened modernity as mere modes of thought, empty shells with no inherent or essential content—not even the rudimentary notion of "rationalization" is attributed to them. Modernity, then, for Rodríguez Juliá is a question of which of among competing modes of thought will emerge victorious, and what discursive techniques are used to acquire and maintain power.

The predominance of technology in the novel attests to a modernity whose content has either been emptied or altered beyond recognition. Reason in the Enlightenment is always predicated on clear perception; perception, enhanced or hindered by the innumerable hallucinogenic substances and magnifying devices in the text, is precisely the category that is called into question. Technology involves not only the development of machines intended to heighten perception; there is in the text a running commentary on the proper techniques for writing chronicles. Both of these technologies—writing-machines and perception-machines—are juxtaposed very early in the novel. The first appearance of them in the novel is the *orejuda*, a huge architectonic structure in the form of a human ear, in the middle of which the child hostage, Niño Avilés, recently rescued from a shipwreck, is placed. The inventor of the *orejuda* is a British engineer, Robert Smith, who, we learn, deserted from the English Armada during the siege of a Caribbean Island in 1762—a date that resonates historically with the British occupation of Havana. However, the inventions of this European engineer of the eighteenth century are not intended to "enlighten" the populace. Rather, we are told explicitly that the Archbishop Larra ordered the construction of the *orejuda* in order to "foment even further fear and superstition" (37). Moreover, this diabolical engineer is author of a "strange book" entitled *Treatise on Machines for the Premises of Power*, "a collection of drawings for the construction of fabulous machines of torture, espionage and psychological terror" (37). Thus the importation to the Caribbean of eighteenth-century European technology and knowledge is not associated with what we traditionally consider Enlightenment knowledge, where the function of technology is to heighten clarity through perception, thereby dispelling "fear and superstition," since fear and superstition are precisely the purpose of this technology. The *orejuda* is, in fact, a strange inversion of Foucault's panopticon, an observation that reinforces the importance of the novel's eighteenth-century setting. Both devices share a complex parallel between physical center and periphery. In the panopticon, the center is the seat from which images emanating from the periphery are perceived. In the *orejuda*, the center *manufactures* the sensory data—the Niño's ear-splintering cries intended for perception by the exterior. Smith's immense ear-shaped edifice is not designed to capture sounds for surveillance, but rather, in an odd reversal of the real architecture of the human ear, amplifies and transmits the continual cries of the child to the general population:

> The child would cry and the furious echo would fall into that sound box until it escaped through the twists and turns carved into the walls, always amplifying itself, as though fleeing from its own monstrosity. And then the frenetic

> cries would become even greater and unleash themselves upon the entire city, suddenly vomited up, day and night, through those impassible and gigantic stone snail shells with which the architect adorned the façade of the black enclosure. And may I and my children be cursed to hell if that machine was not capable of launching the cries of the child Avilés up to a distance of ten leagues, and, I would say, even more. (14)

The panopticon and the *orejuda* have in common a certain relationship with power in which, regardless of the specific mechanism, the center is the seat of hegemony. It might be argued that, through this imaginary technological invention, Rodríguez Juliá is allegorically articulating a fairly standard critique of the Enlightenment. According to this critique, the technological advancements that the Enlightenment occasioned by promoting scientific experimentation are used in a way that oppresses humanity rather than promotes its well-being.[28] The allegorical or emblematic power that Carpentier attributes to the guillotine in *Explosion in a Cathedral* could be said to serve a similar function.

But, in fact, Rodríguez Juliá goes beyond this common critique; at the center of the *orejuda* there is not a sinister presence that recuperates the Enlightenment as an alibi for consolidating hegemony. The center is an empty place or signifier. Rubén Ríos Avila, speaking about Baltasar, the protagonist of another Rodríguez Juliá narration about the eighteenth century (which I will discuss presently), points out that his "monstrosity" is, in fact, the result of the convergence and inbreeding of irreconcilable historical trajectories.[29] Another aspect of this monstrosity in Rodríguez Juliá's depiction of the eighteenth century consists of the absent, or at least invisible, center of a foundational discourse of modernity. The figure of the Niño Avilés, the epic bone of contention of warring factions, is placed at the core of the *orejuda*, and is a deceptive source of the cries that so mystify and terrorize the population. And yet the child itself almost never makes an appearance in the novel. The Archbishop Larra orders the infant's face covered with a handkerchief as soon as he is rescued from the sea. Once rescued, the Archbishop Larra ventures to lift the veil covering the child's face, and yet the chronicler reporting the scene cannot give a report attesting to his visage: "The fearsome guard formed a ring around the Bishop. Larra unveiled the countenance of the infant. No one could see, then, the distress caused by the child's furious visage in the Bishop's temperament" (13).

In fact, the *countenance* of the Niño Avilés can be considered absent, or as a false center on many levels. The novel's title comes from the aforementioned painting by José Campeche, *El Niño Juan Pantaleón Avilés de Luna Alvarado* (a portrait that appears on the cover of the 1991 edition of the novel published by the University of Puerto Rico Press). Rodríguez Juliá's monograph *Campeche, o Los diablejos de la melancolía (Campeche, or, the Demons of Melancholy)* contains an extended commentary on this moving portrait that depicts an armless child with shrunken and misshapen legs and a melancholy countenance. And yet Rodríguez Juliá seems once again to be toying with the conventions of literary intuition since nowhere in the novel is Niño Avilés actually described in these terms. In fact, this fallacy of importing the pictoric Avilés into the novel is committed practically without exception by critics, who repeatedly refer to the *novel's* Avilés as deformed in the same way as in the painting.[30] It is not until the latter part of the novel, in the "secret diary" of Trespalacios (the commander of the Spanish forces besieging San Juan in order to squash the black rebellion led by Obatal), that the connection between the two Avilés, the plastic and the literary, is suggested: "Last night I dreamed that the Child Avilés grew up and became a man; but as he grew his members became smaller, shrinking to the point of disappearing. The poor child was lame, then, and was unable to walk or grasp things, since he was a man with a trunk only" (373). The fact that Trespalacios has this vision of Avilés in a *dream* confirms, in fact, that this is not a description of the figure in the novel's "waking life." Thus even the most rudimentary external source for interpreting the novel, Campeche's portrait, becomes an illicit extratextual referent, not unlike Rodríguez Juliá's birth date, with which the narrator closes the prologue. The only physical or visual characteristic of the Niño (reported secondhand) are his teeth, which "shined resplendently above the waves" (12), a detail that, in perfect keeping with Rodríguez Juliá's literary subterfuge, is absent from Campeche's unsmiling portrait.

The Niño Avilés can be characterized, then, as a producer of effects while paradoxically proving to be their absent or at least invisible source, an arrangement that Rodríguez Juliá seems to be equating allegorically with the emergence of modernity in the Caribbean. Thus manifestations of this modernity no longer possess an ideological center around which to orbit. Trespalacios's study, or "flying observation chamber," also has all the hallmarks of scientific experimentation: navigational instruments, levers and pulleys, test tubes, flasks, ball bearings, etc. And yet the flasks and test tubes contain hallucinogenic powders or snuffs, "rapés," and the entire experience in the "flying study" is soon transformed into an undisguised drug trip having little to do with clarity of perception:

> Coming out of this thurible were four tubes, very similar to those used in hookahs. Each of the four tubes tapered into a small hole in the form of a phallus, but which was inserted into the nose rather than the mouth. In the end curiosity was mightier than prudence, and when everything was prepared, I inserted the little phalli into my nose and breathed in the vapors that were carried though the tube. (91)

The drug experience, meticulously described, carries the narrator to a Roman coliseum, where he wanders through a series of labyrinthine and Borgesian staircases. After an immense fall through empty space, facing skyward, Gracián finds himself scaling a sticky surface, which ends up being the iris of Trespalacios's eyeball, the latter now having been transformed into a colossus. After scaling this orb, Gracián peers down into Trespalacios's pupil and sees a washed-out landscape depicting the port of San Juan. The morning following this hallucinogenic experience, Gracián and Trespalacios are still in the flying office, now peering through "*catalejos*," telescopes, at the enemy camp. This camp, inhabited by the rebel slaves led by Obatal, is described in terms no less hallucinatory than the drug trip itself, as an inverted cathedral, its spiraled towers hanging from the sky rather than reaching up toward it. Trespalacios's goal, the overt raison d'être of his military campaign, will be to turn the city right side up, to "return reason to mankind." And yet the contents of this "reason" possessed by Trespalacios are gluttony, farting, drug use, and hallucination. This idea of a world turned upside down, on its head, is repeated in the description of the periscopes used to spy on the enemy camp, which invert their objects for the observers' perception: "In the lower opening of the tube a magnifying lens is placed to focus the light from the two peepholes. This imperfect technique has the disadvantage of inverting the image, placing it upside down, head over heels, so that using this machine is like spying on the curiosities of a world standing on its head" (241). Given these repeated references to inverted images and worlds, it is certainly tempting to read Rodríguez Juliá within the context of Marx and Engels' image of the camera obscura, a metaphor for viewing reality filtered through the lens of ideology: "If in all ideology men and their circumstances appear upside down as in a camera obscura, this phenomenon arises from their historical life-processes just as the inversion of the retina does from their physical life-process."[31] Rodríguez Juliá is possibly toying with such an association. However, the Puerto Rican's inverted world does not seem to be one suffering specifically from the contradictions decried by Marx and Engels. The telos of Marxism is to turn this world back on its feet, to invert the inversion and thus restore things to their rightful state; Trespalacios's military assault has the same stated goal. And yet while Marxism's "right side up" is viewed as the inevitable trajectory of historical forces stemming from the Enlightenment, in Rodríguez Juliá's view of things, there is no such normative standard by which the inversion can be corrected.

The numerous machines in Rodríguez Juliá's narration are in some ways reminiscent of those that appear in Carpentier. Just as the former is frequently calling attention to "monstrous machines" in the text, so the cryptic and beautiful epigraph of *Explosion in a Cathedral*, taken from Esteban's journal while crossing the Atlantic toward America, opens with similar reference: *tonight I saw them hoist the machine anew.*[32] Carpentier's machine (though there is no way to know this as one begins reading the novel) is in fact the guillotine, a Jacobin exportation to Guadeloupe and the New World. Esteban imagines the ship carrying the guillotine as somehow frozen in time, "suspended between yesterday and a tomorrow that were being transported with us."[33] But, in fact, Esteban's machine is not outside of time; to the contrary, in an understanding of history similar to that of Edmundo O'Gorman, the guillotine, the Jacobin symbol par excellence, paradoxically consolidates the Caribbean within the ambit of a European revolutionary historical trajectory. The Caribbean may prove to be the testing ground that effectively deconstructs, reverses or confirms the ethos of revolutionary Europe; for Carpentier, the effect of the miscegenation of these two incompatible entities is a monstrosity. But for Rodríguez Juliá, the notion of monstrosity, certainly one of his keywords, entails a vision not of Caliban trapped in an irresolvable dialectic with Ariel; rather, we must now attempt to imagine an autonomous Caliban, outside the realm of a dualistic dynamic with Ariel, who retains all his monstrosity precisely due to the lack of an origin and a telos. Another of Rodríguez Juliá's novels situated in the eighteenth century, *La renuncia del héroe Baltasar* (*The Renunciation*), provides an elaboration on this view of historical monstrosity.

Monstrosity and Renunciation

In our discussions of both Arenas and Rodríguez Juliá, Carpentier has often been upheld as a point of departure, a model against which the particular visions of a Caribbean postmodernity have been articulated. Though the genealogical connection in the Hispanic Caribbean to C. L. R. James's understanding of modernity (and its link to the Enlightenment) may be much less direct, there is in Rodríguez Juliá what seems to be a strong resemblance to James's portrait of Toussaint L'Ouverture and the black masses, "the beloved flock," in Rodríguez Juliá's language. *La renuncia del héroe Baltasar* (1974) illustrates with greater succinctness the author's peculiar vision of a Caribbean modernity cut off from any particular origin or telos, of a Caliban that has broken away from the historical or dialectical engagement with Ariel.

The novel takes the form of a series of three lectures in which the historian, certainly the same Alejandro Cadalso who was the narrative organizing principle of the longer novel,[34] presents to the public a reconstruction of Baltasar's arranged marriage and its aftermath, which requires, as in the prologue to *La noche oscura del Niño Avilés*, an impressive amount of deciphering and comparing of archival documents and missives in search of both veridical and apocryphal clues in handwriting, repetitions, turns of phrases, and other textual clues. And, as in the longer novel, this historical deciphering in *The Renunciation* rests on the interpretations of prior interpretations, including the pictorial depictions and verse descriptions.

Baltasar is the son of Ramón Montañez, a legendary slave rebel, and his renunciation entails a clean break from both black rebel ancestry as well as from his newfound access to white power. He washes his hands entirely of both the "black masses" from which he descends and the white power structure that has enlisted him as a lackey, a token to represent the illusory possibility of upward mobility to the discontented black masses. This illusory tokenism is attempted by marrying Baltasar to Josefina Prats, the white daughter of an eminent statesman, General Prats, the "Secretary of the Government." This unholy union, engineered by the Machiavellian Archbishop Larra, is intended to quell the masses of discontented slaves: "Baltasar Montañez would create in the black population the false illusion of freedom and social mobility. The intention was to slow or stop the revolutionary impulse by setting up the figure of a popular hero who would reconcile two opposed classes."[35] There is a hitch in this scheme, though, which is that the father of the sacrificial bride, General Prats, refuses to go along with the plan, and is subsequently stripped of his office and imprisoned. The first of the historian's three lectures deals with General Prats's absence from his daughter's wedding, an absence that is discovered by the historian-narrator by comparing testimonial chronicles of the event. In the first such testimonial, written only days after the wedding ceremony, there is no mention of the presence of General Prats. The absence of the father of the bride at his daughter's wedding, indicating an internal discord, would hinder the Machiavellian efficacy of the arranged union and amount to a potential embarrassment. In a later chronicle describing the ceremony, the general's presence is now overenthusiastically depicted. This contradiction leads our historian-narrator to the following conclusion about the first chronicle, which made a voluntary omission of any reference to the father of the bride: "It is clear that Bishop Larra was beside himself when he read this first report. Its omission of Prats' name is tantamount to an accusatory finger" (16). This revealing and effective figure of speech—that an absence or omission can be at the same time an index, an "accusatory finger"—is one that in large part captures the play of textuality in Rodríguez Juliá's narrations. At the center of his texts about the eighteenth century, there is often this question of a disputed presence, a discursive center that is in fact an empty place, whether it be the presence (or absence) of General Prats at his daughter's wedding, the central location of the rarely seen Niño Avilés at the center of the "*orejuda*," or the very existence of Nueva Venecia itself. This hinge between absence and presence gives way to a dizzying propagation of texts, of still more indices, whose testimonials unwittingly supplant that very center to which they supposedly attest.

As I have mentioned, the historian-narrator of this shorter novel by Rodríguez Juliá's, though never named explicitly, is undoubtedly the same historian and archivist who signs off on the prologue to *La noche oscura*, Alejandro Cadalso. His ideas and turns of phrase, such as "what the French call *la condition humaine*" and "human nature," sound quaint today, and are further evidence of one of Rodriguez Juliá's favorite tactics, which is to represent history as a something that is always at least doubly removed from the present moment. Another of these ideas from an earlier moment in the twentieth century is the reference to Miguel de Unamuno's "intrahistoria." And yet the allusion to Unamuno might have more than a passing significance. If, in *San Manuel Bueno, mártir* (Saint Manuel, the Good, Martyr, 1930), the story of a parish priest who has lost his faith but persists in preaching the gospel to his parishioners, the Unamunian hero Manuel's doctrine with regard to the masses or "pueblo" is "opium, opium, let them have opium, and let them sleep, and let them dream,"[36] then this bears a resemblance to Baltasar's scam marriage, which is intended to drug or sedate the people: "The marriage was intended to offer up a sort of fairy-tale figure which would tranquilize, which would sedate, which would *dope*, black indignation" (6). Unamuno's "opium" is an undisguised reference and response to Marx's opiate of the masses. We have no reason to doubt that this was in fact Unamuno's political position, that a people sedated with the narcotic of religious faith will actually achieve a greater happiness, despite their lack of autonomy, than a sovereign, enlightened populace that has shirked outside authority and has taken control of its own destiny. The risk of the Enlightenment, for Unamuno, is dramatized in the figure of Manuel himself, whose lack of faith results in an unbearable solitude. This improbable digression about *San Manuel Bueno, mártir* may in fact be quite relevant to the entire discussion of the Enlightenment. We have seen in numerous discussions of the passage how Carpentier's conclusion of *The Kingdom of This World* perhaps represents a quasi-Unamunian position on this score, though with qualifications. His position, at least in that particular text, seems to be that emancipation from tyranny and oppression may never come, but that man's redemption is nonetheless his faith in the eminence of that emancipation. The opposing view, taken by C. L. R. James, is that faith alone, as embodied in the unspeakable torments of the Saint Domingue slaves, is no route to happiness or redemption, and that the sole solution is nothing less than full Enlightenment, autonomy over one's own institutions at all costs. James's "tragedy" is in polar opposition to Unamuno's, then, since it is precisely Toussaint's "faith" in the good will of the French authorities as the agents of "civilization" that brings about his calamitous downfall. This binary arrangement, which is similar to the Caliban/Ariel dualism, is a historical structure from which Rodríguez Juliá will attempt to portray a mad alternative, a letristic reality that eschews the very structures that lend meaning to history. Monstrosity and renunciation, embodied in the figures of El Niño Avilés and Baltasar, are Rodríguez Juliá's most powerful themes, since they express not only an absent origin but a radical refusal of history itself.

And just as the Unamunian or Carpenterian view is subtly imported into the text, so some of the descriptions of Baltasar and his father's legacy of rebellion are oddly reminiscent, in an inverse way, of James's descriptions of Toussaint. This historian-narrator describes Baltasar's writing style in the following terms:

> The style is Baltasar's: verbose, rhetorical, slightly pompous, the result of a perhaps over-rapid cultural assimilation. We should recall in this regard that Baltasar was a man of very little learning before he married doña Josefina. His great intelligence—one might almost call it true Genius—allowed him to acquire, within a very few years, tremendous culture, but this legacy, untried by the slow years of tempering, was in truth a pathetic caricature of erudition. (18)

This extended commentary bears a resemblance to James's similar fixation on Toussaint's style, which I discussed at length in chapter 2. Of course, James's criterion is quite the contrary, that anything Toussaint had to say about politics or Enlightenment bore the indelible stamp of his background in slavery, which lent him a fluency and insight that was lacking from whatever the *philosophes* had to say on the subject. Baltasar, according to our rather conservative historian, was too precipitously assimilated into Occidental culture, and therefore his mastery of the forms of Western discourse suffers from an overly exuberant perfection.[37] Moreover, and this would be inconceivable in James's description of Toussaint, Baltasar is described as parodying the enlightened style of eighteenth-century Spanish prose. This reference to parody is perhaps an allegorical self-reference on the part of Rodríguez Juliá to his own genre of historical writing and the relationship it bears to the prior practitioners of this genre.

Baltasar and Toussaint, those two brilliant figures who rose from backgrounds of slavery to positions of eminent power, have styles that are described in contrary terms, but this opposition amounts to different sides of the same coin. Baltasar's renunciation, in its most profound sense, will consist of a rejection of this framework altogether in an attempt to forge a new reality that is, in fact, a form of madness, a theological delirium similar to that of Bishop Trespalacios in the final section of *El Niño Avilés*. Baltasar's condemnation by the Inquisition and subsequent imprisonment unleash the very violence that Larra's scheme was intended to suppress, a violence that, in keeping with Rodríguez Juliá's narrative audacity, is described without sparing the reader any details.[38] Larra makes every attempt to restore Baltasar to his position of power;

he obtains an Inquisitional pardon and attempts to woo him with orgies and feasts. But Baltasar renounces this restoration of his former privileges and does nothing to stop the rebelling masses of slaves who are devastating the island. Three slave leaders attempt to rescue him (we are reminded of Dessalines, Christophe, and Pétion, the leaders of the Haitian Revolution after Toussaint's arrest), but we soon realize that the rebelling slaves and their aspirations of freedom are one of the targets of Baltasar's renunciation: "But they erred in their pretended horrors, for it was don Baltasar himself, whom they intended to steal away, which sounded the alarm" (127–28).

Baltasar's treacherous betrayal of his rescuers (described as "kidnappers" by the colonial chronicle) is yet another noteworthy renunciation. He renounces not so much the struggle of the island's slaves, but rather, by refusing to cooperate with the colonial authorities to stop the violence, he renounces instead an entire model of historical reality molded by hegemony and resistance. That Baltasar stands apart from this structure is confirmed by the Caliban-Ariel embrace once the "hero" steps outside this framework. Larra, whose life work has consisted of maintaining a political and historical economy of masters and slaves, now searches for his dialectical counterpart as though seeking reassurance in the recognizable structure of historical meaning. Speaking about the betrayed rescuers, Larra reveals that his adversarial relationship with them at least reassures him of a stable historical reality, one that has been jarred by Baltasar's renunciations: "But I confess that they did wish great good for their race and their people, and that this harsh, pitiless man has exacted from them and their ambitions a terrible price in blood" (130).

This momentary fraternity between the two poles in the structure of historical meaning—hegemony and resistance, masters and slaves—is brought about by the emergence of Baltasar as a wild card in the arrangement. Though Carpentier hesitates at the crucial moment in *The Kingdom of This World*, there is a moment of what we could call a Sartrean synthesis in which Carpentier's fascination with and objectification of négritude is transcended in favor of Ti Noël's vision of a raceless society. If this ascending triangular or pyramidal structure is the spatial model that represents the movement or architecture of history, then Rodríguez Juliá will attempt to portray an inversion of this structure. Those bizarre architectonic formations in both his novels about the eighteenth century—inverted cathedrals and staircases extending into infinite space—are the tropic equivalent of, to use Rodríguez Juliá's own language, the dark side ("el lado oscuro") of dialectics, of historical structures. Baltasar's renunciation unleashes not only an orgiastic massacre, it is an attempt to achieve a kind of freedom through the destruction of all creation: "the destruction of all creation, which is supreme freedom" (133). Baltasar's renunciation is therefore the diametrical contrary of Ti Noël's revelation, an inverse triangular structure that is an attempt on the part of the historical imagination to effectively "destroy" the very edifices by which we have traditionally given meaning to history. In this sense, Rodríguez Juliá, perhaps even more than Carpentier dared, attempts a negatively dialectic space unrestrained by the limitations of either the cogito or *Aufklärung.* By re-creating within a hollow shell of recognizable formal conventions—the historian's lecture, a chronicle—events and places that never existed, but that could have, since oblivion is part of the Caribbean condition that the Rodríguez Juliá is allegorizing, the Puerto Rican author in a sense moves beyond Carpentier, Chauvet, Condé, and Arenas in the radicalness of his historical imagination, since these Caribbean authors at least anchor their view of history in a recognizable figure whose existence can be corroborated. Rodríguez Juliá's doubly excised history, a result of a foreign past (Spanish colonialism) and a co-opted present (globalization or U.S. neocolonialism) clears a path for an untethered historical imagination and at the same times provides gratification for the author's historical libido, so to speak: a desire to recast an image of the Caribbeanization of Puerto Rico rather than the reverse.

Conclusions

Before and After, Here and There

The writers studied in this monograph abounding in the discernment of binary structures contribute to a critique of this historical framework. By approaching the question of the Enlightenment in the Caribbean through the modern historical imagination, the very idea of the Enlightenment is partially dismantled or deconstructed, not only as something that the Caribbean and Latin America may or may not have "had," but also as a unified or homogeneous philosophical school or historical period in the first place. Moreover, the insertion of this regional factor moves to a new terrain, as it were, the very notion of the Enlightenment, so that now certain contradictory dynamics emerge, such as center and periphery, the universal notion of *Menschheit* versus the division of humanity into leaders and masses, which enhance our understanding of *Aufklärung* in a general sense. Certainly the seeds of these discrepancies or contradictions, as Foucault noted, were already present and troubling in Kant's inaugural essay. But rereading Kant's doctrine about humanity's maturity or immaturity *through* modern Caribbean writers explodes these antinomies into outright paradoxes that emerge in all their complexity when read through the lens of the historical imagination.

The extended essay on Alejo Carpentier set a tone and precedent in this study for speaking about contradictions, oppositions, and binary tensions. With Carpentier serving as a kind of prototype of writing from the Caribbean about the Enlightenment, this cognitive framework of opposition or contradiction is a productive one for characterizing not only the ways in which other writers approach and interpret similar material, but also how their writing amounts to a discursive or even literal response to Carpentier's edifice of historical representation. C. L. R. James belongs to a different, though not distant, linguistic and cultural heritage; and, moreover, *The Black Jacobins* is more an orthodox history than a fictional account of the events of the Haitian Revolution. And yet the fact that these notable cultural and contextual differences exist renders the real similarities and parallels between Carpentier's treatment of the Enlightenment and James's, and especially the respective contradictions that emerge from their writing, that much more noteworthy.

I have argued that the binary tensions in the work of Carpentier did not originate with his writing about the eighteenth century in the Caribbean, but were already present in incipient form in his first novel, *Ecue-Yamba-O*. The fault, in both senses, that Juan Marinello discerned in that novel—the "crack," or *rajadura*, between the narrator and the Afro-Cuban personages that he attempts to represent, between an outside observer and a profound interior—is a productive notion not only for speaking about Carpentier but about the other writers studied here. For Carpentier, the remedy for the ideological fissure in his narration was not somehow to erase or repair it, but rather to thematize it as a polar division that arose from the conditions of history itself. In *The Kingdom of This World*, the Cuban author explores the almost static encounter of an Occident whose notion of temporality and progress is oriented toward the past (Benjamin's angel of history is the fitting image) and an Afro-Cuban ethos for which music and temporality are messianically oriented toward the future. In my reading, one of the Carpenterian moments of greatest discursive tension is Ti Noël's revelation in the closing passages of *The Kingdom of This World*. The old Haitian, having been enslaved and mistreated by the emperor Henri Christophe, realizes in a kind of narrative crescendo that tyranny is not an exclusive practice of the white race. On more than one occasion, I have referred back to Ti Noël's unfinished revelation as a paradigmatic scene. In Carpentier's text, despite the fact that he had gone to such great lengths to establish irresolvable opposition as the thematic structure of his narration, Ti Noël stands at the doorstep of a dialectic, a transcendence of the terms of the opposition between Afro-Cuban temporality and the Enlightenment. Dialectics would be one possible remedy or response to Marinello's fault line or crack, and yet, in what could be viewed as a regression, cyclical nature in the form of an apocalyptic cyclone rather than the elevation human consciousness determines Ti Noël's final destiny.

There is also a quasi-dialectical moment in C. L. R. James's *The Black Jacobins*, but, like Carpentier, James hesitates at the foot of this precipice. If Carpentier enlists the Enlightenment to strengthen his favorite paradigm of mutual opposition, James's relationship to the idea of the

Enlightenment is in some ways even more conflicted. For Carpentier, one of the "uses" of the Enlightenment is as a device conducive to the framing of vignettes within which characters are faced with paradoxical situations or impossible choices, all stemming from the historical moment in which they find themselves. One such vignette takes place in *Explosion in a Cathedral*, when, back in Cuba and disenchanted with the course of the French Revolution, Esteban experiences a sense of profound alienation upon coming face to face with the text of his own translation of Rousseau's *The Social Contract*, a text that has contributed to fomenting his sister Sofía's revolutionary fervor. Reinaldo Arenas aptly points out that Carpentier's characters suffer from a kind of paralysis, but it is not only the overly abundant historical detail in a material sense that encumbers their movement; the deluge of conflicting historical forces also paralyzes their choices and alliances.

Whereas for Carpentier it is Ti Noël whose revelation suggests the possibility of a dialectic in which race is transcended, for James the figure of Toussaint L'Ouverture promises a bridge reconciling a host of hostile contradictions or oppositions. Toussaint, through his erudite knowledge of political economy and the writings of Abbé Raynal, is someone fully fluent in the rhetoric and discourse of the Enlightenment; and due to his past in slavery he was able to more fully absorb or comprehend the precepts of the Enlightenment leading to freedom and autonomy. Born a slave in Saint Domingue, Toussaint was for that reason more enlightened, comprehended more fully the master/slave dialectic, according to James, than the inventors of the Enlightenment, and embodied the promise of a kind of mythic bridge joining the antinomies of leader and masses, master and slave. And yet it becomes clear that, in fact, this promised synthesis fails on two counts. Toussaint holds the French and their cultural milieu in too high a regard and is too eager to conciliate them at the expense of the "black masses." Moreover, this "flaw" is mirrored by James's own treatment of Toussaint since his interpretation of the Haitian Revolution borrows too heavily from European tragedy—a generic grafting that only solidifies the chasm between James and the black masses that constitute his privileged historical subject. Instead of synthesis, what emerges are more highly complex antitheses, namely between the "barbaric" and illiterate Dessalines, who flinches neither at rupturing all ties with France nor at slaughtering the remaining whites in Haiti, and a civilized Toussaint, whose admiration of the styles and tenets of the French Enlightenment amounted to a continued subjection and a deferred autonomy.

James, Carpentier, and Marie Chauvet link the fate of Caribbean modernity to the Enlightenment, in the same mode that Habermas has discerned eighteenth-century philosophy as a modernity: "Enlightenment thinkers of the cast of mind of Condorcet still had the extravagant expectation that the arts and sciences would promote not only the control of natural forces but also understanding of the world and the self, moral progress, the justice of institutions and even the happiness of human beings."[1] In Kant's definition of the Enlightenment, the question of who and where remained ambiguous; Habermas's description reproduces this ambiguity regarding the subject of the Enlightenment. James's critique involves a reversal, so that the lofty aims Habermas attributes to Condorcet—that is, the general improvement of civilization stemming from enhanced knowledge—come (close) to fruition in Haiti though they fail in postrevolutionary imperial France. Carpentier seems to delight in the utter incongruity between modes of Enlightenment thought and the Afro-Caribbean world to which he claims problematic access. His polarization of the two worlds results in a contrapuntal approach that nevertheless implies an implicit normative subjectivity, the common ground upon which these polarities can be cast, or, to employ a Carpenterian metaphor, the musical staff upon which the contrapuntal motifs can be transcribed.

Marie Chauvet would appear initially to buy into Condorcet's view of the Enlightenment program, but the contradictions occasioned by a society that can produce slavery on the one hand and opera and theater on the other implode upon each other in the Haitian author's portrayal of a talented biracial girl in the days leading up to the beginning of the Haitian Revolution. And yet, though the protagonist and perhaps the author struggle with this historical contradiction—that a civilization is capable of producing great art on the one hand and the institution of slavery on the other—it is one that is resolved novelistically, as it were, when Minette offers her dying voice in the service of the Haitian Revolution. In this context, one is reminded of the relevance of Walter Benjamin's observation that every monument of civilization is at the same time a testament of barbarity. Chauvet seems to have taken this axiom to heart by the time she wrote her triptych *Amour, colère et folie*, a work that allegorizes the brutality of the period of the Duvalier regime in Haiti through an approach that is astounding in its departure from the strategies employed in Chauvet's earlier novel. In *Amour*, the reader beholds the sacrificial and oneiric embrace between victimizer and victim, between Calédu and Claire, as an almost (de)mythologizing gesture intended to purge the narrator of historical traumas related to sexuality, class, and race. True, as Maryse Condé points out, killing the sadistic local commander Calédu would not have been enough to stop the march of Haitian history, but by fantasizing about such a gesture Chauvet reveals an enduring and evolving engagement with the forces of historical oppression, thereby implying an elusive horizon of freedom from these forces. This implied horizon leads me to question J. Michael Dash's and others' qualification of Chauvet as a postmodern writer.

Surely the works of Maryse Condé, Reinaldo Arenas, and Edgardo Rodríguez Juliá belong to a generation of Caribbean writing that, even if one is hesitant to employ the term "postmodern," bears unmistakable resemblances to that cultural, aesthetic, and ideological moment that has been acknowledged by Lyotard and Jameson as being the quasi-successor to modernity. The most notable of these resemblances is the absence of the notorious *grand récit*, the totalizing and overarching historical narrative. And yet I believe it feasible to discuss the postmodernity of these writers with a contextual specificity without recurring only in a general and diffuse manner to commonplace notions of postmodernity. The idea not only of the absence of a *grand récit*, or master narrative, but also the decentering of the subject along with propagation of the signifier and deferral of the signified might all be characteristics easily applied to Caribbean writing. Raymond Williams's observation about postmodern literature in Latin American in general undeniably characterizes, at least in part, recent writing in the Caribbean as well: "As frequently happens in postmodern texts, the reality of texts, of fiction, or of storytelling predominate over the empirical reality and often subvert it. These are fictional worlds that inevitably revert back to language as their principal subjects."[2] And yet the contextual specificity of Caribbean historical imagination, at least as discussed here, needs to be located in the tenor of the response to an earlier generation of foundational writers as well as an attitude toward questions of revolution and historicity in general. If Carpentier's commitment to Marxism is not articulated as directly and passionately as James's engagement, both of these key Caribbean figures partake in the idea of Enlightenment historicity, which posits a historico-political denouement, a notion of historical progression whose current trajectory and degree of self-consciousness began in the historical period corresponding to the Enlightenment.

There could be said to exist certain utopic elements in the works of Condé, Rodríguez Juliá, and Arenas, but probably in the more literal sense of not belonging to any particular place. Maryse Condé's historico-fictive text *I, Tituba, Black Witch of Salem*, while pertaining to a literary tradition disparate from, though contiguous to, that of her male Hispanic counterparts, nevertheless articulates a vision of the Caribbean postmodern historical imagination. Though her text is perhaps more in dialogue with her Francophone predecessors and contemporaries such as Capécia, Fanon, Glissant, Chamoiseau, Confiant, and Bernabé than with Carpentier and James, the historical structures that in large part overdetermine her historical imagination reveal noteworthy similarities to her Anglophone and Hispanic forbears. These structural similarities stem from, among other things, the Enlightenment's understanding of historical consciousness and the difficulty of critiquing it without simultaneously participating in and therefore propagating it. These structural dilemmas of the Caribbean critique of the Enlightenment, along with the specific Caribbean historical and cultural motifs that resonate so strongly between Condé's text and Carpentier's (not to mention Condé's direct evocation of Carpentier in *Traversée de la mangrove*), contribute to building a convincing case regarding the unity of Caribbean literary expression.

Condé's postmodern expression might be described as tentative, insofar as it still partakes in more traditional notions of social progress and historicity even while parodying these notions. Her theatrical text *In the Time of the Revolution* reveals that Condé was willing to engage directly the same raw historical material that so preoccupied James and Carpentier, even if she challenges her predecessors' way of viewing this material. Condé's wild card for disrupting more traditional modes of understanding is gender: a subjective factor that is glaringly absent from Carpentier and James and that is perhaps surprisingly not a determining factor even in Marie Chauvet's historical depiction in *Dance on the Volcano* (though gender is certainly one of the central axes of *Amour, colère et folie*). And yet Condé, by her own confession, parodies the commonplaces of feminist literature as well as the key moments of Caribbean history, and therefore casts a skeptical gaze on narratives of liberation. In a conversation with Françoise Pfaff, Condé comments on French Caribbean women writers' depiction of gender and why we may view it as something distinct and apart from the modernist narratives of liberation or even feminism: "What they express is very different from what men express. They don't write about political demands or political consciousness that leads to struggle, nor do they talk about feminism as defined in the West. These women seem interested in matters commonly defined as 'intimist' but that are in fact societal problems."[3] This distinction between "intimist" concerns that for Condé fall into the realm of social problems rather than the wide sweep of a historical narrative might be one of the keys to distinguishing between the modernist moment in the Caribbean historical imagination and the generations that followed.

The marriage of history and narrative necessitates a denouement, a resolution of the conflicts and oppositions that are the narrative engine of history. And yet one of the points of distinction between the practitioners of what we might call modernist historicity and their successors in the Caribbean is that for the latter group their revision of historical narrative consists of a suppression of final resolutions or syntheses. Reinaldo Arenas's antihistorical novel (or, in his own words, "simply a novel") *El mundo alucinante* expresses a synchronic impossibility or denial of historical objectivity. For Arenas, it is not a question of mutual opposition between Afro-Cuban and Occidental culture, but rather the persistence of a concerted Cartesian subjectivity that continuously foils the would-be historian's access to the object of study. If we return on one final occasion to the seminal moment in Carpentier of Ti Noël's revelation, in which the narrator prescribes that man's greatness lies in his continuously frustrated attempt at self-betterment, then the comparable moment in Arenas is the response Fray Servando elicits from Carlos IV, who informs him that it is useless to try to alter "precisely that which forms you." The circumstances from which the friar so longs to escape happen to be the very same that constitute the conditions of his being. This situation leads to a profoundly negative revelation in which Fray Servando longs to have never existed, but then realizes that, if granted, such a wish would cancel out the possibility of all longing in the first place. Arenas seems to aspire to the depiction of a subjectivity that is outside of or before history. This floating subject is allegorized by Fray Servando's anguish toward the novel's end: "The friar had a moment's doubt. He was afraid, seized with fear. Afraid that at the end of that vast country he was to travel, no-one would be awaiting him. Afraid to float forever in a vast emptiness and nothing, whirling through a vacant time, through an inalterable solitude that contained not even the solace of belief, the consolation of a simple faith" (238). Cartesian doubt (on the same page, Arenas refers to "the night that made Emmanuel Kant doubt"), which permeates Arenas's historical novel, is reiterated in this citation. But whereas, for Descartes, doubt is transformed into a launching pad for recovering a more inviolable certitude in which even temporality and memory are generally trustworthy indicators, Arenas retains and lingers in this realm of doubt in its purely negative moment. The image of Fray Servando floating in empty space and time, wounded by an unbearable solitude, is mirrored of course by the narrator whose own subjective solitude excludes any possibility of an "authentic" historical account. If Carpentier reified or relocated his own ideological fissure as a generalized historical condition, then Arenas reverses the procedure and exposes the fraudulent nature of so-called historical objectivity, recuperating the idea of history firmly back into the realm of the subject.

Writing *El mundo alucinante* in the 1960s, Reinaldo Arenas could be said to be a founder of the postmodern historical imagination in the Caribbean. The defiant quality of Arenas's utopic vision is well expressed by Emir Rodríguez-Monegal: "He is truly counterrevolutionary because his texts mock the progressive view of history and deconstruct our views of reality. . . . Arenas is the only voice to come out of Cuba in recent years that truly questions the official version of reality, political or otherwise."[4] We have seen that much of his machinery for representing history in *El mundo alucinante* is, in fact, a parodic expression with Carpentier as its principal target. Parody, following Jameson, seems more appropriately characteristic of a kind of modernism than of postmodernism since it suggests a corrective or normalizing model against which the ridiculed object is compared.[5] The absence of this normative horizon is more characteristic of pastiche, which is clearly the case in the works of Rodríguez Juliá. If Arenas, in his contestatory or parodic gesture, is still locked into a dialogue or dynamic with Carpentier's modernity but has initiated a kind of conceptual breaking away from those models, then Rodríguez Juliá finds a narrative space that is a virtual carte blanche for the postmodern historical imagination.

Condé inserts the character of Hester Prynne from *The Scarlet Letter* in juxtaposition with historical, "real" characters, such as Tituba herself, and therefore posits a postmodern indistinguishability between fictional personages and historical ones. And yet the point of this juxtaposition between Hester and Tituba is an imagined feminine solidarity that amounts to an alternative vision of historical subjectivity and agency. Rodríguez Juliá employs a similar technique, though his fictional trompe l'oeil is not the commingling of historical and fictional characters but rather the reproduction of historical discursive forms that are nevertheless void of historical content. With the lecture by an eminent (if old-fashioned) historian to a historical society or group of students and the footnote leading us to apocryphal textual sources—in both *El Niño Avilés* and *The Renunciation*—the Puerto Rican author reminds us that at the core of historical events (even fictional ones, such as the founding of the lacustrine city Nueva Venecia or the politically arranged marriage between a Baltasar, a black leader, and the white daughter of a distinguished politician), there is a text (a missive, a testimonial) of questionable authenticity. If Condé alters the machinery of the Caribbean historical imagination by inserting gender into its inner workings, then for Rodríguez Juliá, texts rather than sex are the foundation and simultaneous negation of historical objectivity.

Rather than a framework of opposition, which informs the modern works by Carpentier and James, Rodríguez Juliá's postmodern historical vision is more precisely characterized by *renunciation*. I have pointed out that though Carpentier's narration may at times include anachronisms, such as references to Marx and Engels's nineteenth-century specter in a narration taking place in the eighteenth century, these anachronisms in fact reinforce the single and implacable trajectory of history, of a telos. The mélange of temporal references and anachronisms in Rodríguez Juliá is not intended as a response to Carpentier's strict adherence to chronology but rather as genuine reconceptualization of Caribbean temporality in which a generational oblivion renders the past "improper" or absent. This leaves the author free to reinvent the past. If a possible Borgesian model for Arenas is arguably "The Garden of the Forking Paths," in which a subject confronted with multiple narrative possibilities can choose them all simultaneously or sequentially, then perhaps for Rodriguez Juliá the fitting parable is "The Aleph," in which the entirety of the universe—including the transformation of history into a viewable landscape—is glimpsed from unlimited and multitudinous vantage points. The Aleph in Jewish mysticism, Borges explains, is the missing key that would permit a holistic comprehension of the universe, further suggesting the analogy with Rodríguez Juliá, for whom the center of historical narration—the existence of Niño Avilés or the city of Nueva Venecia—is also missing or absent, populated instead by a historical oblivion or a self-generating series of contradictory and labyrinthine textual indices.

It is only fitting that we should speak here yet again of a paradigmatic dialectical moment; in speaking about Rodríguez Juliá, however, rather than Ti Noël's revelation, the most appropriate episode comes from C. L. R. James and the potential offered by Toussaint L'Ouverture of a bridge between opposing factions. Toussaint's failure means that enlightened modernity's binary oppositions of leaders and masses, center and periphery, remain stubbornly in place. Rodríguez Juliá's Baltasar is also invested with a similar hope, that he will act as a kind of liaison between whites and blacks in eighteenth-century Puerto Rico and save the island from the destruction of an imminent race war. But whereas Toussaint and Baltasar are both in a position promising a potential synthesis or resolution of conflict, Baltasar renounces this very structure of historical meaning, bows out of the game entirely, unleashing a wave of violence and destruction. If the appropriate spatial metaphor to describe the dialectic of masses and leaders is the pyramid, then Baltasar's renunciation inverts this spatial model into a negative and upside-down edifice, a structure that is mirrored by the architectonic designs in Rodríguez Juliá's text. The Puerto Rican author thus allegorizes a dismantling of a framework that lent meaning to history in the first place and clears a negative space to explore the "dark side" of historical narration.

The six writers studied here represent disparate traditions in twentieth-century Caribbean writing in English, French, and Spanish. If this brand of expression of the historical imagination amounts to genre or subgenre of historical writing, as I have been arguing, then these writers certainly do not exhaust a widening circle of constellation that can be extended throughout the Caribbean and beyond. Other works that cannot be discussed here but that fit nicely into the conversation are (in no particular order) *L'isolé soleil*, by Daniel Maximin; John de Pool's *Bolívar en Curaçao*; *La tragédie du Roi Christophe* and *Toussaint Louverture*, by Aimé Césaire; *Nobele wilden*, by Frank Martinus Arion; *La isla de Robinson*, by Arturo Uslar Pietri; *El corazón de Voltaire*, by Luis López Nieves; *Monsieur Toussaint* and *Le quatrième siècle*, by Édouard Glissant; *El mar de lentejas*, by Antonio Benítez-Rojo; *La tejedora de coronas*, by Germán Espinosa; *Los pañamanes*, by Fanny Buitrago; *Texaco*, by Patrick Chamoiseau; *El general en su laberinto*, by Gabriel García Márquez; *In the Name of Salomé*, by Julia Alvarez; *The Loss of El Dorado*, by V. S. Naipaul; *Natives of My Person*, by George Lamming; and *Unburnable*, by Marie-Elena John.

Gutiérrez Alea's Historical Imagination

In the introduction, I observed that attitudes toward the ideas of revolution and social progress in general, and, in the specifically Caribbean context, toward the Cuban Revolution in particular, might serve as a gauge for determining the dividing line, the generational break between the modern and the postmodern in the Caribbean historical imagination. One way to demonstrate this way of thinking in the Caribbean is to observe the ideological shifts in one of the films by the great Cuban filmmaker Tomás Gutiérrez Alea. In addition to his well-known films *The Death of a Bureaucrat* (1966), *Memories of Underdevelopment* (1968),

Strawberry and Chocolate (1993), and *Guantanamera* (1995), Gutiérrez Alea is also the director of a film that resonates with the thematic framework of this study: *The Last Supper* (1976). This film is perhaps the most successful cultural product of the 1970s in Cuba, a decade that, following the impressive burst of creative energy in the 1960s, caps what has been described by Ambrosio Fornet as the "quinquenio gris," or "colorless five years," of Cuban culture.[6] No doubt part of the explanation for this sudden paucity of cultural creativity in the 1970s was the official crackdown on any cultural expression that could even remotely be interpreted as critical of the revolutionary regime. This censorial apparatus can be summed up in Fidel Castro's pronouncement in his 1961 "Words to Intellectuals": "Within the Revolution everything is permitted; against the Revolution, nothing."[7] The Conference on Education and Culture in 1971 institutionalized these rigid parameters of cultural expression.

Gutiérrez Alea, paralleling a move by fellow Cuban artist Alejo Carpentier—according to Arenas, the literary idol of the Cuban Revolution—turned toward historical representation in *The Last Supper.* If Carpentier had availed himself of historical narration of eighteenth-century Caribbean society in *The Kingdom of This World* to avoid the psychological and ideological pitfalls that plagued his first novel, *Ecue-Yamba-O*, it seems plausible that in order to eschew the narrow confines of the revolutionary censorship in the mid-1970s, Gutiérrez Alea turned to a prior epoch; in so doing, he achieved one of his greatest films and perhaps the crowning cultural achievement of the "drab years" of the Cuban 1970s.

The motifs of *The Last Supper* are entirely resonant with this tradition and subgenre of historical representation: the film depicts a Cuban colonial sugar plantation in which all the recognizable signposts of the Caribbean historical imagination are present: the eighteenth-century setting, the masses of slaves, the sugar plantation with its imported technological innovations from Europe, the "enlightened" yet oppressive slave owner, and, finally, the bloody slave rebellion with its attendant massacres, reprisals, and atrocities. Through a depiction of Cuba in the eighteenth century, Gutiérrez Alea employs a quasi-Carpenterian vision of the march of history, in which the decadent old order headed by the "sugarocracy" and the church will be overthrown by forces that Gutiérrez Alea no doubt saw as the precursors leading to Maceo, Martí, and finally the Cuban Revolution itself.

Based quite literally on historical events that Manuel Moreno Fraginals discusses in his seminal *The Sugar Mill*, a deeply religious, aristocratic plantation owner (played by Nelson Villagra) wishes to re-create the scene of the Last Supper (casting himself in the role of Christ) and chooses twelve of the plantation's slaves to partake in a Holy Week feast that turns from a solemn catechistic repast into a decadent bacchanalia reminiscent of similar scenes in Buñuel's *Viridiana*. Unfortunately for the count, the indulgence toward the slaves only whets their appetites for more freedom, and on the following day, Good Friday, they burn down the sugar mill. One difference between the historical events that Moreno Fraginals documents and their representation in Gutiérrez Alea's film is, as Paul A. Schroeder astutely points out, that the cinematic depiction moves the historical events forward from the 1780s to the 1790s.[8] The intended effect of this shift could not be clearer. By setting the events in the 1790s and the wake of the Haitian Revolution (which is referred to repeatedly throughout the film), Gutiérrez Alea is clearly constellating this historical event with the unfolding of Cuban history and nationhood. Perhaps as many as thirty thousand French refugees came to Cuba after the rebellion in Saint Domingue began, and in addition to their culture and mores (which Carpentier discusses in *Music in Cuba*), they also brought to the Spanish colony the knowledge and practice of plantation sugar production on a large scale.[9]

Though *The Last Supper* at times incorporates an anticlerical parodic expression that seems to resonate just as strongly with Rodríguez Juliá and Arenas as with Carpentier or James, in fact, the film's vision of historical unfolding is clearly more in line with the latter figures than with the postmodern generation of writers who were Gutiérrez Alea's contemporaries. True to the Spanish, rather than French, colonial context, *The Last Supper* focuses more on the untenable principles of "enlightened" Catholicism as a justification of modern slavery, rather than on the philosophical principles of the Enlightenment, strictly speaking. Despite the count's powdered wig, an unmistakable symbol (or metonymy) for the century of Enlightenment, enlightened modernity is represented in the film not by ideologies of freedom and the ideas of the *philosophes*, but rather by the exigencies of the modern sugar plantation and how they push to the breaking point the hypocritical humanism of colonial Christianity, which had so seamlessly integrated slavery into its purview.

This conflict is embodied in the two characters of Gaspar Duclé, the plantation's sugar engineer, who is surely meant to represent one of the thousands of French refugees from Saint Domingue, and the parish priest. These two metonymic characters engage in a contrapuntal dialogue highly evocative of Fernando Ortiz's *Cuban Counterpoint of Tobacco and Sugar.* Duclé, the sugar mill's resident expert, posits parallels between the mysterious processes of creating sugar, with its "transmutations" from dark *guarapo*, or cane syrup, into pristine white crystals, and the rites and mysteries of Christian sacrament. Referring to the final product, the French engineer remarks to the priest, "The sugar has been purged by fire, just like the just souls in purgatory, isn't that so, Father?"[10] But the priest, uncomfortable with the increasingly dehumanizing effects that the rigorous demands of sugar production are having on the social and spiritual life of the community, responds, "Unfortunately, not all the souls in purgatory are purified."

But these playful Ortizian parallelisms between sugar production and the mysterious rites of the sacrament are no sooner posited than discarded. The plantation owner informs Duclé that he is planning on modernizing the mill with a new type of sugar press from England. The engineer responds: "There's no question that the horizontal sugar mill will become the standard method. But that kind of mill will require more cane. And more black slaves will be needed. And the time will come when there will be more blacks than whites." Duclé's apprehensions are justified. He then refers to Saint Domingue, where there were also more blacks than whites. This is the key moment in the film in which Gutiérrez Alea demonstrates dramatically what C. L. R. James stated unequivocally: that sugar-plantation slavery was not a feudal, premodern institution but rather a practice on the very cusp of modernity. And this realization aligns Gutiérrez Alea—at least the Gutiérrez Alea of *The Last Supper*—with James and Carpentier in his representation of this inaugurating moment of Caribbean modernity. What is absent from Gutiérrez Alea's vision of this historical moment—in what no doubt is a historically accurate omission—is precisely the *thought* of the Enlightenment. In a kind of Adornian nightmare of nonreflexivity, modernity is defined by the instrumentality of human reason, attested to by the division of labor within this sugar-producing society: the plantation owner who provides the capital, the engineer who possesses the technical and organization knowledge, the slaves who supply the labor, the parish priest who brings a tepid moral alibi for the entire operation, and finally the overseer whose brutality supplies the indispensable ideological antidote to the priest's Christian humanism, which, if implemented, would gravely threaten the quota of sugar production. If the Enlightenment is present in this world, it is so only to the degree that, to reiterate a quote from

Horkheimer and Adorno, "Enlightenment behaves toward things as a dictator toward men."[11]

If Reinaldo Arenas criticizes Carpentier because he paralyzes his characters with a surfeit of materially historical verisimilitude, Karen Jaehne sensitively observes that Gutiérrez Alea, in contrast, "has mastered the art of recreating a historical atmosphere without confining it to the aestheticism of 'period' movies."[12] Nevertheless, despite the elegant sparseness of Gutiérrez Alea's cinematic set in contrast to the sumptuousness of Carpentier's period descriptions, there are clear and resonant Carpenterian echoes in *The Last Supper.* One of those permitted to sit at the master's table for the reenactment of Jesus's final meal with his twelve apostles is the old slave Pascual (who identifies himself as a *cuartado*, or indentured servant, with one year of labor remaining), who, once the wine begins to flow and inhibitions to dissipate, timidly approaches the master and requests his freedom. The count reflects, and with an air of deep humanistic satisfaction, concedes: "You are free, Pascual." But it is too late for the frail, doubled-over old slave to profit from his freedom and, though he attempts to depart the premises, soon returns, realizing that he has no home other than the despised sugar mill. Drawing even greater satisfaction from the parable that has played out before the eyes of the other slaves, the master admonishes Pascual that true happiness is not to be found in freedom but rather in resignation and silent suffering. Pascual's predicament is the same as that of Carpentier's Ti Noël (Pascual almost seems like the very visual image of Carpentier's protagonist in his later years), who comes to know freedom when he is so old that he can only think to return "like an eel to the mud in which it was spawned," to the plantation of his erstwhile master Lenormand de Mézy.

In a powerful moment of the film, the count, in order to demonstrate to Pascual and the other slaves that the happiness occasioned by freedom is illusory, recounts the parable of Saint Francis of Assisi's "perfect joy," which consists of suffering the blows and torments of oppression with resignation in silent homage to the sufferings of Christ. Material wealth, fame, and even knowledge and wisdom offer only fleeting glimpses of happiness, according to the master's explication, but "pain and sorrow are the only things that are truly ours." The count explicitly opposes Saint Francis's true happiness to the imperfect satisfactions of freedom, since the old slave Pascual, even though granted his freedom, was still unhappy. Needless to say, this dismissal of freedom as an illusory source of happiness is in opposition to the supreme values of the Enlightenment.

Therefore, in an example of the historical imagination that we might qualify as a hybrid of James and Carpentier, Gutiérrez Alea seems to be suggesting that the slaves in the film, and not the Creoles or Europeans, are the true practitioners of Enlightenment philosophy. Despite the count's extended and dramatic demonstration of Saint Francis's perfect joy, the slave Ambrosio responds not only with comic bathos but also an effective rebuttal to the moral of the tale: "Let me see if I understand. When the overseer beats me, slave should be happy?"

Throughout the meal with the slaves, the count, who has aggrandized himself into the role of Jesus dining with his apostles, makes allegorical references to biblical episodes. For example, he explains to the slaves, "Christ assembled with his disciples, because he knew that he was going to die." One of the slaves at the table responds, "Please don't die, Master; Master good!" When the count speaks of the blood and the flesh of Christ, an astonished slave asks, "They ate him?" (It is then pointed out, much to the count's discomfiture, that one of the slaves gathered at the table is a "Carabalí" and practices cannibalism.) This humorous device is a virtual repetition of Carpentier's technique for deploying his preferred motif, the temporal incompatibility of the Occidental and Afro-Cuban worldviews. But with Gutiérrez Alea, as with Carpentier, the point is not to show that the black slave is simply incapable of understanding the play of temporality in Occidental representation or unable to grasp the dual referentiality of allegory. To the contrary, by stripping allegory of its temporally retrograde field of reference and insisting on an immediate application in the present, the slaves gathered around the master's table render the biblical parables transparent, and effectively "deconstruct" their allegorical (and hegemonic) function.

The morning after the feast, Good Friday dawns (reminiscent of yet another Carpenterian device of providing a liturgical setting for the unfolding of his narration), and the conflict that has been building throughout the film—between a humanistic Catholicism and the unrelenting machine of sugar production—comes into open combat. Though the slaves had been promised a day without labor on Good Friday, the plantation's overseer, Manuel, enforces the true intent of the master and compels them back to work, much to the consternation of the priest. At that moment, the slave rebellion begins in earnest. They take the overseer hostage, and, when it becomes clear that the count has had a change of heart regarding his leniency and compassion, proceed to burn down the plantation.

A contrast between two of the slaves provides an interesting parallel to the differences between Toussaint and Dessalines that I discussed in chapter 2 in reference to C. L. R James. Bangoché identifies himself at the master's table as a king from Guinea who had sold many slaves, but when defeated by an enemy, was in turn sold into slavery himself. Like Toussaint, Bangoché has been on both sides of the slave trade and entertains certain notions of grandeur. On the other hand, the film's hero is Sebastián, the runaway slave who, as the film begins is captured, beaten, and has his ear amputated and fed to the dogs before the eyes of the retching count. Wearing a bloody bandage around his head in meaningful contradistinction to the count's powdered wig, Sebastián is the only slave at the master's table who refuses to enter into dialogue with the count. In a moment—perhaps the film's climax—with obvious Hegelian implications, we see the count and Sebastián in a silent face-to-face showdown. The count asks the ailing slave, "Sebastián, who am I? Come, recognize me." After a palpable silence of almost twenty seconds, with the gradual zoom on the two figures adding to the intensity of the scene, Sebastián abruptly spits in the master's face. This gesture, or refusal, of "recognition," in lieu of words, marks Sebastián as Caliban, with Bangoché, who deems himself worthy of eating at the master's table, as Ariel. Appropriately, Sebastián is the only slave who, in the film's denouement, knows how to achieve freedom, comparable to Dessalines, whose investment in "civilization," according to C. L. R. James, was so negligible he was able to make a clean break from colonialism while Toussaint hesitated.

The charade of a tolerant, enlightened Christian humanism is stripped away when the count appears in the final scenes without the symbolic powdered wig. Once the dead, both white and black, are gathered in the chapel for last rites, the count protests the presence of the cadavers of the murdered slaves: "Get them out of here immediately!" The priest responds, "Sir, this is a church, and in death we are all . . . " The count completes the thought: "Equal? Were you going to say 'equal,' Father? Well what happened in Saint Domingue will not happen here. This is not Saint Domingue!" He then singles out the old slave Pascual, huddling in a corner of the chapel, whom he had "freed" the night before, to be murdered along with the others who had gathered at the master's table so that their heads may be displayed as a warning to those who might wish to reenact in Cuba what happened in Saint Domingue. And in the film's penultimate scene, we see the chilling image of eleven decapitated heads impaled on stakes. The one headless stake corresponds to Sebastián, the Caliban who spit in the master's face, who in the closing images is seen running through the woods toward freedom. Sebastián had told the other slaves that with his powers he would be able transform himself into a bird, a horse, a stone, and we see these images as Sebastián runs, machete in hand, to the top of a mountain. Though Sebastián had never read Abbé Raynal or Condorcet, he no doubt represents for Gutiérrez Alea the character who best embodies the Enlightenment ideals of freedom and self-reliance.

In this study, I have referred on several occasions to Carpentier's vision of history, especially in *Explosion in a Cathedral*, as telic (rather than ludic), as leading inexorably toward the historical denouement of the present. The same could be said about Gutiérrez Alea in *The Last Supper*. A good example of this historical "foreshadowing" of the future occurs toward the beginning of the film, when the parish priest has gathered some of the slaves into the chapel for a catechism. The priest explains what heaven is and why it is so desirable: "In heaven no one says this is mine and this is yours, because in heaven everything belongs to everyone and there is always enough of everything. Doesn't this sound like a good thing, a great thing? Doesn't this make you want to go to heaven?" During this celestial description, the viewer sees close-ups of the incredulous faces of the slaves. From the film's authorial point of view, a perspective that includes the present moment, the real reference of the catechism is clear. The objectives of the Cuban Revolution, as seen by Gutiérrez Alea, would be to create the reality that the priest describes not in the afterlife beyond but rather in the kingdom of *this* world.

But this depiction of the eighteenth century was Gutiérrez Alea's only cinematic excursion into the century of the Enlightenment. Like Marie Chauvet, who turned from historical fiction in *Dance on the Volcano* to an "intimist" tale, to echo the language of Maryse Condé, of sexuality in *Amour, colère et folie*, Gutiérrez Alea's 1993 film *Strawberry and Chocolate* enacts the ideological shift to a postmodern vision that I have discussed. In it, the Cuban director directs his attention to a more personal narrative involving sexual orientation and its disharmony with the traditional view of the Cuban revolutionary.

Gutiérrez Alea's well-known *Memories of Underdevelopment* (1968) provided a study in alienation, but one would hesitate to characterize it as postmodern since the understood authorial perspective of this film is the Cuban Revolution. In this film, the alienated bourgeois protagonist, Sergio, makes a pronouncement regarding a fleeting girlfriend that expands into a judgment on the Cuban people:

> One of the things that disconcerts me the most about people is their inability to maintain a feeling, an idea without dispersion. . . . That's one of the

> signs of underdevelopment: inability to accumulate experience and develop. It's pure alienation, as Ortega would say. It's difficult to find a woman here molded by feelings and culture. The atmosphere is too soft. All the talent of the Cuban is wasted in adapting to the moment. The people aren't consistent. And they always need someone to think for them.[13]

Sergio's judgment here seems to have an uncanny similarity to Kant's formulation that the Enlightenment entails an exit or emergence from one's self-imposed tutelage or immaturity. In the introduction, I discussed the rhetorical ambiguity surrounding the word *Menschheit*; a similar rhetorical slippage occurs here in Sergio's declaration in which a single Cuban woman (Elena) becomes a synecdoche for the Cuban people and their condition of "underdevelopment." Kant's concept of immaturity has now evolved into an articulation of underdevelopment, in which the Cuban, and by extension, Caribbean, people[14] (in Sergio's judgment) are unable to avail themselves of either personal or historical experience in order to progress. It seems rather clear that Gutiérrez Alea's response to Sergio is the Cuban Revolution itself, and the people's solidarity in the film's final scenes, as the masses prepare for an impending U.S. invasion during the Cuban Missile Crisis, is in stark contrast to Sergio's secluded and solitary anxiety.[15] For Gutiérrez Alea, the Cuban Revolution represents precisely a rebuttal to Sergio (and Kant) and amounts to a maturation, a cumulative availing of historical experience and a seizing of self-determination.

In *Strawberry and Chocolate*, which appeared some twenty-five years after *Memories of Underdevelopment*, the film's authorial consciousness, so to speak, is now clearly aligned with the protagonist rather than opposed to him. If, in *The Last Supper*, Gutiérrez Alea portrayed in detail aspects of African culture and mythology in Cuba (even if the historical veracity of these details was somewhat speculative)[16] and incorporated these characteristics into a wide-lens view of the unfolding of Cuban nationhood, in *Strawberry and Chocolate* Diego, an openly gay man in the Cuba of the early 1970s, has no such traditionally viewed role in Cuba. Diego's isolation in the film correlates rhetorically to the absence of historical narrative of the gay subject in Cuban history.[17] In the film's conclusion, Diego, dismissed from his job, persecuted by the authorities, and isolated, is forced against his will to emigrate, revealing another side of the Cuban emigration that is a far cry from "the stupid Cuban bourgeoisie" that Sergio belittles in *Memories*.

Gutiérrez Alea's commiseration with this state of affair signals an ideological transition and a shift to a postmodern expression in the Caribbean. From a depiction of the comeuppance of the Cuban masses pitted against a bourgeois notion of individualist subjectivity embodied in Sergio in *Memories of Underdevelopment* to a portrait of a slave rebellion in *The Last Supper* as a spark or origin of the Cuban national unfolding, the 1990s portrait of Diego in *Strawberry and Chocolate* (significantly, though the film was released in 1993, at the beginning of the austerity measures of the Cuban "Special Period," the film takes place in the early 1970s) is not a portrait painted with wide historical strokes, but rather an "intimist" depiction of a social problem. Diego's departure from Cuba is no longer a symptom of a binary state of Cuban affairs that pitted patriots against traitors, revolutionaries against *gusanos*. The question of emigration in the Caribbean has ruptured many of the notions and contradictions of modernity, so that we may now in fact speak of a Caribbean Diaspora so vast that it at last defies that very founding opposition between center and periphery. We are left instead with a demographic and cultural situation that explodes the notion of a fixed geography and replaces it instead with a floating economy of a here-there, *acá-allá*, dynamic of which Carpentier was so fond in his later works.[18]

Notes

Introduction

1. Alonso, *The Burden of Modernity.*
2. Todorov, *Le siècle des lumières*, 22–26.
3. Muthu, *Enlightenment against Empire*, 13, 259.
4. "These forces, varying among the empires, produced political autonomy differently on different islands, transmitted democracy at different times and with different intensities, produced rebellion or resistance among planters to imperial power, led to management of the maritime part of the system with different kinds of market politics and administrative apparatuses, and produced environments in which slave sugar production was introduced easily or with great difficulty. And they varied over time, which produced higher degrees of entrenchment of slave societies on the early-developed islands, produced societies that had, and had not, experienced the French Revolution, and produced an environment for plantation growth in which planters would buy slaves, contract Asian labor, or hire free proletarians moving among islands, depending on the historical situation" (Stinchcombe, *Sugar Island Slavery in the Age of Enlightenment*, 8).
5. Foucault, "What Is Enlightenment?" 33.
6. Kant, "An Answer to the Question, What Is Enlightenment?" in *Kant's Political Writings*, 54.
7. Foucault, "What Is Enlightenment?" 33. Intriguingly, the translator of Ernst Cassirer's classic study renders *Ausgang* as "exodus" (Cassirer, *The Philosophy of the Enlightenment*, 163).
8. Jameson, "The Realist Floor-Plan," 373.
9. Žižek, *The Sublime Object of Ideology*, 80.
10. Ibid.
11. Sala-Molins, *The Dark Side of Light*, 16.
12. Ibid., 11.
13. Ibid., 8.
14. Nesbitt, *Universal Emancipation*, 217n.

15. Foucault, "What Is Enlightenment?" 35.
16. Todorov, *L'esprit des lumières*, 31.
17. Muthu, *Enlightenment against Empire*, 130.
18. Nesbitt, *Universal Emancipation*, 103.
19. Muthu, *Enlightenment against Empire*, 123.
20. Fischer, *Modernity Disavowed*, 2–4.
21. Fischer also points to more recent thinkers such as Hannah Arendt, Marshall Berman, and Jürgen Habermas who do not take slavery fully into account in their understanding of the modernity's evolution. Despite an excellent extended discussion of Paul Gilroy's *The Black Atlantic*, Fischer, in my view, gives short shrift to Caribbean thinkers who *do* indeed fully incorporate slavery and racism into their articulation of modernity, such as José Martí, C. L. R. James, Frantz Fanon, and others.
22. Buck-Morss, *Hegel, Haiti and University History*, 42.
23. Fischer, *Modernity Disavowed*, 11.
24. Nesbitt does not actually suggest that the *philosophes* were required reading for the slaves in order for them to envisage freedom. He does imply that according to Kant's conceptualization of humans as cultural, reasoning beings, the slaves were interpellated or imagined readers of Kant.
25. Trouillot, *Silencing the Past*.
26. Buck-Morss, *Hegel, Haiti and Universal History*, 50. Buck-Morss is quoting from Trouillot.
27. Ibid., 73.
28. Dussel, *The Invention of the Americas*, 20.
29. Trouillot, *Silencing the Past*, 80.
30. Eze, *Race and Enlightenment*, 3.
31. Dussel, *The Invention of the Americas*, 20.
32. Kant quoted in Eze, *Race and the Enlightenment*, 64.
33. Ibid, 63.
34. Ibid, 64.
35. Ibid, 8.
36. Trouillot, *Silencing the Past*, 78.
37. Ibid., 52, final emphasis added.
38. Muthu, *Enlightenment against Empire*, 147.
39. Ibid., 183.
40. Kant quoted in Muthu, *Enlightenment against Empire*, 187–88. In a constellation intended to expand upon my assertion that this issue is relevant for Caribbean history and culture, Silvio Torres-Saillant responds in a "Kantian" manner to Doris Sommer's criticism of Pedro Mir's *Cuando amaban la tierras comuneras*. For Sommer, Mir's celebration of the "soil" is "reminiscent of a 'Volkish Romanticism'" and has "reactionary implications." Torres-Saillant responds: "Sommer's position fails to consider the role of the land in the development of the Dominican nation. One need only delve in the pages of the country's

historical experience to find that this land has historically suffered through the impending threat of occupation, annexation, or of being mortgaged by foreign imperial forces" (Torres-Saillant, *Caribbean Poetics*, 267–68).

41. Martínez, *La Ilustración en América*, 34–37.
42. Harris, *Absolutism and Enlightenment*, 262.
43. Paz, *Los hijos del limo*.
44. Arciniegas, *Caribbean: Sea of the New World*, 268
45. Ibid., 275.
46. Hussey, "Traces of French Enlightenment in Colonial Hispanic America," 34.
47. Harris, *Absolutism and Enlightenment*, 262.
48. Hussey, "Traces of French Enlightenment in Colonial Hispanic America," 25.
49. Ibid., 28.
50. Arciniegas, *Caribbean: Sea of the New World*, 273.
51. Trouillot, *Silencing the Past*, 81, 85.
52. Fischer, *Modernity Disavowed*, 42.
53. Hussey, "Traces of French Enlightenment in Colonial Hispanic America," 26.
54. Whitaker, "Changing and Unchanging Interpretations of the Enlightenment in Spanish America," 256–71. Whitaker concludes that the most noteworthy development in the study of the Enlightenment in Latin America is the emergence of and further need for regional studies in a move away from overly broad generalizations concerning the Enlightenment in Latin America as a whole.
55. Arciniegas, "La Ilustración en Latinoamérica," 51. It should be noted that the meeting between Pétion and Bolívar in Haiti would represent a special triumph of enlightened thought for C. L. R. James. James, though, dialecticizes his thought so that this triumph also transforms the form and content of the Enlightenment itself: "Toussaint L'Ouverture and the Haitian slaves brought into the world more than the abolition of slavery. When Latin Americans saw that small and insignificant Haiti could win and keep independence they began to think that they ought to be able to do the same. Pétion, the ruler of Haiti, nursed back to health the sick and defeated Bolívar, gave him money, arms and a printing press to help in the campaign which ended in the freedom of the Five States" (James, *The Black Jacobins*, 411).
56. Paz, *The Labyrinth of Solitude*, 117–18.
57. Beverly, *Against Literature*, 10–12.
58. O'Gorman, *La invención de América*, 159.
59. See Joan Dayan's reading of the Code Noir as an Enlightenment text ("Codes of Law and Bodies of Color," 41–67).
60. Gikandi, *Writing in Limbo*, 3.
61. Arciniegas, *Caribbean: Sea of the New World*, 275.
62. There is still no better discussion of these "contradictions"—both per-

sonal and intellectual—than in Roberto González Echevarría's *Alejo Carpentier: The Pilgrim at Home* (see esp. 19–33). Perhaps the most anecdotally provocative of these contradictions is the fact that Carpentier, whose father was French, had a speech impediment that gave his Spanish what seemed to be a strong French accent. He was regularly taken to be a foreigner in Cuba.

63. Wilson-Tagoe, writing about the historical imagination in the Anglophone Caribbean or West Indian imagination, describes an evolution of historicity away from theological concerns to dialectics, which nevertheless retains the trace of a former transcendence: "The movement was towards transcendence, a religious goal which, though challenged by Renaissance and rationalist philosophers, remains fundamental to European historical thought. For what the secular philosophical traditions really did was replace the religious motive with a rationalist explanation. This perspective, which envisioned the laws of history as dictated by dialectics, implied that the meaning of history lay in this world and that a certain metaphysical determinism held the key to this meaning." This description, even its language ("this world") is certainly evocative of Carpentier's historical imagination as well (Wilson-Tagoe, *Historical Thought and Literary Representation in West Indian Literature*, 15).

64. Dayan, *Haiti, History and the Gods*, 182–86.

65. Quoted in Beverly and Oviedo, introduction to *The Postmodernism Debate in Latin America*, 2.

66. Quoted in Fornet, introduction to *El siglo de las luces*, by Alejo Carpentier, 54.

67. Larsen, "Postmodernism and Imperialism," 111.

68. Phaf, "Caribbean Imagination and Nation-Building in Antillean and Surinamese Literature," 155.

69. Ibid., 70 n. 30.

70. Price, *Alabi's World.*

71. van Neck-Yoder, "Introduction."

72. Phaf, "Caribbean Imagination and Nation-Building in Antillean and Surinamese Literature," 157.

1. Carpentier and the Temporalities of Mutual Exclusion

1. Moreiras, "Hybridity and Double Consciousness," 375.
2. Fanon, *The Wretched of the Earth*, 41.
3. Coronil, "Transculturation and the Politics of Theory," ix–lvi.
4. Marinello, "Una novela cubana," 171.
5. Benítez-Rojo, "Alejo Carpentier," 269–83.
6. Carpentier, "Problemática de la actual novela latinoamericana," 11–12.
7. In her reading of *The Kingdom of This World*, Barbara J. Webb formulates Carpentier's fissure in another manner: "Since [Carpentier] does not share the religious beliefs of the slaves, how then can he portray the "marvelous" aspects of the Saint Domingue uprising without resorting to the same literary

"tricks" for which he criticized the surrealists?" (Webb, *Myth and History in Caribbean Fiction*, 31).

8. Carpentier, *Ecue-Yamba-O*, 10. See Robin Moore's *Nationalizing Blackness*, 191–213, for a very informative review of Carpentier's activity in the vanguardist movement in Cuba.

9. Coronil, "Transculturation and the Politics of Theory," xliv.

10. Birkenmaier, *Alejo Carpentier y la cultura del surrealismo en América Latina*, 62.

11. Emery, *The Anthropological Imagination in Latin American Literature*, 33.

12. Ibid., 9.

13. Leante, "Confesiones sencillas de un escritor barroco," 22.

14. Carpentier quoted in Ambrosio Fornet, introduction to *El siglo de las luces*, 57.

15. González Echevarría, *Alejo Carpentier*, 80.

16. Leante, "Confesiones sencillas de un escritor barroco," 22.

17. Carpentier, *Ecue-Yamba-O*, 36–37.

18. Ibid., 40.

19. Ortiz, *La música afrocubana*, 166–67.

20. Birkenmaier, *Alejo Carpentier y la cultura del surrealismo en América Latina*, 63.

21. Kwabena Nketia, "African Music," 586.

22. In *Phaedrus*, Socrates says: "Other people use writing to record the past, but this invention has killed the faculty of memory among them. They do not feel the past anymore, for writing lacks the warmth of the human voice. With them everybody thinks he knows, whereas learning should be a secret" (quoted in Peek, "The Power of Words in African Arts," 43).

23. Birkenmaier, *Alejo Carpentier y la cultura del surrealismo en América Latina*, 63.

24. Foucault, *The Order of Things*, 56.

25. Carpentier, *Ecue-Yamba-O*, 97.

26. "In the black world, time is subject not to history but to liturgy, ensuring the rhythmic processes of life and preserving them" (González Echevarría, *Alejo Carpentier*, 84).

27. Carpentier, *Ecue-Yamba-O*, 11.

28. Or, according to Sokoloff, Carpentier had not yet decided between the rhetorical strategies of metonymy or metaphor (Noemi B. Sokoloff, "The Discourse of Contradiction: Metaphor, Metonymy and *El reino de este mundo*").

29. Verba, *Music and the French Enlightenment*, 77.

30. See ibid. for an overview of these issues.

31. Ibid., 42.

32. González Echevarría, *Alejo Carpentier*, 84; Birkenmaier, *Alejo Carpentier y la cultura del surrealismo en América Latina*, 100–116.

33. Carpentier, *Music in Cuba*. 61.

34. Ibid., 39.

35. Ibid., 163–64.

36. Smith, "Ausencia de Toussaint," 206.

37. Volek, "Análisis e interpretación de *El reino de este mundo* de Alejo Carpentier," 158.

38. Carpentier, *The Kingdom of This World*, trans. Harriet de Onís. Page numbers from this edition will be cited parenthetically in the chapter text.

39. Benítez Rojo, "Alejo Carpentier: Entre la música y la historia."

40. This process is reversed in Carpentier's short story "Viaje a la semilla" ("Journey Back to the Source"). Since time moves in reverse fashion in this story, the more modern waltz succumbs to the older minuet.

41. Soliman's inability to comprehend the statue of Pauline Bonaparte as representation is another instance of this. He is almost driven mad by the form that his hands recognize so well but that now houses an alien content.

42. Quoted in Verba, *The Music of the French Enlightenment*, 77.

43. Jonassaint, "De la complexité caraïbéenne," 37–58.

44. Benjamin, "Theses on the Philosophy of History," in *Illuminations*, 254–64.

45. Carpentier, Prologue to *El reino de este mundo*, 13.

46. And yet, complicating this dualism, we find that nature's apocalyptic leveling was foreshadowed by Ti Noël, who predicted early in the novel that a cyclone would complete the destructive work of men: "Un día daría la señal del gran levantamiento, y los Señores de Allá, encabezados por Damballah, por el Amo de los Caminos y por Ogún de los Hierros, traerían el rayo y el trueno, para desencadenar el ciclón que completaría la obra de los hombres" (33).

47. Carpentier, *Baroque Concerto*, 111.

48. Smith, "Ausencia de Toussaint," 279.

49. Ibid., 279.

2. Enlightened Hesitations

1. James, "Lectures on the Black Jacobins," 72.

2. James, *Beyond a Boundary*, 53.

3. See Kevin Meehan's compelling essay on James's direct and indirect political engagement with African American culture and politics (Meehan, "To Shake This Nation as Nothing Before Has Shaken It").

4. See Worcester, *C. L. R. James*.

5. James would later write about Trotsky: "the full, the complete significance of the creative power of the proletariat in the construction of the socialist economy always eluded him" (quoted in Worcester, *C. L. R. James*, 63; see also Bogues, *Caliban's Freedom*, 29–33).

6. Rabbitt, "C. L. R. James's Figuring of Toussaint-Louverture," 128.

7. James, *The Black Jacobins*, 291–92. Page numbers from this edition will be cited parenthetically in the chapter text.

8. Horkheimer and Adorno, *Dialectic of Enlightenment*, 43–80.

9. Quoted in James, *Black Jacobins*, 338n.

10. Spivak, "Can the Subaltern Speak?" 271–313. Spivak's enduring essay has relevance to the topic discussed in this chapter.

11. James, "Lectures on the Black Jacobins," 108.

12. Kant, *Kant's Political Writings*, 55.

13. Quoted in Scott, *Conscripts of Modernity*, 122.

14. Quoted in Rojas Osorio, "El impacto de la ilustración en el pensamiento latinoamericano." Carpentier also represents this colonial hypocrisy in *The Kingdom of This World*, when M. Lenormand de Mézy deplores the slaves' lack of demonstrative mourning when Mackandal is executed: "[He] commented with his devout wife on the Negroes' lack of feelings at the torture of one of their own—drawing therefrom a number of philosophical considerations on the inequality of the human races which he planned in a speech larded with Latin quotations" (Carpentier, *The Kingdom of This World*, 53).

15. Gay, *The Enlightenment*, 6.

16. James, "Lectures on the Black Jacobins," 78.

17. Scott, *Conscripts of Modernity*, 169.

18. Ibid, 99–101.

19. Trouillot, *Silencing the Past*, 85.

20. Buck-Morss, *Hegel, Haiti and Universal History*, 21.

21. Quoted in Lüsebrink, "Mise en fiction et conceptualization de la Révolution Haitienne: La genèse d'un discours littéraire (1789–1848)," 228.

22. David Scott ponders outright if this is indeed the case: "I regard as dissolvable and worthy of dissolution . . . the humanist assumption of a preconstituted slave Will to Resist or Will to Freedom" (Scott, *Conscripts of Modernity*, 122).

23. James, "Lectures on the Black Jacobins," 80.

24. The "Moses paradigm" is in keeping with "tragic structure" of *The Black Jacobins*, and yet James never makes the comparison. The absence of a theological metaphor was certainly intentional, as can be inferred by James's defensive response in "Dialectical Materialism and the Fate of Humanity": "Our anti-dialecticians believe the negation of negation and the inevitability of socialism are religion. But when one attempts to penetrate into *their* philosophy of history, one increasingly meets a vacuum or the most arbitrary combinations of historical phenomena, tied together by bits of string, by subjective analysis and a crude determinism which even sometimes has the presumption to call itself Marxism" (James, *C. L. R. James Reader*, 177). The entire question of James's "theological historiography" is most relevant to the text analyzed here.

25. Scott, *Conscripts of Modernity*, 123.

26. Nesbitt, *Universal Emancipation*, 45.

27. Ortiz, *Cuban Counterpoint*, 103.

28. Sala-Molins, *The Dark Side of Light*, 16.

29. Said, *Culture and Imperialism*, 253.

30. It is worth pointing out, however, that in James's theater version of *The Black Jacobins*, Dessalines is portrayed as more ambivalent regarding European culture. In the play, he requests that his paramour recite verses from Racine. I will comment more specifically on this scene in the next chapter.

31. Lamming continues: "It is not by accident that a document so rich in facts, so beautiful in narrative organisation, should have remained out of print for over twenty years" (Lamming, *The Pleasures of Exile*, 119).

32. See Fernandez Retamar, *Caliban and Other Essays.*

33. The obvious analogy, as the title of the appendix suggests, is between Castro and Toussaint, but there are parallels with Dessalines as well (for example the "purging" of the bourgeoisie and the resulting "brain-drain" or shortage of technical and managerial expertise), an extended discussion of which could be illuminating. Disappointingly, the title notwithstanding, James has little to say about the Cuban Revolution in this somewhat rambling appendix. The following passage typifies James's elusive approach to the question: "I do not propose to plunge this appendix into the turbulent waters of controversy about Cuba. I have written about the West Indies in general and Cuba is the most West Indian island in the West Indies. That suffices" (411). James is equally inscrutable, considering his prolific output, as regards Latin America in general, especially for a Marxist who grew up just miles off the coast of Venezuela. Santiago Colás has dealt with this issue valiantly in his essay "Silence and Dialectics: Speculation on C. L. R. James and Latin America" (Farred, *Rethinking C. L. R. James,* 131–63). The present chapter, too, by juxtaposing James and Carpentier, may be considered an attempt to bring James into the mix of questions concerning Latin American cultural studies. I will revisit the question of the Cuban Revolution and its significance in the Caribbean historical imagination in the conclusion.

34. Trouillot, *Silencing the Past*, 43.

35. Quoted in Dubois and Garrigus, *Slave Revolution in the Caribbean*, 168, emphasis added

36. Ibid., 188.

37. Muthu, *Enlightenment against Empire*, 87.

38. Dubois and Garrigus, *Slave Revolution in the Caribbean*, 108.

39. Ibid., 192.

40. "It was somewhat disappointing for me at first to discover how ideas were abandoned by Carpentier without being explored to the fullest; how, in other words, philosophical positions were loosely and episodically taken in his journalistic work, often to explain or justify his fictions. . . . But as Carpentier and modern Latin American writers denounced Western tradition, their search for a Latin American consciousness and mode of expression became, paradoxically, more European" (González Echevarría, *Alejo Carpentier*, 19).

41. Carpentier, *Afirmación literaria americanista*, 12.

42. As we shall see in later chapters, both Reinaldo Arenas and Edgardo Rodríguez Juliá avail themselves of real historical figures as well, but with radically different intentions. Arenas's preferred figure, Fray Servando, was a Mexican revolutionary theologian whose story is well known. This gives Arenas's "hallucinatory" version of Fray Servando's biography a polemical or contestatory edge concerning the nature of historical writing in general. On the other hand, Rodríguez Julia's point of departure for his historical fantasy is already a text: a painted portrait from nineteenth-century Puerto Rico.

43. Bernard Moitt reproaches James on these grounds: "A reading of *The Black Jacobins* suggests, however, that James either ignored or disregarded works written at a much earlier time . . . which may well have given him valuable insights into slavery. One may therefore take James to task for not reading more of the general literature that would have sharpened his understanding of the nuances of slavery in the French Antilles" (Moitt, "Transcending Linguistic and Cultural Frontiers in Caribbean Historiography," 138). James could be defended on the grounds that he was attempting to write an account of the Haitian Revolution, not a sociology of slavery, but Moitt's criticism is consistent with my observation that James's "masses"—comprised of none other than these slaves—are too monolithic and idealized. Moitt also points out that "James's portrait of slavery in San Domingo is too broad and general. It does not illustrate the complexity of slavery in the French Antilles."

44. Said, *Culture and Imperialism*, 253.

3. Conflicted Epiphanies

1. Dayan, *Haiti, History and the God*, 303 n. 75.

2. Scharfman, "Theorizing Terror," 230.

3. Dayan, *Haiti, History and the Gods*, 119–20.

4. The novel has been discussed in the context of Freud's *Beyond the Pleasure Principle* in Serrano, "La dérive du plaisir."

5. Scharfman, "Theorizing Terror," 244.

6. Dash, *The Other America*, 18.

7. Dayan, *Haiti, History and the Gods*, 83.

8. Ibid., 84.

9. Chauvet, *Dance on the Volcano*, trans. Salvator Attanasio, 1. Originally published as *La danse sur le volcan* in 1957. Page numbers from the translated edition will be cited parenthetically in the chapter text.

10. "The reader must be warned that the story he is going to read is based on rigorous documentation which not only respects the historical truth of the events, the names of the characters (even the minor ones), of the places, and even of the streets, but which also conceals under its apparently non-chronological facade a minute collation of dates and chronologies" (Carpentier, prologue to *The Kingdom of This World*).

11. Fouchard quotes an eighteenth-century travelogue: "Saint Domingue is dancing upon a volcano. Its masters and lords amuse themselves. Meanwhile, how many of them are concerned with the slave's sufferings?" (Fouchard, *Le Théâtre à St-Domingue* 351).

12. Fouchard wonders about this historical figure, "Was Mesplès ever a good person in his entire life?" (Fouchard, *Le Théâtre à St-Domingue*, 164).

13. Ibid., 304.

14. According to Joan Dayan, "Chauvet occupied a very privileged position as a beautiful, light-skinned member of the Port-au-Prince bourgeoisie" (Dayan, *Haiti, History and the Gods*, 119).

15. Fouchard, *Le Théâtre à St-Domingue*, 331.

16. The original French also emphasizes the act of seeing: "Tout cela à cause de ce dos saignant qu'elle avait sous les yeux et qui semblait être venu là, exprès, pour lui faire voir, si jamais elle l'avait oublié, comment pouvait être un dos d'esclave quand il avait subi la peine du fouet" (Chauvet, *La Danse sur le volcan*, 38).

17. James, *The Black Jacobins*, 74.

18. Fouchard, *Le Théâtre à St-Domingue*, 344. Fouchard speculates that the historical Minette and Lise probably lost their lives in this fire. Most other sources report this catastrophic fire as occurring in October 1791.

19. James, *The Black Jacobins*, 129.

20. Chancy, *Framing Silence*.

21. Pétion would go on to succeed Dessalines as leader of the southern part of the independent republic while Christophe controlled the north. In 1815, he gave succor to a defeated and ailing Simón Bolívar and supplied him with arms and a printing press (James, *The Black Jacobins*, 411; see also Dubois, *Avengers of the New World*, 303).

22. Dayan, *Haiti, History and the Gods*, 154–55.

23. The fictional Lapointe, with his fierce hatred of the slaves and repudiation of the whites, might have been modeled after the *affranchi* leader André Rigaud, who opposed Toussaint in the so-called "War of the Knives": "Rigaud was undoubtedly narrow-minded. He wore always a brown wig with straight hair to give him an appearance as close to that of a white man as possible. This sensitiveness to color is usually accompanied in active men by great bitterness against the oppressing race, and the narrowness of Rigaud's organization and his exclusion of whites and blacks from all positions of power undoubtedly owed something to his personal character. But fundamentally it lay in the very circumstances of the Mulattoes. They were hopelessly outnumbered by the blacks" (James, *The Black Jacobins*, 181).

24. González Echevarría, "Literature of the Hispanic Caribbean," 1–19.

25. Two excellent examples (among many) of this device can be found in Gabriel García Márquez's *Chronicle of a Death Foretold* (*Crónica de una muerte*

anunciada) as well as his short story “The Last Voyage of the Ghost Ship” (“El último viaje del buque fantasma”).

26. “At the Cap they issued an order that forbade this degraded class from wearing shoes. They then appeared in sandles [*sic*], with diamonds on the toes of their feet” (quoted in Dayan, *Haiti, History and the Gods*, 179; Dayan is quoting Madame Laurette Aimée Mozard Nicodami Ravinet’s *Mémoires d’une Créole du Port-au-Prince*).

27. Ibid., 170–86.

28. James, *The Black Jacobins*, 37.

29. The racial resentment inspired by Minette’s ascendancy—however verisimilitudinous—is Chauvet’s novelistic invention and does not seem to figure in Fouchard’s history.

30. See Meehan, “Titid ak pep la se marasa,” as well as Aristide’s own *In the Parish of the Poor.*

31. Löwy, “The Historical Meaning of Christianity of Liberation in Latin America,” 351–52.

32. See Fouchard, *Le Théâtre à St-Domingue*, 348.

33. James, *The Black Jacobins*, 124.

34. Serrano, “Deux romans de Marie Vieux-Chauvet,” 101.

35. Cited in Lüsebrink, “Mise en fiction et conceptualization de la Révolution Haitienne,” 228.

36. Fick, *The Making of Haiti*, 40–45.

37. James, “The Black Jacobins,” in *The C. L. R. James Reader*, 106.

38. Fouchard, *Le Théâtre à St-Domingue*, 321, emphasis added.

39. Ibid., 343–44.

40. Scharfman, “Theorizing Terror,” 240.

4. Alliances and Enmities in Maryse Condé’s Historical Imagination

1. Condé, *La parole des femmes*, 101.

2. Ibid., 100.

3. Condé, “The Stealers of Fire,” 163.

4. Condé, *I, Tituba, Black Witch of Salem*, trans. Richard Philcox, 3. Page numbers from this translation will be cited parenthetically in the chapter text.

5. Condé, *Traversée de la mangrove*, 219.

6. Dash, *The Other America*, 18.

7. Jean Jonassaint’s discussion of Chauvet’s *Amour* further convinces me that it may be premature to speak of this fine *récit* as “postmodern.” Jonassaint refers to Chauvet’s use of the French language in *Amour* as “un français pur, de France,” which he sees as against the grain of the predominant Haitian tradition of the time. This linguistic trait is strikingly reminiscent of the references to

"impeccable" French in *Dance on the Volcano* (Jonassaint, "De la complexité caraïbéenne," 54).

8. Condé, *In the Time of Revolution*, 454–93.

9. González Echevarría, "Literature of the Hispanic Caribbean," 4.

10. Lukács, *The Historical Novel*, 20.

11. Nesbitt, *Voicing Memory*, 201.

12. Glissant, *Caribbean Discourse*, 66.

13. See ibid., 49–50.

14. Ibid., 200.

15. Condé, *In the Time of Revolution*, 490 n. 3. The name "Zephyr" is attributed to a Haitian writer, Jacques Stephen Alexis.

16. Nesbitt, *Voicing Memory*, 193.

17. Bécel, "*Moi, Tituba Sorcière . . . Noire de Salem* as a Tale of Petite Marronne," 610.

18. González Echevarría, *Alejo Carpentier*, 237.

19. Whether or not the specific telos of *Explosion in a Cathedral* was the Cuban Revolution remains an interesting and open question (see ibid., 215–22).

20. Debrauwere-Miller, "Au Carrefour de la négritude et du Judaïsme," 223–33.

21. Fanon, *Black Skin, White Masks*, 115.

22. Ibid., 42.

23. Condé, "Order, Disorder, Freedom, and the West Indian Writer," 161.

24. Bécel, "*Moi, Tituba Sorcière . . . Noire de Salem* as a Tale of Petite Marronne," 612.

25. Nevertheless, this generalization about Caribbean literature cannot be considered universal. Derek Walcott describes in sumptuous detail the *Ramleela*, the festive celebration of the Hindu epic the *Ramayana*, as an example of historical memory and continuity in the Caribbean that is in opposition to the more accepted idea of historical rupture and fragmentation (Walcott, *The Antilles*).

26. Benjamin, *Illuminations*, 83.

27. Condé, "Order, Disorder, Freedom, and the West Indian Writer," 151–65.

28. For further discussion of efforts to transform the patriarchal roots of nationalist narratives in the Caribbean, see Meehan, "Romance and Revolution."

5. Cuban Cogito

1. "Though coherent, Diderot's political philosophy is inherently unstable, indeed explosive: if legitimate government is rooted in the principle of the 'general will,' then just and justifiable government is practically realizable only under an enlightened philosopher-king" (Israel, *Radical Enlightenment*, 79).

2. Horkheimer and Adorno, *Dialectic of Enlightenment*, 9.

3. Ibid., xv, 4.

4. A. González, "Una alegoría puertorriqueña," 584.

5. Arenas, *El mundo alucinante*, 22. Page numbers from Andrew Hurley's translation, *The Ill-fated Peregrinations of Fray Servando*, will be cited parenthetically in the chapter text. Nevertheless, due to its relative succinctness, I will continue to give the novel's title in the original Spanish.

6. See especially Eduardo G. González, "A razón de santo: Ultimos lances de fray Servando," and Pagni, "Palabra y subversión en *El mundo alucinante.*"

7. For the question of the influence (or lack thereof) of the Cuban Revolution on *Explosion in a Cathedral*, see Gonzalez Echevarría, *Alejo Carpentier*, 217–22.

8. Arenas, *Antes que anochezca*, 98.

9. Barrientos, "Reynaldo Arenas, Alejo Carpentier y la nueva novela hispanoamericana," 20.

10. Arenas, prologue to *El mundo alucinante*, 19.

11. The Venezuelan author Arturo Uslar Pietri attempts something along these lines in his *La isla de Robinson*, which depicts the historical figure Simón Rodríguez (1771–1854) as an enthusiastic proponent of the Enlightenment well into the nineteenth century. The historical Fray Servando and Rodríguez worked together in Paris and founded a Spanish-teaching school there.

12. Consider the kind of revolutionary fervor expressed by Sofía and Carlos when a jaded Esteban returns to Cuba from France in *Explosion in a Cathedral.*

13. Rotker, "Editor's Introduction," xxiv.

14. Ibid., xxv–xxviii.

15. Jameson, "The Realist Floor-Plan," 374.

16. Lourdes Tomás Fernández de Castro, *Fray Servando alucinado*; Perla Rozencvaig, *Reinaldo Arenas*; Elzbieta Sklodowska, "*El mundo alucinante*: Historia y ficción"; Pagni, "Palabra y subversión en *El mundo alucinante.*" Though it is not the main thrust of her argument, Tomás makes some insightful observations on this score, pointing out, for example, that "Gaceta" in Servando's *Memorias* becomes *Gaceta* in Arenas's version, referring specifically to a contemporary Cuban publication.

17. For an important article on this intertextuality, see Borinsky, "Re-escribir y escribir." In addition to Tomás and Rozencvaig, see also Eduardo C. Bejar, La textualidad de Reinaldo Arenas: Juegos de la escritura posmoderna. Barrientos's "Reynaldo Arenas, Alejo Carpentier y la nueva novela hispanoamericana" is particularly useful for understanding the precise textual correspondences taking place between Arenas and his historiographical predecessors.

18. Rozencvaig, "Reinaldo Arenas: Entrevista," 44.

19. See Barrientos, "Reynaldo Arenas, Alejo Carpentier y la nueva novela hispanoamericana."

20. Tomás, *Fray Servando alucinado*, 34.

21. Marengo, "*El mundo alucinante* y *El Siglo de las luces*," 113.

22. Quoted in Cerzo, "Del 'Discurso' al 'Recurso del Método,'" emphasis added.

23. Ibid., 97–98.
24. Derrida, "Cogito and the History of Madness," 56.
25. González Echevarría, *Alejo Carpentier*, 264.
26. Arenas, *Antes que anochezca*, 326.
27. This textual practice was paralleled by the identitarian vicissitudes in Arenas's life. As Rodríguez-Monegal observes, "Not even the spelling of his name is certain" (Rodríguez-Monegal, "The Labyrinthine World of Reinaldo Arenas," 126). One could also read his entire doctrine of gay sexuality articulated in *Antes que anochezca* as a "search for the opposite" in a similar framework.
28. Barrientos, "Reynaldo Arenas, Alejo Carpentier y la nueva novela hispanoamericana," 49.
29. Carpentier, *The Kingdom of This World*, 175.
30. Foucault, *History of Madness*, 537. Quoted in Eduardo G. González, "A razón de santo: Ultimos lances de Fray Servando," 601.
31. Descartes, "Meditations on First Philosophy," 15.
32. Ibid., 14.
33. Borinsky, "Re-escribir y escribir: Arenas, Menard, Borges, Cervantes, Fray Servando," 27. As we shall see in the following chapter, this conversion of temporality into a spatial, and specifically horizontal or expanding, metaphor is a trope of Caribbean postmodernity.
34. Rodríguez-Monegal, "The Labyrinthine World of Reinaldo Arenas," 128.
35. Descartes, "Meditations on First Philosophy," 13.
36. So much so that it seems likely that Bosch's *The Garden of Earthly Delights* is a clear source for the king's gardens.
37. Arenas, prologue to *El mundo alucinante*, 23.

6. Heightened Perceptions

1. Rodríguez Juliá, "Puerto Rico y el Caribe: Historia de una marginalidad," 513.
2. Torres-Saillant, *Caribbean Poetics*, 67.
3. Rodríguez Juliá, "Puerto Rico y el Caribe," 518.
4. Ibid., 518–20, emphasis added.
5. Nesbitt, *Voicing Memory*, 193.
6. R. González, *La historia puertorriqueña de Rodríguez Juliá*, xiv.
7. A. González, "Una alegoría de la cultura puertorriqueña," 584.
8. Rodríguez Juliá, "At the Middle of the Road," 126.
9. Camayd-Freixas, "Penetrating Texts," 17.
10. A. González, "Una alegoría puertorriqueña," 584.
11. Benítez-Rojo, *The Repeating Island*, 243.
12. Camayd-Freixas, "Penetrating Texts."
13. Benítez-Rojo, *The Repeating Island*, 258–59.

14. Camayd-Freixas, "Penetrating Texts," 10.

15. Rodríguez Juliá, *La noche oscura del Niño Avilés*, ix. Page numbers from this novel will be cited parenthetically in the chapter text.

16. He finds the triptych "among forgotten stacks of folios and discarded easels." This phrase bears an uncanny resemblance to Carpentier's language in *Music in Cuba* when he claims to have stumbled upon the scores of Esteban Salas "discovered in a forgotten drawer" (Carpentier, *La música en Cuba*, 12).

17. Jameson, "On Literary and Cultural Import-Substitution in the Third World," 182. "The canonical joke about this retrospective illusion, this projection of the present back into a past, for which that present was as yet utterly undreamed of, turns on the paradox of the birth date. . . . This is a thought mode most exquisitely parodied by that character of Raymond Roussel, who claimed to have seen, in a small provincial museum, under glass, 'the skull of Voltaire as a child'" (182).

18. See González Echevarría, *Alejo Carpentier*, 244.

19. Hutcheon, *A Theory of Parody*, 67.

20. Walcott, "The Muse of History," 37.

21. San José Vásquez, *Las luces de un siglo*, 193.

22. Rubén González, *La historia puertorriqueña de Rodríguez Juliá*, 68.

23. Franco, "The Nation as Imagined Community," 211.

24. Ríos Ávila, "La invención de un autor," 208.

25. Camayd-Freixas, "Penetrating Texts," 10.

26. A. González, "Una alegoría puertorriqueña," 584.

27. de Man, *Blindness and Insight*, 189.

28. See Todorov, *L'Esprit des lumières*, 27–41, for a discussion of this and other "détournements" of Enlightenment philosophy.

29. Ríos Ávila, "La invención de un autor," 208.

30. Soto-Crespo, "The Pains of Memory," for a discussion of the role of painting in this and other novels by Rodríguez Juliá.

31. Marx and Engels, *The German Ideology*, 37–38.

32. Carpentier, *El siglo de las luces*, 85.

33. Ibid., 7.

34. In a brief but insightful article, Jaime L. Martell-Morales identifies the narrator as Cadalso and situates historically the series of lectures in the 1930s, in which "the culturalist discourses were institutionalized as official versions of Puerto Rican history" (Martell-Morales "La heterotopía en la obra de Edgardo Rodríguez Juliá," 34).

35. Rodríguez Juliá, *The Renunciation*, trans. Andrew Hurley, 9. Page numbers from this translation of *La renuncia del héroe Baltasar* will be cited parenthetically in the chapter text.

36. Unamuno, *San Manuel Bueno, mártir*, 90.

37. This particular accusation against the slave who assimilates too well the forms of European or Creole discourse is an old one in the Caribbean. Car-

pentier, in *La música en Cuba*, speaks about "los negros catedráticos," the emancipated slaves who learned to perfection the turns of speech of the creole aristocracy in nineteenth-century Cuba. One particular work that makes of fun of the supposed pretensions of this class is Joaquín Lorenzo Luaces, *Los negros catedráticos*.

38. For example: "Lying upon the mansion's great divan we found don Rafael's naked torso, which had been placed in a most obscene posture, with its backside in the air, and tied to it—oh God!—the head of his faithful Negro overseer. So extreme had been the unspeakable barbarity committed here that almost the entire tongue of the unfortunate servant—a good black man, one of those who accept with blessed patience and docility their condition, and give thanks to God for the great favor which He has bestowed upon them, of living among a race which rears them up to Christianity and humanity . . . —into that part of his master's body which decorum begs me not to name" (93).

Conclusions

1. Habermas, "Modernity—An Incomplete Project," 9.
2. Williams, *The Postmodern Novel in Latin America*, 37.
3. Condé and Pfaff, *Conversations with Maryse Condé*, 37–38.
4. Rodríguez-Monegal, "The Labyrinthine World of Reinaldo Arenas," 131.
5. Interestingly, Barbara J. Webb discerns the seeds of parody already in *El reino*: "[T]he manifestations of the marvelous in *El reino* are often ironic, verging on caricature and parody" (Webb, *Myth and History in Caribbean Fiction*, 37).
6. Fornet, *Las máscaras del tiempo*, 21.
7. Castro, *Palabras a los intelectuales*, 13.
8. Schroeder, *Tomás Gutiérrez Alea*, 79.
9. Ibid., 79.
10. Gutiérrez Alea, *La última cena*.
11. Horkheimer and Adorno, *Dialectic of Enlightenment*, 9.
12. Jaehne, "*The Last Supper* by Tomas Gutiérrez Alea," 53.
13. Gutiérrez Alea, *Memorias del subdesarrollo*.
14. In one of Sergio's most comical and cynical moments, he observes that in postrevolutionary Cuba, Havana, which used to be known as the Paris of the Caribbean, now more resembles a "Tegucigalpa of the Caribbean."
15. For an analysis of Leo Brouwer's musical score that accompanies and provides an interpretation of these scenes in *Memorias*, see my essay "Reading Caribbean Music."
16. "Here Alea met with the sad fact that, compared to the amount of historical information available to accurately reconstruct the worldview, gestures, and speech of the Count, there existed almost no information on how slaves in eighteenth century Cuba thought, talked or acted. Luckily, Alea was able to enlist the help of Tomás González and María Eugenia Haya, who contributed

immensely to the film's veracity and complexity by researching and integrating into the script important aspects of African folklore and mythology" (Schroeder, *Tomás Gutiérrez Alea*, 83–83).

17. For an attempt to reconstruct this elusive history and link it explicitly to the narratives of Cuban nationhood, see Bejel, *Gay Cuban Nation*.

18. A recent example of this expression of an unrooted Caribbean spatial imagination is Junot Díaz's *The Brief Wondrous Life of Oscar Wao*. In this remarkable novel, the "intimist" portrait of the characters occupies the body of the text while the "historical" commentary on the reign of Trujillo in the Dominican Republic occupies the extended footnotes.

Works Cited

Abbad y Lasierra, Iñigo. *Historia geográfica, civil y política de la isla de San Juan Bautista de Puerto Rico.* Rio Piedras: Universidad de Puerto Rico, Editorial Universitaria, 1966.

Aldridge, A. Owen. "The Enlightenment in the Americas." In *Actes du VIIe Congrès de l'Association Internationale de Littérature Comparée*, 59–67. Stuttgart: Kunst und Wissen, 1980.

Alonso, Carlos J. *The Burden of Modernity: The Rhetoric of Cultural Discourse in Spanish America.* New York: Oxford University Press, 1998.

———. "The Mourning After: García Marquez, Fuentes and the Meaning of Postmodernity in Spanish America." *MLN* 109, no. 22 (1994): 52–67.

———. *The Spanish American Regional Novel: Modernity and Autochthony.* New York: Cambridge University Press, 1990.

Arciniegas, Germán. *Caribbean: Sea of the New World.* Miami: Ian Randle, 2004.

———. "La Ilustración en Latinoamérica." In *Mélange à la mémoire de Jean Sarrailh*, 29–55. Paris: Centre de Recherches de L'Institut d'Etudes Hispaniques, 1966.

Arenas, Reinaldo. *Antes que anochezca.* Barcelona: Tusquets, 1996.

———. *Hallucinations.* Translated by Gordon Brotherston. New York: Harper and Row, 1968

———. *The Ill-fated Peregrinations of Fray Servando.* Translated by Andrew Hurley. New York: Avon, 1987

———. *El mundo alucinante.* Barcelona: Tusquets, 1997.

Aristide, Jean-Bertrand, and Amy Wilentz. *In the Parish of the Poor: Writings from Haiti.* Maryknoll, N.Y.: Orbis, 1990.

Barrientos, Juan José. "Reynaldo Arenas, Alejo Carpentier y la nueva novela hispanoamericana." In *Historia, ficción y metaficción en la novela latinoamericana contemporánea*, edited by Mignon Domínguez, 49–67. Buenos Aires: Corregidor, 1996.

Bécel, Pascale. "*Moi, Tituba Sorcière . . . Noire de Salem* as a Tale of Petite

Marronne," in "Maryse Condé," special issue, *Callaloo* 18, no. 3 (Summer 1995): 608–15.

Bejar, Eduardo C. *La textualidad de Reinaldo Arenas: Juegos de la escritura posmoderna*. Madrid: Editorial Playor, 1987.

Bejel, Emilio. *Gay Cuban Nation*. Chicago: University of Chicago Press, 2001.

Benítez Rojo, Antonio. "Alejo Carpentier: Entre la música y la historia." *La Torre* 8, no. 31 (1994): 269–83.

———. *The Repeating Island: The Caribbean and the Postmodern Perspective*. Translated by James E. Maraniss. Durham, N.C.: Duke University Press, 1992.

Benjamin, Walter. *Illuminations*. Edited by Hannah Arendt. Translated by Harry Zone. New York: Schocken, 1969.

Beverly, John. *Against Literature*, Minneapolis: University of Minnesota Press, 1993.

Beverly, John, and José Oviedo. Introduction to *The Postmodernism Debate in Latin America*, 2–17. Durham, N.C.: Duke University Press, 1995.

Birkenmaier, Anke. *Alejo Carpentier y la cultura del surrealismo en América Latina*. Madrid: Iberoamericana (Vervuert), 2006.

Bogues, Anthony. *Caliban's Freedom: The Early Political Thought of C. L. R. James*. Chicago: Pluto Press, 1997.

Borinsky, Alicia. "Re-escribir y escribir: Arenas, Menard, Borges, Cervantes, Fray Servando." *Revista Iberoamericana* 41, no. 92–93 (1975): 605–16.

Buck-Morss, Susan. *Hegel, Haiti and Universal History*. Pittsburgh: University of Pittsburgh Press, 2009.

Camayd-Freixas, Erik. "Penetrating Texts: Testimonial Pseudo Chronicles in *La noche oscura del Niño Avilés* by Edgardo Rodríguez Juliá Seen from Sigüenza y Gongora´s *Infortunios de Alonso Ramírez*." Paper presented at the First International Conference on Caribbean Literature. Nassau, Bahamas, November 6, 1998.

Carpentier, Alejo. *Afirmación literaria americanista*. Caracas: Ediciones de la Facultad de Humanidades y Educación, Universidad Central de Venezuela, 1978.

———. *Baroque Concerto*. Translated by Asa Zatz. London: Andre Deutsch, 1991.

———. *Concierto barroco*. Mexico City: Siglo Veintiuno, 1987.

———. *Ecue-Yamba-O*. Madrid: Alianza Editorial, 1989.

———. *The Kingdom of This World*. Translated by Harriet de Onís. New York: Farrar, Straus and Giroux, 1989.

———. *Music in Cuba*. Edited by Timothy Brennan. Translated by Alan West-Durán. Minneapolis: University of Minnesota Press, 2001.

———. *La música en Cuba*. Mexico City: Fondo de Cultura Económica, 1946

———. "Problemática de la actual novela latinoamericana." In *Tientos y diferencia*. Montevideo: Editorial Arca, n.d.

———. Prologue to *El reino de este mundo*. Santiago, Chile: Editorial Universitaria, 1967.

———. *El recurso del método*. Mexico City: Siglo Veintiuno Editores, 1974.

———. *El reino de este mundo*. Barcelona: Seix Barral, 1986.

———. *El siglo de las luces*. Edited by Ambrosio Fornet. Madrid: Cátedra, 1982.

———. "Viaje a la semilla." In *Guerra del tiempo y otros relatos*. Madrid: Alianza, 1988.

Cassirer, Ernst. *The Philosophy of the Enlightenment*. Translated by Fritz C. A. Koelln and James P. Pettegrove. Boston: Beacon Press, 1951.

Castro, Fidel. *Palabras a los intelectuales*. Havana: National Cultural Council, 1961.

Cerzo, María del C. "Del 'Discurso' al 'Recurso del Método': Descartes y Carpentier." *Sin nombre* 12, no. 2 (July–September1981) : 96–106.

Césaire, Aimé. *Toussaint L'Ouverture: La révolution française et le problème colonial*. Paris: Présence Africaine, 1981.

Chancy, Myriam J. A. *Framing Silence: Revolutionary Novels by Haitian Women*. New Brunswick, N.J.: Rutgers University Press, 1997.

Chauvet, Marie. *Amour, colère et folie*. Paris: Gallimard, 1968.

———. *Dance on the Volcano*. Translated by Salvator Attanasio. New York: William Sloan, 1959.

———. *La danse sur le volcan*. Paris: Librarie Plon, 1957.

Condé, Maryse. *I, Tituba, Black Witch of Salem*. Translated by Richard Philcox. New York: Ballantine, 1992.

———. *In the Time of the Revolution*. Translated by Doris Y. Kadish and Jean-Pierre Piriou. *Callaloo* 25, no. 2 (2002) : 454–93.

———. *Moi, Tituba sorcière . . . Noire de Salem*. Paris: Mercure de France, 1986.

———. "Order, Disorder, Freedom, and the West Indian Writer." *Yale French Studies* 97 (2000) : 151–65.

———. *La parole des femmes: Essai sur des romancières des Antilles de langue française*. Paris: L'Harmattan, 1979.

———. *Segou: Les murailles de terre*. Paris: Pocket, 2005.

———. "The Stealers of Fire." *Journal of Black Studies* 35, no. 2 (November 2004) : 154–64.

———. *Traversée de la mangrove*. Paris : Mercure de France, 1989.

Condé, Maryse, and Françoise Pfaff. *Conversations with Maryse Condé*. Lincoln: University of Nebraska Press, 1996.

Coronil, Fernando. "Transculturation and the Politics of Theory: Countering the Center, Cuban Counterpoint." Introduction to *Cuban Counterpoint: Tobacco and Sugar*, by Fernando Ortiz, translated by Harriet de Onís, ix–lvi. Durham, N.C.: Duke University Press, 1995.

Cudjoe, Selwyn R. *Resistance and Caribbean Literature.* Athens: Ohio University Press, 1980.

Dash, J. Michael. *The Other America: Caribbean Literature in a New World Context.* Charlottesville: University Press of Virginia, 1998.

Dayan, Joan. "Codes of Law and Bodies of Color." In *Penser la créolité*, edited by Maryse Condé and Madeleine Cottenet-Hage. Paris: Karthala, 1995.

———. *Haiti, History and the Gods.* Berkeley and Los Angeles: University of California Press, 1998.

de Man, Paul. *The Resistance to Theory.* Minneapolis: University of Minnesota Press, 1986.

———. "The Rhetoric of Temporality." In *Blindness and Insight: Essays in the Rhetoric of Contemporary Criticism.* Minneapolis: University of Minnesota Press, 1971.

Debrauwere-Miller, Nathalie. "Au Carrefour de la négritude et du Judaïsme: *Moi: Tituba sorcière . . . noire de Salem.*" *Romanic Review* 90, no. 2 (March 1999): 223–33.

Derrida, Jacques. "Cogito and the History of Madness." In *Writing and Difference*, by Derrida, translated by Alan Bass. Chicago: University of Chicago Press, 1978.

Descartes, René. "Meditations on First Philosophy." Translated by John Cottingham, Robert Stoothoff, and Dugald Murdoch. In *The Philosophical Writings of Descates,* vol. 2. Cambridge: Cambridge University Press, 1984.

Díaz, Junot. *The Brief Wondrous Life of Oscar Wao.* New York: Riverhead, 2007

Dubois, Laurent. *Avengers of the New World: The Story of the Haitian Revolution.* Cambridge: Belknap Press of Harvard University Press, 2004.

Dubois, Laurent, and John D. Garrigus. *Slave Revolution in the Caribbean, 1789–1804: A Brief History with Documents.* Boston: Bedford/St. Martin's, 2006.

Dussel, Enrique. *The Invention of the Americas: Eclipse of "the Other" and the Myth of Modernity.* Translated by Michael D. Barber. New York: Continuum, 1995.

Emery, Amy Fass. *The Anthropological Imagination in Latin American Literature.* Columbia: University of Missouri Press, 1996.

Eugenio Martínez, María Ángeles. *La Ilustración en América (siglo XVIII): Pelucas y casacas en los trópicos.* Madrid: Anaya, 1988.

Eze, Emmanuel Chukwudi. *Race and the Enlightenment: A Reader.* Cambridge, Mass.: Blackwell, 1997.

Fanon, Frantz. *Black Skin, White Masks.* Translated by Charles Lam Markmann. New York: Grove Weidenfeld, 1967.

———. *Peau noire, masques blancs.* Paris: Éditions du Seuil, 1971.

———. *The Wretched of the Earth.* New York: Grove Press, 1963.

Farred, Grant, ed. *Rethinking C. L. R. James.* Cambridge: Blackwell, 1996.

Fernandez Retamar, Roberto. *Caliban and Other Essays.* Translated by Edward

Baker. Minneapolis: University of Minnesota Press, 1989.
Fick, Carolyn. *The Making of Haiti: The Saint Domingue Revolution from Below*. Knoxville: University of Tennessee Press, 1990.
Fischer, Sibylle. *Modernity Disavowed: Haiti and the Cultures of Slavery in the Age of Revolution*. Durham, N.C.: Duke University Press, 2004.
Fornet, Ambrosio. Introduction to *El siglo de las luces*, by Alejo Carpentier, 13–57. Madrid: Cátedra, 1982.
———. *Las máscaras del tiempo*. Havana: Letras Cubanas, 1995.
Foucault, Michel. *History of Madness*. Translated by Jean Khalfa and Jonathan Murphy. London: Routledge, 2006.
———. *The Order of Things*. New York: Vintage, 1973.
———. *Surveiller et punir: Naissance de la prison*. Paris: Gallimard, 1975.
———. "What Is an Author?" In *The Foucault Reader*, edited by Paul Rabinow. New York: Pantheon, 1984.
———. "What Is Enlightenment?" In *The Foucault Reader*, edited by Paul Rabinow. New York: Pantheon, 1984.
Fouchard, Jean. *The Haitian Maroons: Liberty or Death*. Translated by A. Faulkner Watts. New York: Edward W. Blyden Press, 1981.
———. *Le théâtre à St-Domingue*. Port-au-Prince: Imprimerie de l'État, 1955.
Franco, Jean. "The Nation as Imagined Community." In *The New Historicism*, edited by H. Aram Veeser, 204–12. New York: Routledge, 1989.
García Canclini, Néstor. *Culturas híbridas: Estrategias para entrary y salir de la modernidad*. Mexico City: Grijalbo, 1989.
García Márquez, Gabriel. *El general en su laberinto*. Buenos Aires: Editorial Sudamericana, 1989.
Gay, Peter. *The Enlightenment: An Interpretation: The Rise of Modern Paganism*. New York: Knopf, 1966.
Gikandi, Simon. *Writing in Limbo: Modernism and Caribbean Literature*. Ithaca, N.Y.: Cornell University Press, 1992.
Gilroy, Paul. *The Black Atlantic*. Cambridge: Harvard University Press, 1993.
Glissant, Édouard. *Caribbean Discourse*. Translated by J. Michael Dash. Charlottesville: University Press of Virginia, 1989.
Goldman, Lucien. *The Philosophy of the Enlightenment*. Translated by Henry Maas. Cambridge: MIT Press, 1973.
González, Aníbal. "Una alegoría puertorriqueña: *La noche oscura del Niño Avilés* de Edgardo Rodríguez Juliá." *Revista iberoamericana* 52, no. 135–36. (September–April 1986): 583–90.
González, Eduardo G. "A razón de santo: Ultimos lances de Fray Servando." *Revista Iberoamericana* 41 (1975): 93–603.
González, Rubén. *La historia puertorriqueña de Rodríguez Juliá*. San Juan: Editorial de la Universidad de Puerto Rico, 1997.
González Echevarría, Roberto. *Alejo Carpentier: The Pilgrim at Home*. 1977. Austin: University of Texas Press, 1990.

———. "Literature of the Hispanic Caribbean." *Latin American Literary Review* 8, no. 16 (Spring–Summer 1980): 1–19.

Gutiérrez Alea, Tomas. *La última cena*. ICAIC, 1976.

Gutiérrez Alea, Tomas, and Senel Paz. *Fresa y chocolate*. ICAIC, 1993.

Gutiérrez Alea, Tomas, and Edmundo Desnoes. *Memorias del subdesarrollo*. ICAIC, 1968.

Habermas, Jürgen. "Modernity—An Incomplete Project." In *The Anti-Aesthetic: Essays on Postmodern Culture*, edited by Hal Foster Port Townsend, 3–15. Washington: Bay Press, 1983.

Harris, Ronald Walter. *Absolutism and Enlightenment, 1660–1789*. London: Blandford, 1967.

Harvey, Salley. *Carpentier's Proustian Fiction: The Influence of Marcel Proust on Alejo Carpentier*. London: Tamesis, 1994.

Hegel, Georg Wilhelm Friedrich. *Lectures on the Philosophy of World History*. Translated by H. B. Nisbet. New York: Cambridge University Press, 1975.

Horkheimer, Max, and Theodor W. Adorno. *Dialectic of Enlightenment*. Translated by John Cumming. New York: Continuum, 1972.

Hussey, Roland D. "Traces of French Enlightenment in Colonial Hispanic America. *Latin America and the Enlightenment*," edited by Arthur P. Whitaker. New York: D. Appleton-Century, 1942.

Hutcheon, Linda. *A Theory of Parody: The Teachings of Twentieth-Century Art Forms*. New York: Methuen, 1985.

Israel, Jonathan I. *Radical Enlightenment: Philosophy and the Making of Modernity, 1650–1750*. Oxford: Oxford University Press, 2001.

James, C. L. R. *Beyond a Boundary*. Durham, N.C.: Duke University Press, 1993.

———. *The Black Jacobins: Toussaint L'Ouverture and the San Domingo Revolution*. New York: Vintage, 1963.

———. *The C. L. R. James Reader*. Edited by Anna Grimshaw. Cambridge; Mass.: Blackwell, 1992.

———. "Lectures on the Black Jacobins." *Small Axe* 8 (September 2000): 65–112.

Jameson, Fredric. "Nostalgia for the Present." *South Atlantic Quarterly* 88, no. 2 (1989): 517–37.

———. "On Literary and Cultural Import-Substitution in the Third World." In *The Real Thing: Testimonial Discourse and Latin America*, edited by Georg M. Gugelberger, 172–91. Durham, N.C.: Duke University Press, 1996.

———. "Postmodernism and Consumer Society." In *The Anti-Aesthetic: Essays on Postmodern Culture*, edited by Hal Foster. Port Townsend, Wash.: Bay Press, 1983. 111–25.

———. "The Realist Floor-Plan." In *On Signs*, edited by Marshall Blonsky, 370–80. Baltimore: Johns Hopkins University Press, 1985.

———. "Third-World Literature in the Era of Multinational Capitalism." *Social Text* 15 (Fall 1986): 65–88.

Jaehne, Karen. "The Last Supper by Tomás Gutiérrez Alea." *Film Quarterly* 33, no. 1 (Autumn 1979): 48–53.

Jonassaint, Jean. "De la complexité caraïbéenne: Notes sur une impasse théorique." *Francofonia* 49 (2005) : 37–58.

Judovitz, Dalia. "Derrida and Descartes: Economizing Thought." In *Derrida and Deconstruction*, edited by Hugh J. Silverman, 40–58. New York: Routledge, 1989.

Kant, Immanuel. *Kant's Political Writings*. Translated and edited by Hans Reiss. New York: Cambridge University Press, 1970.

Kwabena Nketia, J. H. "African Music." In *Peoples and Cultures of Africa: An Anthropological Reader*, edited by Elliot P. Skinner. New York: Doubleday/Natural History Press, 1973.

Lamming, George. *Natives of My Person*. New York: Allison and Busby, 1971.

———. *The Pleasures of Exile*. Ann Arbor: University of Michigan Press, 1991.

Larsen, Neil. "Postmodernism and Imperialism: Theory and Politics in Latin America." In *The Postmodern Debate in Latin America*, edited by John Beverly, José Oviedo, and Michael Aronna. Durham, N.C.: Duke University Press, 1995.

Leante, César. "Confesiones sencillas de un escritor barroco." In *Homenaje a Alejo Carpentier: Variaciones interpretativas en torno de su obra*, edited by Helmy F. Giacoman. New York: Las Américas, 1970.

Lorenzo Luaces, Joaquín. *Los negros catedráticos*. In *Teatro del siglo XIX*. Havana: Editorial Letras Cubanas, 1986.

Löwy, Michael. "The Historical Meaning of Christianity of Liberation in Latin America." In *Coloniality at Large: Latin America and the Postcolonial Debate*, edited by Enrique Dussel, Mabel Moraña, and Carlos Jáuregui. Translated by Paul B. Miller, 350–59. Durham, N.C.: Duke University Press, 2008.

Lukacs, Georg. *The Historical Novel*. Translated by Hannah Mitchell and Stanley Mitchell. Middlesex, U.K.: Penguin, 1969.

Lüsebrink, Hans-Jürgen. "Mise en fiction et conceptualization de la Révolution Haitienne: La genèse d'un discours littéraire (1789–1848)," in *Proceedings of the Tenth Congress of the International Comparative Literature Association, New York 1982*, ed. Anna Balakian (New York: Garland, 1985), 228–33.

Lyotard, Jean-François. *La condition postmoderne: Rapport sur le savoir*. Paris: Éditions de Minuit, 1979.

———. *The Differend: Phrases in Dispute*. Translated by Georges Van Den Abbeele. Minneapolis: University Minnesota Press, 1988.

Marengo, María del Carmen. "*El mundo alucinante* y *El Siglo de las luces*: Problemas de realismo en la representación de la historia." In *Voces e ideologías: Estudios bajtinianos*, edited by Aran de Meriles. Córdoba, Argentina: Alcion, 1996.

Marinello, Juan. "Una novela cubana." In *Literatura Hispanoamericana*. Mexico City: UNAM, 1937.

Martell-Morales, Jaime L. "La heterotopía en la obra de Edgardo Rodríguez Juliá." *Acta Literaria* 31 (2005): 33–46.

Marx, Karl, and Frederick Engels. *The Communist Manifesto.* New York: Penguin, 1998.

———. *The German Ideology.* London: Lawrence and Wishart, 1965.

Meehan, Kevin. "Romance and Revolution: Reading Women's Narratives of Caribbean Decolonization." *Tulsa Studies in Women's Literature* 25, no. 2 (Fall 2006): 291–305.

———. "'Titid ak pep la se marasa': Jean-Bertrand Aristide and the New National Romance in Haiti." In *Caribbean Romances: The Politics of Regional Representation*, edited by Belinda J. Edmondson, 205–22. Charlottesville: University Press of Virginia, 1999.

———. "'To Shake This Nation as Nothing Before Has Shaken It': C. L. R. James, Radical Fieldwork, and African American Popular Culture." In *Displacements and Transformations in Caribbean Cultures*, edited by Lizabeth Paravisini-Gebert and Ivette Romero-Cesareo, 76–99. Gainesville: University Press of Florida, 2008.

Memorias del subdesarrollo. Directed by Tomás Gutiérrez Alea. Perf. Sergio Corrieri. ICAIC, 1968.

Miller, Paul B. "Enlightened Hesitations: Tragic Heroes and Black Masses in C. L. R. James's *The Black Jacobins.*" *MLN* 116 (2001): 1069–90.

———. "Reading Cuban Music: Reflections on the Music of Leo Brouwer." In *Music, Writing, and Cultural Unity in the Caribbean*, edited by Timothy J. Reiss, 59–74. Trenton, N.J.: Africa World Press, 2004.

Moitt, Bernard. "Transcending Linguistic and Cultural Frontiers in Caribbean Historiography: C. L. R. James, French Sources, and Slavery in San Domingo." In *C. L. R. James: His Intellectual Legacies*, edited by Selwyn R. Cudjoe and William E. Cain. Amherst: University of Massachusetts Press, 1995.

Moore, Robin. *Nationalizing Blackness: Afrocubanismo and Artistic Revolution in Havana, 1920–1940.* Pitt Latin American series. Pittsburgh: University of Pittsburgh Press, 1997.

Moreau de Saint-Méry, M. L. E. *Description topographique, physique, civile, politique et historique de la partie française de l'Isle de Saint-Domingue.* Paris: Société française d'histoire d'outre-mer, 1984.

Moreiras, Alberto. "Hybridity and Double Consciousness." *Cultural Studies* 13, no. 3 (1999): 373–407.

Moreno Fraginals, Manuel. *The Sugarmill: The Socioeconomic Complex of Sugar in Cuba, 1760–1860.* New York: Monthly Review Press, 1976.

Muthu, Sankar. *Enlightenment against Empire.* Princeton, N.J.: Princeton University Press, 2003.

Neck-Yoder, Hilda van. "Introduction." Callaloo 21, no. 3 (1998): 441–46.

Nesbitt, Nick. *Universal Emancipation: The Haitian Revolution and the Radical Enlightenment.* Charlottesville: University of Virginia Press, 2008.

———. *Voicing Memory: History and Subjectivity in French Caribbean Literature.* Charlottesville: University of Virginia Press, 2003.

O'Gorman, Edmundo. *La invención de América.* México: Fondo de Cultura Económica, 1958.

Ortega y Gasset, José. *La rebelión de las masas.* Madrid: Espasa Calpe 1986.

Ortiz, Altagracia. *Eighteenth-Century Reforms in the Caribbean.* Teaneck, N.J.: Fairleigh Dickinson University Press, 1983.

Ortiz, Fernando. *Cuban Counterpoint: Tobacco and Sugar.* Translated by Harriet de Onís. Durham, N.C.: Duke University Press, 1995.

———. *Historia de una pelea cubana contra los demonios.* Madrid: Ediciones ERRE, 1973.

———. *La música afrocubana.* Madrid: Júcar, 1974.

———. *Los negros curros.* Havana: Editorial de Ciencias Sociales, 1986.

Pagni, Andrea. "Palabra y subversión en *El mundo alucinante.*" In *La escritura de la memoria Reinaldo Arenas: Textos, estudios, documentación*, edited by Ottmar Ette, 139–48. Frankfurt: Vervuert, 1991.

Paz, Octavio. *Los hijos del limo.* Barcelona: Seix Barral, 1981.

———. *The Labyrinth of Solitude: Life and Thought in Mexico.* New York: Grove Press, 1961.

Peek, Philip M. "The Power of Words in African Arts." *Journal of American Folklore* 94, no. 371 (January–March 1981): 19–43.

Pérez, Louis A., ed. *Historiography in the Revolution: A Bibliography of Cuban Scholarship, 1959–1979.* New York: Garland, 1982.

Phaf, Ineke. "Caribbean Imagination and Nation-Building in Antillean and Surinamese Literature." *Callaloo* 34 (Winter 1988): 148–71.

Price, Richard. *Alabi's World.* Baltimore: Johns Hopkins University Press, 1990.

Quijano, Aníbal. "Modernity, Identity and Utopia in Latin America." In *The Postmodern Debate in Latin America*, edited by John Beverly, José Oviedo, and Michael Aronna, 200–216. Durham, N.C.: Duke University Press, 1995.

Rabbitt, Kara M. "C. L. R. James's Figuring of Toussaint-Louverture: *The Black Jacobins* and the Literary Hero." In *C.L.R. James: His Intellectual Legacies*, edited by Selwyn R. Cudjoe and William E. Cain, 118–35. Amherst: University of Massachusetts Press, 1995.

Ríos Ávila, Rubén. "La invención de un autor: Escritura y poder en Edgardo Rodríguez Juliá." *Revista Iberoamericana* 162–63 (1993): 203–19.

Rodríguez Juliá, Edgardo. "At the Middle of the Road." In *Images and Identities: The Puerto Rican in the Two World Contexts*, edited by Asela Rodríguez de Laguna. New Brunswick, N.J.: Transaction, 1987.

———. *Campeche, o los diablejos de la melancolía.* San Juan: Instituto de Cultura Puertorriqueña, 1986.

———. *La noche oscura del Niño Avilés.* San Juan: Editorial de la Universidad de Puerto Rico, 1991.

———. "Puerto Rico y el Caribe: Historia de una marginalidad." *Torre: Revista de la Universidad de Puerto Rico* 3, no. 2 (1989): 513–29.

———. *La renuncia del héroe Baltasar.* 1974. Rio Piedras, Puerto Rico[?]: Editorial Cultural, 1986.

———. *The Renunciation.* Translated by Andrew Hurley. New York: Four Walls Eight Windows, 1997.

Rodríguez-Monegal, Emir. "The Labyrinthine World of Reinaldo Arenas." *Latin American Literary Review* 8, no. 16 (Spring–Summer 1980): 126–31.

Rojas Osorio, Carlos. "El impacto de la Ilustración en el pensamiento latinoamericano." Special issue, *La Torre* (1991): 139–56.

Rotker, Susana. "Editor's Introduction." In *The Memoirs of Fray Servando Teresa de Mier*, edited by Susana Rotker, translated by Helen Lane, xxiii–lxiv. New York: Oxford University Press, 1998,

Rousseau, Jean-Jacques. *Essai sur l'origine des langues.* Edited by Jean Starobinski. Folio/Essais Series 135. Paris: Gallimard, 1990.

Rozencvaig, Perla. "Reinaldo Arenas: Entrevista." *Hispamérica* 28 (1981): 41–28.

———. *Reinaldo Arenas: Narrativa de Transgresión.* Mexico City: Editorial Oasis, 1986.

Said, Edward W. *Culture and Imperialism.* New York: Knopf, 1993.

Sala-Molins, Louis. *The Dark Side of Light: Slavery and the French Enlightenment.* Translated by John Conteh-Morgan. Minneapolis: University of Minnesota Press, 1992.

San José Vázquez, Eduardo. *Las luces del siglo: Ilustración y modernidad en el Caribe: La novela histórica hispanoamericana del siglo XX.* Alicante, Spain: Universitat d'Alacant, 2008.

Sarrailh, Jean. *L'Espagne éclairée de la seconde moitié du XVIIIe siècle.* Paris: Impr. nationale, 1954.

Sartre, Jean-Paul. "Orphée Noir." In *Situations III*, by Sartre. Paris: Gallimard, 1949.

Scarboro, Anne Armstrong. Afterword to *I, Tituba, Black Witch of Salem*, by Maryse Condé, translated by Richard Philcox. New York: Ballantine, 1992.

Scharfman, Ronnie. "Theorizing Terror: The Discourse of Violence in Marie Chauvet's *Amour Colère Folie.*" In *Postcolonial Subjects: Francophone Women Writers*, edited by Mary Jean Matthews Green et al., 229–45. Minneapolis: University of Minnesota Press, 1996.

Schroeder Paul A. *Tomás Gutiérrez Alea: Dialectics of a Filmmaker.* New York: Routledge, 2002.

Scott, David. *Conscripts of Modernity: The Tragedy of Colonial Enlightenment.* Durham, N.C.: Duke University Press, 2004.

Serrano, Lucienne J. "La dérive du plaisir dans *La Danse sur le volcan* et *Amour, colère et folie* de Marie Vieux-Chauvet." *Francofonia: Studi e ricerche sulle literature di lingua francese* 25, no. 49 (2005): 95–113.

Sklodowska, Elzbieta. "*El mundo alucinante*: Historia y ficción." In *Reinaldo*

Arenas: Alucinaciones, fantasía y realidad, edited by Julio E Hernández-Miyares and Perla Rozencvaig. Glenview, Ill.: Scott, Foresman, Montesinos, 1990.

Smith, Verity. "Ausencia de Toussaint: Interpretación y falseamiento de la historia en *El reino de este mundo*." In *Historia y ficción en la narrativa hispanoamericana*, edited by Roberto González Echevarría, 275–82. Caracas: Monte Avila Editores, 1984.

———. "'Capítulo de novela' y la génesis de *El reino de este mundo*." *Bulletin Hispanique* 86, no. 1–2 (1984): 205–14.

Sokoloff, Naomi B. "The Discourse of Contradiction: Metaphor, Metonymy and *El reino de este mundo*." Modern Language Studies 16:1 (1986): 39-53.

Sommer, Doris. "No Secrets." In *The Real Thing: Testimonial Discourse and Latin America*, edited by Georg M. Gugelberger, 130–57. Durham, N.C.: Duke University Press, 1996.

Sorel, Andrés. "El mundo novelístico de Alejo Carpentier." In *Homenaje a Alejo Carpentier: Variaciones interpretativas en torno de su obra*, edited by Helmy F. Giacoman. New York: Las Américas, 1970.

Soto-Crespo, Ramon E. "'The Pains of Memory': Mourning the Nation in Puerto Rican Art and Literature. *MLN* 117, no. 2 (March 2002): 449–80.

Spivak, Gayatri Chakravorty. "Can the Subaltern Speak?" In *Marxism and the Interpretation of Culture*, edited by Cary Nelson and Lawrence Grossberg, 271–313. Chicago: University of Illinois Press, 1988.

Stinchcombe, Arthur L. *Sugar Island Slavery in the Age of Enlightenment: The Political Economy of the Caribbean World*. Princeton, N.J.: Princeton University Press, 1995.

Subirats, Eduardo. *La Ilustración insuficiente*. Madrid: Taurus, 1981.

Todorov, Tzvetan. *L'esprit des lumières*. Paris: Robert Laffont, 2006.

Tomás Fernández de Castro, Lourdes. *Fray Servando alucinado*. Miami: Instituto de Estudios Ibéricos, 1994.

Torres-Saillant, Silvio. *Caribbean Poetics: Toward an Aesthetic of West Indian Literature*. Cambridge: Cambridge University Press, 1997.

La última cena. Directed by Tomás Gutiérrez Alea. Perf. Nelson Villagra. ICAIC, 1976.

Trouillot, Michel-Rolph. *Silencing the Past: Power and the Production of History*. Boston: Beacon Press, 1995.

Unamuno, Miguel de. *San Manuel Bueno, martír*. Madrid: Castalia, 1984.

Uslar Pietri, Arturo. *La isla de Robinson*. Barcelona: Seix Barral, 1981.

Verba, Cynthia. *Music and the French Enlightenment*. Oxford: Clarendon Press, 1993.

Volek, Emil. "Análisis e interpretación de *El reino de este mundo* de Alejo Carpentier." In *Homenaje a Alejo Carpentier: Variaciones interpretativas en torno a su obra*, edited by Helmy G. Giacoman. New York: Las Americas, 1970.

Walcott, Derek. *The Antilles: Fragments of Epic Memory. The Nobel Lecture.* New York: Farrar, Straus and Giroux, 1993.
———. "The Muse of History." In *What the Twilight Says*, 36–64. New York: Farrar, Straus and Giroux, 1998.
Webb, Barbara J. *Myth and History in Caribbean Fiction: Alejo Carpentier, Wilson Harris, and Édouard Glissant.* Amherst: University of Massachusetts Press, 1992.
Whitaker, Arthur P. "Changing and Unchanging Interpretations of the Enlightenment in Spanish America." *Proceedings of the American Philosophical Society* 114, no. 4 (1970): 256–71.
White, Hayden. *Metahistory.* Baltimore: Johns Hopkins University Press, 1973.
Williams, Raymond L. *The Postmodern Novel in Latin America: Politics, Culture, and the Crisis of Truth.* New York: St. Martin's Press, 1996.
Wilson-Tagoe, Nana. *Historical Thought and Literary Representation in West Indian Literature.* Gainesville: University Press of Florida, 1998.
Wittgenstein, Ludwig. *Tractatus logico-philosophicus.* Translated by D. F. Pears and B. F. McGuinness. London: Routledge, 1974.
Worcester, Kent. *C. L. R. James: A Political Biography.* Albany: State University of New York Press, 1996.
Žižek, Slavoj. *The Sublime Object of Ideology.* New York: Verso, 1989.

Index

New World Studies

Vera M. Kutzinski, *Sugar's Secrets: Race and the Erotics of Cuban Nationalism*

Richard D. E. Burton and Fred Reno, editors, *French and West Indian: Martinique, Guadeloupe, and French Guiana Today*

A. James Arnold, editor, *Monsters, Tricksters, and Sacred Cows: Animal Tales and American Identities*

J. Michael Dash, *The Other America: Caribbean Literature in a New World Context*

Isabel Alvarez Borland, *Cuban-American Literature of Exile: From Person to Persona*

Belinda J. Edmondson, editor, *Caribbean Romances: The Politics of Regional Representation*

Steven V. Hunsaker, *Autobiography and National Identity in the Americas*

Celia M. Britton, *Edouard Glissant and Postcolonial Theory: Strategies of Language and Resistance*

Mary Peabody Mann, *Juanita: A Romance of Real Life in Cuba Fifty Years Ago*
Edited and with an introduction by Patricia M. Ard

George B. Handley, *Postslavery Literatures in the Americas: Family Portraits in Black and White*

Faith Smith, *Creole Recitations: John Jacob Thomas and Colonial Formation in the Late Nineteenth-Century Caribbean*

Ian Gregory Strachan, *Paradise and Plantation: Tourism and Culture in the Anglophone Caribbean*

Nick Nesbitt, *Voicing Memory: History and Subjectivity in French Caribbean Literature*

Charles W. Pollard, *New World Modernisms: T. S. Eliot, Derek Walcott, and Kamau Brathwaite*

Carine M. Mardorossian, *Reclaiming Difference: Caribbean Women Rewrite Postcolonialism*

Luís Madureira. *Cannibal Modernities: Postcoloniality and the Avant-garde in Caribbean and Brazilian Literature*

Elizabeth M. DeLoughrey, Renée K. Gosson, and George B. Handley, editors, *Caribbean Literature and the Environment: Between Nature and Culture*

Flora González Mandri, *Guarding Cultural Memory: Afro-Cuban Women in Literature and the Arts*

Miguel Arnedo-Gómez, *Writing Rumba: The Afrocubanista Movement in Poetry*

Jessica Adams, Michael P. Bibler, and Cécile Accilien, editors, *Just Below South: Intercultural Performance in the Caribbean and the U.S. South*

Valérie Loichot, *Orphan Narratives: The Postplantation Literature of Faulkner, Glissant, Morrison, and Saint-John Perse*

Sarah Phillips Casteel, *Second Arrivals: Landscape and Belonging in Contemporary Writing of the Americas*

Guillermina De Ferrari, *Vulnerable States: Bodies of Memory in Contemporary Caribbean Fiction*

Claudia Sadowski-Smith, *Border Fictions: Globalization, Empire, and Writing at the Boundaries of the United States*

Doris L. Garraway, editor, *Tree of Liberty: Cultural Legacies of the Haitian Revolution in the Atlantic World*

Dawn Fulton, *Signs of Dissent: Maryse Conde and Postcolonial Criticism*

Nick Nesbitt, *Universal Emancipation: The Haitian Revolution and the Radical Enlightenment*

Michael G. Malouf, *Transatlantic Solidarities: Irish Nationalism and Caribbean Poetics*

Maria Cristina Fumagalli, *Caribbean Perspectives on Modernity: Returning the Gaze*

Vivian Nun Halloran, *Exhibiting Slavery: The Caribbean Postmodern Novel as Museum*

Paul B. Miller, *Elusive Origins: The Enlightenment in the Modern Caribbean Historical Imagination*